Neither
Fire
Nor
Steel:

Sir Christopher Hatton

A representation of a suit of armor for use in ceremonial tilts, made for Sir Christopher Hatton by Jacob Halder. Victoria and Albert Museum, London.

Alice Gilmore Vines

Neither
Fire
Nor
Steel:

Sir Christopher Hatton

Nelson-Hall
Chicago

Library of Congress Cataloging in Publication Data

Vines, Alice Gilmore.
    Neither fire nor steel.

    Bibliography: p.
    Includes index.
    1. Hatton, Christopher, Sir, 1540-1591.   2.   States-
men—Great Britain—Biography. 3. Great Britain—History—Elizabeth, 1558-1603. I. Title.
DA358.H3V56   942.05′5′0942 [B]   77-21424
ISBN 0-88229-372-9

Manufactured in the United States of America

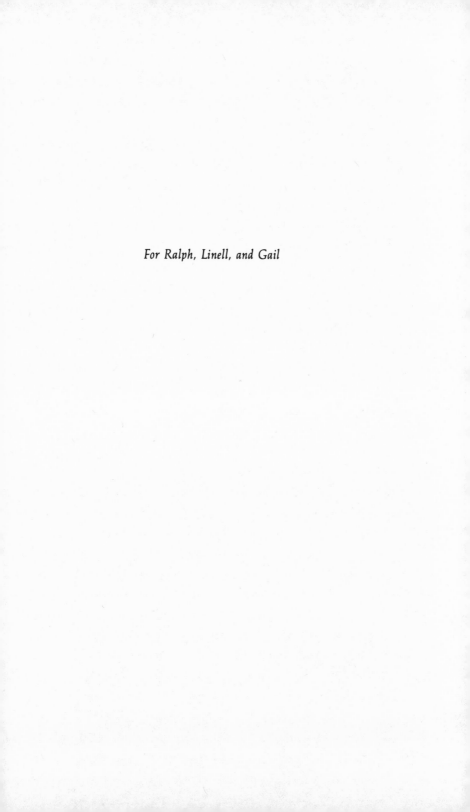

For Ralph, Linell, and Gail

Contents

acknowledgments

I thank Dr. Ronald Pollitt of the Department of History, University of Cincinnati, for his valued criticisms of this work in its early form, and Dr. Eugene August of the Department of English, University of Dayton, for his reading of the manuscript, advice, and great friendship when he was in the midst of his own writing. And above all, I owe an incalculable debt to my husband, Ralph, who not only has encouraged my work for years but was an eagle-eyed proofreader and invaluable editor for this book. Curiously enough, we're still married.

introduction

Christopher Hatton and the Era of Elizabeth

In Elizabethan England the Court of the Queen was the center of political, social, and cultural concerns of the nation. Appropriate to the personal monarchy of the Tudors, attendance upon the Queen was obligatory for the aristocracy and the goal of all those with ambition. The Court was the source of patronage and promotion, exercising a powerful magnetic force. As the monarch was a woman, extra dimensions were added to this attraction. Elizabeth was ruler, Supreme Governor of the Church of England, and an attractive, emotional woman. In the sixteenth century, this Queen was subject to many dangers, but Elizabeth was able to turn her vulnerability into an advantage. In so doing she inspired a unique form of secular devotion in a society that was predominantly masculine.

The attitude towards Elizabeth which was displayed by all those at Court owed something to the old ideals of chivalry, but was enhanced by the fact that she was an unmarried monarch. Elizabeth cultivated this attitude among her courtiers until it grew into what amounted to a personal cult, symbolized by the phrase "Virgin Queen," which was often used in the later years of her reign. She was praised by poets and musicians as Cynthia, the moon goddess, or as the Fair Oriana, and on her Accession Day in November a jousting tournament was held annually in which her champions would vie for a prize from her graceful hands.

The Queen dominated the scene. The masculine Court centered about her consisted of Privy Councillors, peers, senior officials of the Royal Household, members of the various departments of state, and handsome young men hoping to make their fortunes. Often the wives and daughters of these men served as Ladies of the Bedchamber to the Queen. The officials were entitled to food and lodging at Court although their families were not. All of these upper levels of society at Court were attended to by huge numbers of servants who also had servants.

This splendid Court was an attraction for men of all types, drawn either because of ambition or curiosity. (The ranks of the courtiers were constantly fluctuating, losing those who no longer pleased the Queen, and taking on favored newcomers.) A young man hoping to be noticed had to dress in extravagant apparel and be handsome in his own person. However, to make a success of oneself at Court required a good deal more than a fine figure with clothes to match. The Queen valued intelligence, witty conversation, ability to perform in the courtly graces of music and poetry, and energetic performances in the tiltyard. The successful young courtier also needed a delicate intuition as to when to treat Elizabeth as a Queen and when to flatter her as a woman. If the courtier could then persuade her he was in love with her, he might well be on the royal road to success.

Despite the pleasant flattery and courtly graces which were required of Elizabeth's courtiers, her councillors and men appointed to important offices were men of intelligence who often had been trained at Oxford or Cambridge and generally had some legal experience gained at an Inn of Court. It was not easy to incorporate these two characteristics in one person, nor for that person to acquire a suitable temperament to withstand the rigors of Court life. He needed to be fortified against loss of the royal favor, disappointments, and the envy of others. Elizabeth also required the total commitment of the courtier's life. She frowned upon marriage and insisted upon courtiers remaining at Court and accompanying her on uncomfortable progresses through the country each summer. Life and position were fragile when dependent upon the changing favor of the Queen. Christopher Hatton, who spent a lifetime at Court, said that the Queen "did fish for men's souls, and had so sweet a bait that no one could escape her network . . . she caught many poor fish who little knew what snare was laid for them."[1] Elizabeth's godson John Harington wrote, "When she smiled it was pure sunshine that everyone did choose to bask in if they could," but when the Queen was displeased, "the thunder fell in monstrous measure on all-alike."[2]

Living up to Elizabeth's expectations cost a great deal of money, and despite the generous grants attained by many, few actually became rich from Court life. This is evidenced by the careers of the two greatest favorites, the Earl of Leicester, and Christopher Hatton. After a lifetime of royal favor these men died owing the government 34,000 and 42,000 pounds respectively, in addition to other, private debts. Given this insecure, flamboyant, restless Court life, it is easy to understand the comment of one who assessed the scene, granted its magnificence, but concluded, "Blessed are they that can be away and live contented."[3]

One who apparently could not contentedly live away from this magnetic center of English life was Christopher Hatton. He arrived in London in 1560 at twenty years of age. He came from Northamptonshire gentry stock, and followed the usual route of young ambitious men of that time, spending a few years at Oxford and making his way to the Inner Temple as a law student in 1560. He was fortunate in having the physical qualities necessary to be noticed by the Queen; he was tall, dark, and handsome. His many portraits which still exist attest to these qualities. He was also an excellent dancer, and dancing and taking part in masques were essential parts of a gentleman's repertory and were required graces for members of the Inns of Court, one of Hatton's training schools. The custom was to celebrate the Christmas season with revels until Candlemas Day, February 2. In 1561, Hatton played a major part in the revels as a Master of the Games. Masques consisted of a series of short dramatic performances interspersed with dancing, and it is possible that Elizabeth danced with the young Christopher at this time.

Elizabeth wanted men of good looks around her but she also wanted strong evidence of real capacity, and as in Hatton's case, this often took years to display before promotion came. Therefore, although Hatton was noticed, his governmental career was slow to develop. The legend that he was instantly taken into the royal service originated with Hatton's first biographer, Sir Robert Naunton, who had a family hostility towards Hatton. Naunton had married the granddaughter of Sir John Perrot, Hatton's only known enemy. Perhaps this enmity was based on guilt, as there is some evidence that Perrot had seduced Hatton's illegitimate daughter Elizabeth. The Perrot family blamed Hatton for Perrot's death of illness in the Tower of London. Naunton then described Hatton as coming to Court by the galliard, a complicated dance, and that he was a "mere vegetable of the court that sprang up at night and sank again at his noon."4 This biased judgment of Nauntons is highly debatable.

True, Hatton was a fine dancer, but so was the Earl of Oxford, and a peer as well, but nimble footwork did not save him when he proved to be a fool. Hatton's rise was gradual; two and one-half years elapsed before he was made a Gentleman Pensioner in 1564 and several months more passed before he had an official task at Court as a member of a delegation to meet the Scottish ambassador. He took part in ceremonial tilts and was also appointed as a member of a delegation to Scotland. It was not until 1568 that he got his first land grants and it took another year for him to become a Gentleman of the Privy Chamber. In 1571 he got a seat in the House of Commons as a burgess from Higham Ferrers and in 1572 sat for Northamptonshire. Also in 1572 he was appointed to his first really important position as Captain of the Queen's Bodyguard. Thus, between his first notice and his gaining of real position, Hatton had spent over a decade of hard work at Court, during which time his behavior, honesty, loyalty, tact, and gifts to the Queen had been closely scrutinized. He got his rewards, but only after a long apprenticeship.

Few rulers have impressed themselves so forcefully upon English history as Elizabeth. Elizabethan England was *her* England. She made possible its amazing development. She inspired its patriotism, its poetry, and shaped its destiny by the force of her character. When she died in 1603 she left England in a commanding position in Europe. She had inherited a weak and defeated country in 1558; England was in debt and its major forts were in ruins. The French king, Henry II, had one foot in Calais and the other in Edinburgh. In France lived Mary Stuart, a dangerous claimant to Elizabeth's throne.

The first and perhaps most difficult problem Elizabeth faced was that of holding the balance between the assaults of Catholics from without and the clamors of Protestant sectarians from within. This conflict lasted throughout her reign and involved large numbers of people of both high and low estate, people who were beginning to make up their own minds about religion and were therefore less amenable to royal sovereignty in this area.

For the first twenty years of her reign Elizabeth virtually refrained from any action against those who declined to accept the state form of religion. In the north very few clergymen were removed from their positions. Catholic peers continued to enjoy the Queen's favor as long as they remained loyal to her. With the state support withdrawn in 1559, English Catholicism tended to become a nonpublic religion, with Catholic ceremonies conducted in private manors rather than in churches. Therefore the gentry could be held responsible for the loyalty of the priests who essentially became members of the household, as in the Middle Ages. Most English Catholics were grateful for the royal toleration and remained loyal during the crucial period of the attack of the Spanish Armada.

This situation of toleration was endangered in the late

1580s with the arrival of the new priests whose aim was to revive a Catholic clerical establishment. These new seminarians also accepted financial support from foreign powers and in so doing endangered the lives and estates of English Catholics. The government could not stop them from coming into the country and Elizabeth was eventually forced to act.

Another crucial situation was the pressure of the Puritans in the Commons to achieve penal legislation against the Catholics. Although she disliked special legislation or allowing Parliament an initiative in this field, Elizabeth's hand was often forced. As many priests continued to get through the watch at the ports, executions inevitably followed. With the exception of those who engaged in active rebellions against the government, in the thirty years when active Catholics were in danger, about 300 people were executed. This was about the same number of Protestants executed in the five years of Queen Mary's reign. Elizabeth's entire government realized if they lost the battle of the Counter-Reformation they would all be executed. On the whole it seems accurate to conclude that Elizabeth did not bear any hostility towards English Catholics as long as they remained loyal to her.

In her actions towards the Puritans she had firm convictions; she totally disagreed with their views. Elizabeth hated the sermons which the Puritans felt were essential. She acted against the Puritans with uncharacteristic intolerance because she undoubtedly saw them as a threat to monarchical government. She agreed with Archbishop John Whitgift who said, "In the end your Majesty will find that those which now impugn the ecclesiastical jurisdiction will endeavor also to impair the temporal, and to bring even kings and princes under their censure."[5] He was of course exactly correct, as the Stuarts were to learn.

Elizabeth strove with greater success than most to build within England some fabric of sanity and sense, of moderation and internal peace. It was in this vital work of holding the balance that Hatton was to be invaluable to the Queen. His attitude that neither fire nor steel should be used in settling religious matters was characteristic of this man of moderation. And although he was seen by many as an anti-Puritan, he dealt with the Puritans with tact and restraint. At times he opposed the inquisitorial methods of Archbishop Whitgift. During the Queen's later years evangelical Puritanism was driven underground.

In general Elizabeth was supported by the majority of her people in her religious policies. A type of Puritan ministry was popuular with the lower-middle-class and middle-class townsmen, but not with the majority of the English people. Elizabeth refused to allow a joyless Puritan Sunday to be enacted, believing that the common people should be allowed their pleasures. She also refused to allow the Puritans their way in the arts. She supported the theatres of London and religious cycle plays in Coventry when the Puritans wished to abolish both. By appointing a group of players as the "Queen's Men" and encouraging courtiers to establish groups of performers she effectually saved the theatre, including Shakespeare's work.

Elizabeth's major accomplishment was not the victory over Spain but the maintenance of internal peace. This was the supreme accomplishment of the last successful personal monarch of England and in her achievements she had the total dedication and devotion of one Christopher Hatton.

chapter one
The Early Years

Destined to become a longtime favorite of Elizabeth I and an influential member of her government, Christopher Hatton was born in 1540 to Alice and William Hatton of Northamptonshire. Members of the gentry class, the Hattons owned the manor of Holdenby and their son Christopher would build a great house there in the days of his success at Court.

William Hatton died when Christopher was seven, and it is not known when Alice died. Nothing is recorded of the boy's early life until he was admitted to St. Mary's Hall, Oxford, as a Gentleman-Commoner about 1555 or 1556.[1] He left Oxford without taking a degree, a customary practice for young gentlemen of that period. Christopher apparently followed the usual path from Oxford to the Inns of Court in London, for he is next found entered as a member of the Inner Temple on May 26, 1560.[2] There he seems to have lived as a typical student at the Inn, and his conduct was to bring criticism later in his career. One author wrote that he "rather took a bait than made a meal at the Inns of Court whilst he studied the law therein."[3] He is described by an indignant writer of the nineteenth century as spending his time in licentious living, staying out all night, and shirking his studies.[4] Neither of these judgments, however, has supportive evidence.

In Elizabeth's reign the Inns of Court were a proper beginning for any career, not only the law itself. It was customary for gentlemen to join the Inns to learn dancing, acting, and fencing—all qualities essential to advancement at Elizabeth's Court. The location of the Inns made them ideally suited to introduce young men to the exciting world of London, already the mecca of ambition and talent and the kingdom's administrative, commercial, cultural, and political center. At the Inns young men from the country would find good lodgings, proper friends, and be prepared to seize whatever opportunity presented itself.

Hatton had a special talent for dancing and it seems his skill was noticed soon after his arrival in London when he took an important part in the Christmas festivities of the Inner Temple in 1561. As Master of the Games he dressed in green velvet with a hunting horn around his neck.[5] Indeed, contemporaries believed that during a masque his striking looks and grace first attracted the Queen's eye. "Being young and of a comely tallness of body and countenance, he got into such favor with the Queen," William Camden wrote, "that she took him into her band of fifty Gentlemen Pensioners."[6]

However Hatton managed to catch the Queen's eye, he was made a Gentleman Pensioner in 1564. He thus joined a very select group of young men who, besides adding their stately presences to Court ceremonials, were responsible for the Queen's safety. This corps accompanied the Queen on most occasions, especially her annual summer progresses. This post was the first on Hatton's gradual climb to wealth and influence.

Organized by Henry VIII, the Gentlemen Pensioners were chosen from the gentry or "gentlemanly" class in contrast to the Yeomen Guard established by the first Tudor monarch. The high cost of apparel for the Pensioners required considerable income and resources. By order of Henry VIII each man was to have an archer, a lance, and an armed servant. Each Pensioner or "Spear" as they were called because of the golden spear they carried, was also to have three horses available.

Henry Brackenbury wrote of this group:

> . . . the apparel and charges were so great, for there was none of them but they and their horses were apparelled and trapped in cloth of gold, silver and goldsmith's work, and their servants richly apparelled also.[7]

A suit of armor was also required, and there is a warrant in which Elizabeth directed the Master of the Armory ". . . to cause to be made one armor fit for the body of our well-beloved servant, Christopher Hatton, to be delivered to him on his paying the just value thereof."[8] Hatton remained a member of this highly esteemed group until 1577 when be became Vice-Chamberlain and a member of the Privy Council.

As a newcomer at Court, Hatton was given simple assignments such as welcoming the Scottish emissary, Sir James Melville, in September 1564 and conducting him to an audience with the Queen. Likewise Hatton appeared in the ceremonial tournaments staged during noble weddings, visits of foreign dignitaries, and annual entertainments in honor of Elizabeth's accession to the throne. Hatton's first recorded appearance before the Queen in such a joust was in 1565 at Westminster, a tournament celebrating the marriage of Lady Anne Russell to Ambrose Dudley. Dudley, the Earl of Warwick, was the elder brother of Robert Dudley, the Queen's principal favorite at this time, who became the Earl of Leicester. In a tournament held in May, 1571, Hatton appeared as the Black Knight, his horse suitably trimmed with black feathers.[9]

In 1566, as part of the Earl of Bedford's delegation to represent Elizabeth at the baptism of James, the son of Mary, Queen of Scots, and Henry, Lord Darnley, Hatton was part of a diplomatic errand that almost ended in violence. The christening took place at Stirling on Sunday, December 17, 1566, followed on Thursday by a banquet and masque. This extravaganza, produced by Bastian Pages, Mary Stuart's French valet, featured a group of men who had been hired to serve the guests. These men were dressed as satyrs, and carried away with their role, ". . . they put their hands behind them to their tails, which they wagged with their hands in such sort as the Englishmen supposed it had been devised and done in derision of them."[10] The foreign belief that Englishmen had been endowed with tails as punishment for the murder of Thomas Becket was probably the intended allusion. In any event, Hatton and the other Englishmen took offense, turned their backs, and sat down on the floor behind the table. Hatton is reported to have said:

> If it were not in the Queen's presence, he would put a dagger to the heart of that French knave, Bastian, who, he alleged, had done it out of despite that the Queen made more of them than of Frenchmen.[11]

Mary and the Earl of Bedford managed however to soothe the irate Englishmen.

At the conclusion of the mission, the Queen gave gifts to the most important members of the delegation, Hatton receiving a chain with the Queen's picture and a ring. So ended the first of Hatton's contacts with Mary Stuart. He was to meet her again under considerably different circumstances.

It was fortunate for Hatton, who had been put to vast expense by his role at Court, that the Queen now gave him the first of many grants of land. In April, 1568, Elizabeth leased to him the site of the abbey and demesne lands of Sulby in Northamptonshire, nominally in exchange for his manor of Holdenby. But on the same day she leased Holdenby to him for forty years. In July, 1568, he was appointed Keeper of the Park at Eltham in Kent and also of Horne Park in Surrey. In 1569 the chapel farm of Monkton in Pembrokeshire was granted to him.[12] He was also appointed a justice of the peace in Northamptonshire that year.

Hatton continued to receive various grants of land through the years, including a life grant of the office of Remembrancer of First Fruits and Tenths in the Exchequer Office on February 24, 1570. His other grants included the lease for thirty years of a London inn called the "Ship" and the grant of wardship and marriage of his nephew William Underhill.[13] These and many other grants from the Queen permitted Hatton to live in the elaborate fashion required by his position and presence at Court.

In April, 1571, Hatton entered the House of Commons for the town of Higham Ferrers, Northamptonshire. The next year he was appointed Captain of the Queen's Guard and Gentleman of the Privy Chamber. An example of the elegant dress of Hatton in this office is the warrant issued by Elizabeth for the delivery to Hatton of six yards of tawney medley cloth with sufficient black fur for it.[14] He also sat in the House of Commons for the county of Northamptonshire, a seat which he held until he became Lord Chancellor in 1587. In 1577 Hatton became Vice-Chamberlain and a Privy Councillor, both positions of great importance.

As a Privy Councillor Hatton joined the central body of the Elizabethan adminstration. The Privy Council consisted of seventeen to twenty carefully chosen experienced men, mostly officials of the royal household, through whose hands all of the routine business of government passed. Usually the number making vital decisions was only eight or ten or less, and Hatton became one of the inner circle. The council was the executive instrument of the Queen, who appointed its members and delegated authority to it. There was no special meeting place for the Privy Council. They simply met wherever the Queen was residing. The meetings were secret and the Queen did not attend, making her wishes known through one of the members. She often took the council's decision but did not hesitate to follow her own inclination when she differed.

This small influential group of men who saw much of each other were constantly jealous of royal favor and could at times divide into factions. They all felt the need to acquire information from any possible source to strengthen their hand in the debates in council. There are many letters from various adventurers who acted as agents for Hatton in Ireland and Europe. The Councillors associated daily with each other,

> . . . in an atmosphere permitted by overlapping and interlocking ties of kinship, friendship, gratitude, affection, loyalty, and self-interest. On the whole they ruled England with Queen Elizabeth in that climate of understanding which grew out of their having so many more things in common than there were jealousies and feuds dividing them.[15]

The business of the council varied widely. They dealt with the highest matters of state and with small details affecting the private lives of individuals. In addition, they were in positions of authority over the judicial system, the Church, and Parliament. Decisions were made concerning the security of the state and the welfare of subjects. Local Lords Lieutenant, sheriffs, and justices of the peace were all directed by Privy Councillors. The Council received voluminous reports from the country in the forms of reports, letters, and petitions which were answered by directives and instructions. Some judicial cases were relegated to the court of Star Chamber or specially named commissions but the Council remained ". . . the final court of appeal and the co-ordinating center of the political universe."[16]

Hatton, as a major figure in the Council, became very involved with the conciliar duties of guardian of the state. The Council had the power to use torture to force confessions in cases of suspected treason during the 1580s when fears of Catholic infiltration had gripped the government. These prisoners then were tried in the judicial arm of the Council, the Star Chamber, with Privy Councillors sitting as judges. Other judges also attended who were not Privy Councillors, but the Councillors kept their eyes on all facets of political and religious life. Their powers were all-encompassing, covering the areas of breach of public order and problems stemming from violation of proclamations or royal ordinances. The procedure in the Star Chamber differed greatly from common law courts, being composed only of judges who decided the case from written depositions or oral testimony. Often the prisoner was not called to appear until near the end of the trial. It is in this court that Hatton often sat in the 1580s and gained much legal experience. Thus in joining the Privy Council Hatton entered into the center of Elizabethan government, where he would become one of the key figures.

The position of Vice-Chamberlain which Hatton also attained in 1577 was of a very different type from that of Privy Councillor. This post made Hatton a member of the Queen's Household responsible for the smooth operation of the Court. Special work was required to plan for the summer progresses which involved hundreds of people and commensurate supplies. This work required Hatton's presence at Court, where he was in constant attendance upon the Queen. This position would be properly held by a courtier such as Hatton, but he was much more, which his appointment to the Privy Council demonstrated. He began, in this year of 1577, his dual career of favorite of the Queen as well as a trusted, influential politician, a position which he earned by his political ability.

Hatton's position became a unique one. Lord Burghley was always senior adviser to the Queen, but there was little emotional quality between Burghley and Elizabeth. The same situation prevailed with Walsingham, who was very important to the government, but not a royal favorite. Leicester came closest to Hatton's situation, in being the original and special favorite of the Queen, but his political abilities were not as solid as Hatton's, nor did he support the Queen in the later years in the vital maintenance of her religious policy. Leicester was not content to devote his entire personal life to the Queen. As it became obvious she would not marry him, Leicester had several affairs and finally a secret marriage with Lettice Knollys. Hatton alone of the courtiers remained unmarried, centering his emotional life in Elizabeth with an unusual singleness of mind.

As Hatton grew in Elizabeth's favor Leicester was no doubt jealous and there is a story told that he tried to ridicule Hatton's supposed speciality of dancing. Leicester offered to produce a dancing master who excelled Hatton. Elizabeth contemptuously rejected this idea, saying, "Pish, I will not see your man; it is his trade!"[17]

Leicester and Hatton seemed to have settled down into a remarkable tolerance and even friendship as the years went on. They faced together other rivals such as the Earl of Oxford and Walter Raleigh and the threat to their positions of a possible French marriage.

In 1572 Hatton gave Elizabeth the first of the annual conceits in jewelry which so pleased the Queen. The first creation consisted of a ". . . a jewel of . . . gold adorned with rubies and diamonds, and flowers set with rubies, with one pearl pendant, and another at the top."[18] These gifts became more elaborate and costly as the years passed. Hatton always received the largest amount of silver plate, the customary royal gift. His 400 ounces surpassed all other amounts.

Thus Hatton began the vital years of his career, a personal favorite of the Queen and a person of ability who grew with experience into one of the major figures of Elizabethan government.

chapter two

Two Parliaments and Troubled Times

Hatton's first Parliament, that of 1571, had many long-overdue and serious matters to consider. Two problems had been in the forefront of English political life since the accession of Elizabeth in 1558—her marriage, and the naming of a successor, which Parliament felt would attain some stability for the country. These considerations were persistently debated in each Parliament despite the Queen's view that these two topics were to be decided by her alone. Also woven into these areas of political concern was the question of religion. The stalwart Puritans in and out of Parliament were convinced that the safety to practice their religion depended upon the life of Elizabeth and, should there be no heir, the security of a Protestant succession. These concerns were to be permanent subjects of debate and political sparring between the Queen and Parliament.

In the Parliament of 1566 Elizabeth had summarily refused the petition of the members of Parliament concerning the succession. In the speech ending the session, Elizabeth answered the petition:

> Your petition is to deal in the limitation of the succession.
> At this present it is not convenient; nor never shall be without
> some peril unto you and certain danger unto me. . . . But as
> soon as there may be a convenient time, . . . I will deal therein
> for your safety, and offer it unto you as your Prince and head,
> without request; for it is monstrous that the feet should direct
> the head.[1]

In this Parliament Elizabeth had even forbidden debate on
the succession topic but strong reaction persuaded her to
rescind her command. The conclusion of that frustrated Parliament found Elizabeth promising to marry and evading the
matter of naming a successor.

When economic needs became so pressing that another
Parliament was unavoidable, the matter of the royal promise to
actively undertake marriage negotiations had not been fulfilled.
In 1567, the negotiations with Archduke Charles of Austria had
ended. The marriage had failed to materialize largely due to
parliamentary opposition to the Archduke's Catholic religion.

The idea of naming a successor to the throne, who would
logically be Mary, Queen of Scots, had also collapsed due to
surprising events in Scotland. Mary had been following an anti-
English course since her arrival in Scotland in 1561 to begin her
active reign as Queen. Her foremost goal was to be named as
Elizabeth's successor, should Elizabeth not produce an heir.
Mary had married Henry Darnley against Elizabeth's wishes
and produced a son in 1566. Darnley had proved a most un-
satisfactory consort who joined the plot of several nobles to kill
Mary's secretary David Rizzio. This was done most cruelly,
Rizzio being dragged from Mary's side to the outer chamber of
Holyrood Palace in Edinburgh, where he was stabbed repeat-
edly.

Darnley proved an inconstant conspirator and soon became the target of a plot himself. In February, 1567, he died of
strangulation in the garden of Kirk O'Field in Edinburgh. The
house from which he fled to his death was blown up. General
agreement placed the blame on James Hepburn, Earl of Bothwell, with whom Mary soon became intimate. Mary then
pursued a most unwise course; she married the man assigned

the guilt for the death of Darnley, in a Protestant ceremony, with Bothwell still married to another woman. Mary's actions led successively to a rebellion of Scottish nobles, her capture and imprisonment on an island, and her escape and flight into England for refuge.

Mary arrived in England in May, 1568, creating a situation which marked a turning point in Elizabeth's reign. Mary would become and remain until her death in 1587, the focal point of anti-Elizabeth plots and the source of increasing internal and external danger for both Elizabeth and her realm. In these new circumstances all thought of naming Mary in the line of succession ceased. Mary was quickly confined, under the guardianship of the Earl of Shrewsbury, to his castle at Tutbury.

In addition to the problem of Mary, Elizabeth and her government had to evaluate the impact of the beginning of a religious war in France, the revolt of the Netherlands against Spain and the arrival in the Netherlands of the Duke of Alva, and an actual rebellion within England itself.

The first of many conspiracies caused by Mary Stuart's presence within the country had already been uncovered by the time the 1571 Parliament met. The Northern Rebellion of November, 1569, had aimed at the marriage of Mary Stuart to the English Duke of Norfolk. The rebellion coincided with a papal bull of excommunication against Elizabeth in an attempt to aid her enemies by releasing English Catholic subjects from allegiance to their Queen.

The land north of the Trent River was almost an unknown country to the government in London. This area remained more agrarian and feudal than did the rapidly changing area to the south. The great feudal families of Dacre, Percy, and Neville still were the centers of strong local loyalties. In these strongholds of tradition people had from the beginning of Elizabeth's reign proved recalcitrant in the matter of religious change, and the Queen had been reluctant to force change upon them. The Council of the North, the Queen's governing body in northern areas of the kingdom, had similarly closed its eyes to the situation.

Added to the regional discontents, the northern earls had

many private grievances as well as public ones. In public policy they disapproved of the Queen's continued refusal to settle the succession question in favor of Mary Stuart, and of Elizabeth's veto of the marriage of Norfolk to Mary. Added to these points of conflict was their envy of and hostility to the power of William Cecil, the Queen's first secretary.

The Northern Rebellion hoped to dislodge Cecil, to settle the succession in favor of Mary, and restore her to the throne of Scotland with the Duke of Norfolk as her new husband. The plot developed in the minds of Norfolk and the Earl of Arundel, who were soon joined by the Earls of Northumberland, Westmoreland, Pembroke, Leicester, and Derby. The Spanish ambassador, Don Guerau de Spes, also was in contact with this group. This diplomat cherished the illusion that behind these northern earls loomed thousands of discontented Englishmen who would welcome the changes the earls wanted including the re-establishment of a Roman Catholic Church in England.

The plotters were soon to be disillusioned, as no aid came from Spain or France and Elizabeth became aware of their plans. Norfolk was severely warned to cease such planning and Leicester, who had defected from the conspirators, had been pardoned by Elizabeth in the middle of September, 1569. Norfolk retired to his country house at Kenninghall, begged the Queen's pardon, and wrote to his fellow conspirators to attempt to forestall their action. Elizabeth sent word to the Earl of Sussex, the Lord President of the Council at York, to put him on his guard, although he was inclined to take the matter lightly at this time.

Sussex soon learned that the earls feared to retreat now that they had gone this far. Despite Sussex's commands to come before him at York, they met at Westmoreland's castle with their men in armor. On November 15 they entered Durham, held mass in the cathedral, and defied Sussex. While Sussex called his forces together the earls published a proclamation accusing evil persons around the Queen of overthrowing the Catholic religion, abusing the Queen, and seeking the destruction of the nobility. The rebels then marched southward with the probable intention of reaching Tutbury to release Mary Stuart. Mary was quickly removed south to Coventry and the troops of Sussex gathered. A royal force advanced south from the Scottish border as Sussex, supported by Lord Clinton and the Earl of Warwick, pursued the rebels. The rebellious earls, realizing they had lost, disbanded their troops for flight on December 15. The leaders themselves fled into the remote border country where they were able to find refuge. They were pursued by Lord Hunsdon, who defeated the forces of Dacre and prevented the northwest border area of Carlisle from being lost to the enemy.

By February 4, some 500 of the followers of these noblemen had been put to death under martial law and another 129 indicted for treason. Altogether about 800 people died as a result of this plot. There was great loss of cattle, land, and goods. The north was on the verge of starvation, and the Duke of Norfolk was committed to the Tower of London.

Elizabeth decided on a plan which she hoped would rid England of Mary's presence by handing her back to Scotland. Elizabeth sent her ambassador with her new proposal to the members of James' party at Stirling. Unfortunately the Queen's terms were unacceptable to the Scottish commission and Mary was to linger on in England. The terms were certainly severe, including the surrender of James VI for his mother's good behavior. The Scots could not abrogate the abdication forced from Mary in 1567, nor would they give up their king.

It was shortly following these stirring events that the Parliament of 1571 met. William Cecil, now Lord Burghley, took his seat in the House of Lords, thus demonstrating his secure place in Elizabeth's government. Burghley's departure from the House of Commons left an important vacancy in government leadership in Commons, a vacancy Hatton was eventually to fill.

Opening on April 2, the Parliament of 1571 was the first in which each member had to take the oath of the Act of Supremacy, which meant in effect that no member could be a practicing Catholic. This Parliament session had to deal with the leaders of the revolt and consider the papal bull of excommunication of Elizabeth, as well as collect money to pay the costs of suppressing the recent rebellion. The money had quickly been raised by forced loans and now needed to be repaid by a subsidy.

In addition to the legislation needed for taxation, the topic of religion would be a major part of this Parliament's concern. The papal bull and the Northern Rebellion had centered on religious doctrines. But despite the fright occasioned by these two events, Elizabeth continued to maintain her generally broad and lenient view of her subjects' religion. Following the publishing of the papal bull in June, 1570, the Queen had the Lord Keeper declare her continuing policy in the Star Chamber:

> Her Majesty would have all her loving subjects to understand that as long as they shall openly continue in the observation of her laws and shall not willfully and manifestly break them by their open acts, her Majesty's meaning is not to have any of them molested by any inquisition or examination of their consciences in causes of religion. . . ; being very loth to be provoked by the overmuch boldness and willfullness of her subjects to alter her natural clemency into a princely severity.[2]

Despite this statement of the Queen's tolerance, the Puritan Parliament was not in agreement with her. A well-organized group of Puritans in the House of Commons immediately began to discuss a number of bills dealing with reform of the Anglican Church in such matters as the wearing of surplices and the confirmation of children. That these parliamentarians were able to speak so long and freely was due to the lack of any expert political manager on the government bench. The bill which took the most time in debate concerned the requirements for church attendance, which, when passed by both houses, was vetoed by the Queen. In this display of personal rule Elizabeth refused to allow Parliament to force her to renege on her 1570 statement of tolerance. But this would not be the last Puritan campaign to attempt to force the royal hand.

With the religious reformers temporarily quelled the government legislation could now be introduced. This consisted of a treason act, an act to prevent papal bulls coming into the country, and an act for attainder of the northern earls. The treason bill concerned any attempt to harm the Queen or to write to the effect that she was not lawful Queen or that her religion was heretical. It was not severe enough for the Puritans in Commons, who wished to add a clause which concerned the succession. Anyone who claimed a right to the throne during the life of Elizabeth or anyone who aided such a person was to be declared treasonous. After many days of debate and committee work an amended bill was passed. This revision removed the retroactive penalty and stated that James' claim to the throne could not be disallowed by any action of his mother. This bill was obviously aimed at Mary Stuart's claim and her role as catalyst of the Northern Rebellion. Parliament subsequently was to attempt legislation more severe than this, still trying to include a penalty for James, which Elizabeth would never allow. The mildness of this complete bill is even more surprising as the government already had details of a new plot against the Queen, again implicating Mary Stuart.

Having completed most of its assigned work, Parliament was dissolved. The two houses had passed forty-six bills, many of them controversial in nature. Elizabeth was present to close this session, and having had the names of the bills read to her, she approved of forty-one of them. Following the speech of the Speaker, Sir Nicholas Bacon replied for the Queen, thanking the dutiful members for their work and subsidies. But there was criticism of those members who ". . . showed themselves audacious, arrogant, and presumptuous, calling her Majesty's grants, and prerogatives also, into question, contrary to their duty . . . and contrary to the express admonition given in her Majesty's name in the beginning of this Parliament."[3] These men were condemned for their folly in spending time in frivolous speech and ". . . meddling with matters neither pertaining unto them nor within the capacity of their understanding."[4] The discussion of religion was the most serious offense in the Queen's eyes. It was indicated that these matters should only have been debated in Convocation, an assembly of bishops and

clergy of the Church of England. Following these admonitions
the Parliament was dissolved, with Elizabeth no doubt hoping to
find a more amenable group in the next one.

The Queen almost certainly did not imagine that she would
have to burden herself with a new Parliament as soon as she
did. Some details of the new Ridolfi Plot had come into government hands during the last session and more was learned in the
fall of 1571. This conspiracy contained the same plans as the
earlier one—release of Mary Stuart, her marriage to the Duke
of Norfolk, and internal revolt, military aid from the Duke of
Alva, the death of Elizabeth, and the restoration of Catholicism
in England.

Details of this new conspiracy became known in England
just as the government was negotiating a rapprochement with
France involving the marriage of Elizabeth and the Duke of
Anjou. The plot was of Spanish-papal roots, organized by an
Italian, Robert Ridolfi, who had played a small part in the
rebellion in 1569. His grand plan was to combine the dissidents
of England with Spanish invasion forces with the intent to put
Mary and Norfolk on the throne of England. He was overconfident to say the least in believing that he could control the far-
flung areas involved in this plot—Brussels, Madrid, Rome, and
London—without the English government becoming aware of
his maneuvers. Ridolfi also misunderstood the attitude of the
English Catholics, believing that tens of thousands of them
would rise to follow Norfolk and his peers, whom he numbered
at more than sixty.

Ridolfi had no trouble gaining Mary's consent to his plan.
She provided him with letters for the Pope, Philip II, and Alva,
the commander of the Spanish forces in the Low Countries.
Norfolk resisted at first, remembering his recent time in the
Tower and quite rightly doubting that the matter could be kept
secret for long. Nevertheless he eventually allowed himself to
be persuaded by Ridolfi and the Bishop of Ross, Mary's representative in England.

With the conspiracy thus under way in England Ridolfi
went to Europe, where he met determined resistance to his

plans. The Duke of Alva, who had no confidence in Ridolfi, re-fused to be drawn into the grandiose scheme. Philip II relied upon Alva's judgement and Ridolfi's plan now lacked a neces-sary part, the Spanish invasion force. Alva quite correctly realized the increased danger for Mary that the news of such a plot would bring. He also feared an English reaction that would be an incentive for a French-English alliance, with possible French intervention in the Netherlands.

Evidence from many sources concerning the conspiracy was not slow in coming to the Privy Council. Written evidence was obtained when Charles Bailly was arrested at Dover with letters from Ridolfi to the Bishop of Ross, who was soon arrested. Men of the Duke of Norfolk were apprehended with money and letters for Mary's supporters in Scotland. The letters implicated Norfolk once again. He had been released from the Tower in August, 1570, and had given his solemn oath never to consider marriage with Mary or any cause relating to her, and had been placed under house arrest. Nevertheless he had continued to counsel Mary and to send her money, and finally consented to take part in this latest plot to release her, all in contempt of his oath of allegiance to Elizabeth. So he was soon rearrested and taken to the Tower on September 7, 1571. He also caused the arrest of his associates Arundel, Cobham, and Southampton.

In October the Bishop of Ross, under threat of torture, confessed the entire plot and provided the government with evidence to use against Norfolk. The only duke of England was tried for treason in January, 1572, and sentenced to death by his peers on January 16. Despite Norfolk's repeated acts of treason, his trial and sentence, Elizabeth hesitated to sign his death warrant.

Elizabeth was seriously ill in March, 1572, and for five days it was feared she might die. The dangers this possibility pre-sented to the government added to the Council's wish for a Parliament to add its pressure to the Council in the matter of Norfolk. These concerns finally broke down the Queen's resist-ance to the convening of a new Parliament.

Although it was later than usual in the year for a
Parliament to be called, the unusual conditions warranted this
action. It was generally considered too dangerous for a Parliament to be held in the summer months due to the everprevalent
plague. Nevertheless writs for the election went out on March
28, calling a Parliament to meet on May 8. As noted earlier
Hatton was returned from the county of Northamptonshire in
this election. There is no evidence of Hatton having taken an active part in the previous Parliament of 1571.

Hatton had been involved in the examination of Norfolk in
the early part of 1572 and had apparently treated the prisoner
kindly. On January 20 Norfolk wrote of Hatton to his son
Philip, the Earl of Surrey, that "Mr. Hatton is a marvelous constant friend, one that I have been much beholden to. Write to
him and seek his goodwill, and I believe you shall find him assured."[5] When it was believed that Norfolk was to be executed,
as the Queen had finally signed the warrant, Norfolk wrote this
letter which is included in the collection of Hatton's letters.

When the new session of Parliament met on May 8, members were told that the major business concerning them was to
devise some laws for the Queen's safety as rapidly as possible to
avoid being in London during the hot and dangerous months.
The members of Commons chose as their Speaker Robert Bell,
one of the effective members of the previous Parliament. Bell
gave a long speech when he was presented to the Queen which
made light of the uniqueness of a Parliament being called so
soon following another one. He mentioned the major reason for
the convening of Parliament and gave a hint as to the members' attitude toward Mary Stuart. He said, "This error was
crept into the heads of a number: that there was a person in this
land whom no law could touch."[6] His oration concluded, Bell
asked for the usual freedom of speech in the House of Commons without which he maintained no important matter could
be perfected. This was allowed but again with limitations placed
by Sir Nicholas Bacon, the Lord Keeper, responding for the
Queen.

In less than two weeks the Parliament produced two bills

through joint committees and debates in the full houses. Concerning Mary, the first bill involved her execution as a traitor, the second providing only for her exclusion from the succession. The members knew that Elizabeth preferred the second course of action for the time being, although they were horrified and shocked that the Queen would not consider the execution of Mary, which would remove the present danger to Elizabeth's life and the country's security. There followed much emotional debate, culminating in the decision to push ahead in spite of the Queen's attitude, with Thomas Norton shrewdly speaking for the death of Norfolk. In the face of almost unanimous opinion in favor of the execution of Mary, the Queen received a deputation from Parliament on May 26 and prohibited any further discussion of the matter.

An astute member of Commons, Robin Snagge, began at once to speak of the next culprit, the Duke of Norfolk. No prohibition had been placed on discussion about him and Snagge advocated cutting "off the heads of other [of] her enemies, which are already condemned by law. . . "[7] Other members spoke in complete agreement with Snagge and proposed a petition to the Queen. Sir Francis Knollys, the senior Privy Councillor in Commons, tried to stem the tide of accusation. Although he agreed with the members concerning Norfolk he explained that ". . . the disposition of Princes is rather of themselves to do such things than by way of pressing and urging."[8] He urged them to consider that "the execution will be more honorable to her Majesty if the doing thereof came of her free mind without our motion."[9] There were still those who spoke for immediate action but a vote on a final question to simply adjourn for that day was passed.

With pressure from Commons and the Privy Council to dispose of both Mary and Norfolk, Elizabeth realized that one sacrifice was necessary. Accordingly, on Monday morning, June 2, at 7 o'clock before Commons had assembled, the Duke of Norfolk was taken out to execution on Tower Hill.

Commons had one victory but they would be thwarted of another. Elizabeth was saddened by the death of Norfolk and refused to consider the execution of Mary. Commons had to be satisfied with a relatively harmless bill denying Mary's claim to the succession, making advocation of such a claim treasonous, and making provisions for Mary's trial by English peers if she ever again conspired to overthrow Elizabeth. An additional clause made Mary responsible for any rebellion for her cause and in effect made a lynch act against her legal in such an event. Although this act passed both houses, the Queen vetoed it at the conclusion of this session.

The Puritan members of the Commons had not ignored their religious goals in the emotional and dramatic debates over the life and death of Mary and Norfolk. On May 17 a bill was introduced which criticized the *Book of Common Prayer*, and pointed to the prosecutions of godly ministers for slight deviations from it. This act would have allowed the introduction of Calvinistic forms of service and eventually would have destroyed the Anglican Church. Even though the bill was subsequently modified, the Queen would not allow it to pass into law.

On June 30 Elizabeth went to the House of Lords to close Parliament. Although she would not accept the bill presented concerning Mary Stuart she promised Parliament an answer at the Feast of All Saints, November 1. However, this feast came and went and it was four years before a session of Parliament met again. This had been a frustrating period for Commons. They had achieved the elimination of Norfolk but had not succeeded in getting "an axe nor an act"[10] for Mary Stuart.

In addition to the continuing problem of Mary Stuart, Elizabeth's marriage proposals were to be a frequent source of tension throughout much of her reign. It is obvious that Hatton would regard the French negotiations, which covered so many years, with mixed emotions, as he might have hoped to marry Elizabeth himself. Earlier there had been talk of Elizabeth's marriage to the Duke of Anjou, the brother of the King of France, but the difficult problem of religion finally put an end to that speculation. Then Catherine de Medici suggested her third son, Francis, the Duke of Alencon, as an acceptable suitor, since he was less scrupulous than his brother concerning the practice of his religion. It concerned no one that he was over twenty years younger than Elizabeth. These negotiations were to drag on for ten years. Marriage or not, a useful alliance was concluded between the two countries in April, 1572. This was a mutual defense pact against Spain, and it diminished French interference in Scotland. In the same month the revolt against Spain broke out again in the Netherlands, and here the French saw an opportunity to interfere and possibly gain some territory. This Elizabeth could not countenance and Sir Humphrey Gilbert was sent over with instructions to keep the French out of the Netherlands ports.

In addition to these disagreements between allies the news of the St. Bartholomew's Day Massacre on August 24 stirred the Protestants of England to anger and fear. A Catholic uprising or attempt to murder Elizabeth was feared and the Protestant belief in a Catholic conspiracy to wipe them out gained credence. The English fleet put to sea and the coast defenses were activated. Elizabeth responded to this dangerous situation with calmness and restraint. She accepted the official version of the massacre from France but any French marriage in the near future became highly unlikely.

chapter three

Renaissance Man

Hatton's personal relationship with Elizabeth had by 1572 grown into a steady intimacy. Despite this he, as other courtiers, occasionally found himself in the Queen's bad graces. In 1572 he earned the Queen's criticism by his actions concerning the Duke of Norfolk. He wrote Elizabeth an interesting letter defending himself, superscribed with his personal mark illustrating his nickname given by the Queen. Hatton's name was "Lydds," the mark consisted of three triangles, and it is usually found on his letters to Elizabeth. All of the courtiers close to the Queen had been given such names; Leicester's was "Eyes." Because of this combination of names for her two most important favorites, it is possible that an allusion to Elizabeth's motto—*Video et Taceo*, "I see all and am silent"—is intended. The Queen also had other names for Hatton, namely "mutton," and "bellwether."

In this early letter of Hatton to the Queen he defended himself against her royal displeasure. She had complained that he was unthankful, covetous, and ambitious. In a long effusive letter Hatton denies these charges:

. . . the bitterness of my heart in humble complaints I trust you
will hear, for your goodness and justice sake.[1]

As for the charge of unthankfulness, Hatton stated:

. . . I speak the truth before God, that I have most entirely loved
your person and service; to the which, without exception, I have
everlastingly vowed my whole life, liberty, and fortune. Even so
I am yours. . . . This I supposed to have been the true remuner-
ation. . . Neither has the ceremony of thanksgiving any way
wanted, as the world will right-fully witness with me; and
therefore in righteousness I most humbly pray you condemn me
not. Spare your poor prostrate servant from this pronounced
vengeance.[2]

In answering the charge of covetousness Hatton claimed "I have
ever found your largess before my lack . . . if any other way it
appeared, let it be folly and not of evil mind that so I have
erred."[3] He also denied the criticism of ambition, declaring,
"God knows I never sought place but to serve you . . . if ever I
inordinately sought either honor, or riches, place, calling, or
dignity, I pray to God that he might swallow me."[4]

In this letter Hatton mentioned the "late great causes that
most displeased your nobles, as of the Duke of Norfolk and Q.
of S., the Acts of Parliament for religion,"[5] which he claimed
". . . were all laid on my weak shoulders."[6] He beseeched the
Queen not to believe evil tales told of him, ". . . be not led by
lewdness of others to lose your own, that truly loves you."[7] He
concluded with his prayer for her blessing.

The Queen's displeasure with Hatton at this time may also
have been occasioned by his possible interest in another lady. A
reference made by Mary Stuart in a letter intended for Elizabeth indicated that Hatton had been interested in Elizabeth
Cavendish, the daughter of the Earl of Shrewsbury, but had not
dared to court her because of the Queen.[8] Mary wrote from
Sheffield Castle where she was in the custody of the Shrews-
burys. The letter contained allegations supposedly made by
Lady Shrewsbury of the Queen's alleged immoral behavior with

several courtiers. Mary's letter was written in 1584 concerning earlier events and there is no way to verify its contents. The letter was never delivered to the Queen and remains in the Burghley papers. It is just possible that some hint of Hatton's slightly diverted attention may have become known to Elizabeth. If he had any thought of marriage this is the only known evidence of it. Unlike any other important Elizabethan courtier Hatton remained a bachelor, devoting his entire personal life to the Queen.

Gossip concerning Elizabeth's relations with Leicester and Hatton was not confined to the Court. Many rumors of their allegedly scandalous behavior reached the government from the common people. One of the conspirators in the Ridolfi Plot, who confessed to Leicester, quoted a Mr. Mather as saying that the Queen:

> . . . desireth nothing but to feed her own lewd fantasy, and to cut off such of her nobility as were not perfumed and courtlike to please her delicate eye, and place such as were for her turn, meaning dancers, meaning . . . my Lord of Leicester, and one Mr. Hatton, whom he said had more recourse unto her Majesty in her privy chamber than reason would suffer if she were so virtuous and well-inclined as some noiseth her.[9]

Also reported to Burghley by Archbishop Parker were comments made at Dover by a man questioned by the mayor there. This person uttered ". . . most shameful words against her, namely that the Earl of Leicester and Mr. Hatton should be such toward her as the matter is so horrible that they would not write down the words."[10]

A few weeks after the Dover report a perplexing letter was sent from Edward Dyer, a friend and fellow courtier, to Hatton. According to this letter a rival had appeared at Court, and the news caused Hatton to consider taking some action to regain or retain his place in the Queen's favor. The young Earl of Oxford was probably the interloper, as he was rising in royal favor at that time. The identity of the newcomer is not vital but Hatton took the situation so seriously that he considered reproaching the Queen for her lack of constancy.

Approached for advice on the matter, Dyer wrote a letter on October 9 to reinforce the advice he had given in his last discussion with Hatton. Assessing the situation, Dyer bluntly described the folly of upbraiding the Queen concerning her actions. Dyer advised Hatton to take care.

> First of all, you must consider with whom you have to deal, and what we be towards her; who though she do descend very much in her sex as a woman, yet we may not forget her place, and the nature of it as our Sovereign. . . . It is not good for any man straitly to weigh a general disallowance of her doing.[11]

Dyer shrewdly surmised that Elizabeth would dislike any such attitude on Hatton's part and would resent his attempt to influence her choice of courtiers, ". . . and so you may be cast forth to the malice of every envious person, flatterer, and enemy of yours: out of which you shall never recover yourself clearly, neither your friends."[12] Dyer's advice is to carry on as before with no appearance of jealousy, "For though in the beginning when Her Majesty sought you . . . she did bear with rugged dealing of yours, until she had what she fancied, yet now, after satiety and fullness, it will rather hurt than help you. . . ."[13] Following this course Hatton should be in Court with his loyal followers ready to take advantage of any change of heart on the part of the Queen. Dyer warned Hatton not to take the advice of any of his envious acquaintances who might urge him to foolish action merely to see how he would fare. These kinds of friends would urge him to action "to see whether the Queen will make an apple or a crab of you."[14]

This last passage and the passionate letters written by Hatton to the Queen give some basis for the earlier view that Elizabeth and Hatton were indeed lovers. If so the relationship was well-known to the Court, as Dyer's letter indicates several men who would be waiting to see the outcome of Hatton's response to the new rival. The more likely interpretation of all of these letters is that they were simply written in the exaggerated style of flattery most appreciated by the Queen. Hatton's letters excel in this quality, perhaps because he never married and centered his emotional life on the Queen.

Early in May, 1573, Hatton became seriously ill and this ended his period of disgrace with Elizabeth. She could never be severe with her favorites when they were ill. On May 11 in a gossipy letter from Court to his father the Earl of Shrewsbury, Gilbert Talbot wrote: "Hatton is sick still; it is thought he will very hardly recover his disease, for it is doubted it is his kidneys; the Queen goes almost every day to see how he does."[15] Talbot included a comment about Oxford's rise to favor, "if it were not for his fickle head, he would sure pass any of them shortly."[16] He also reported a plan of Leicester's to place Dyer in Hatton's place. "Now is there devices, chiefly by Leicester (as I suppose) and not without Burghley's knowledge, how to make Mr. Edward Dyer as great as ever was Hatton; for now, in this time of Hatton's sickness, the time is convenient."[17] How important Hatton's position was is indicated by this plan to displace him while he was too ill to be effective. It is understandable then that he was very depressed by having to go to a spa in Antwerp. He was given permission on May 29 to go due to his illness. Elizabeth's personal concern is evidenced by the fact that he was accompanied by Dr. Julio, the Court physician. Hatton took leave of Elizabeth on June 3 and kept himself fresh in her mind by a series of ardent letters.

Sir Harris Nicolas wrote, "The style of his correspondence is that of an ardent and successful lover, separated by distance and illness from a mistress, rather than that of a subject to his sovereign."[18]

On June 5 Hatton answered the letters he had received from the Queen. His letters illustrate his relationship with Elizabeth as well as his state of mind while ailing and far from the center of his world at Court. He was obviously distraught at being so far from Elizabeth and described her as ". . . the Sun that gives light unto my sense and soul."[19] He vowed never to go so far again even if it meant death. "I lack that I live by . . .

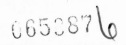

My spirit and soul agree with my body and life, that to serve you is a heaven, but to lack you is more than hell's torment. . . "[20] He begged pardon for such a tedious letter and promised to ". . . wash away the faults of these letters with the drops from your poor Lydds. . . Would God I were with you but for one hour. . . Passion overcomes me. I can write no more. Love me; for I love you."[21] He signed himself her "bondsman everlastingly tied."[22]

On June 17 Hatton wrote again of his health and distress at being away, mentioning the honor he had received because of the high regard for Elizabeth held by the government in Antwerp. He begged her ". . . forget not your Lydds that are so often bathed with tears for your sake. A more wise man may seek you, but a more faithful and worthy can never have you."[23]

In an undated letter but probably of this period Hatton wrote concerning his health. "Your Mutton is black; scarcely will you know your own, so much has this disease dashed me,"[24] he wrote. He again expressed his love for the Queen,

> It might glad you (I speak without presumption), that you live so dearly loved with all sincerity of heart and singleness of choice. I love yourself. I cannot lack you. . . you are the true felicity that in this world I know or find.[25]

Elizabeth had obviously sent him a gift of a jewelled branch, for he wrote, "The branch of the sweetest bush I will wear and bear to my life's end."[26] In an obvious allusion to a well-known rival, the Earl of Oxford, whose crest was a boar, Hatton wrote, "Reserve it to the Sheep, he has no tooth to bite, whereas the Boar's tusk may both rase and tear."[27] The Queen had been ill and Hatton promised to return if needed, regardless of his health. He concluded, "Humbly on the knees of my soul."[28]

On August 10 he wrote in response to a letter from the Queen that it had ". . . warmed my heart's blood with joys above joys."[29] His health had improved and he had achieved a ". . . contentment of mind you give me does most of all re-cure me."[30] He usually concluded with a phrase containing a play on the inintials *E.R.* for *Elizabetha Regina,* such as "All and *EveR* yours."[31]

While in Antwerp, Hatton received an interesting letter from a person who signed himself T.G. With it was a copy of a seditious book printed in Antwerp earlier that year. It was entitled *A Treatise of Treasons against Queen Elizabeth and the Crown of England.* The book refuted the allegations against Mary Stuart and the Duke of Norfolk and attacked Burghley and Sir Nicholas Bacon, the Lord Keeper. They were accused of planning to kill Elizabeth in favor of the Suffolk line descended from Mary, the younger sister of Henry VIII.

The accompanying letter to Hatton asked him to deliver this warning book to Elizabeth and assumed that he was of the Catholic faith, mentioning that he had been baptized in that religion and that he had remained in it for many years. This letter was sent by Hatton not to the Queen but to Burghley, where it remains among his papers at Hatfield.

After regaining his health and the good graces of Elizabeth, Hatton returned to London sometime before October, 1573. On October 11 a Puritan law student at the Middle Temple, Peter Brychett, who regarded Hatton as ". . . a willful Papist, and hinders the glory of God so much as in him lies,"[32] attempted to assassinate him. Luckily for Hatton Brychett did not know him by sight, and attacked John Hawkins, the famous sailor, by mistake while the latter was riding near Temple Bar. Sent to the Tower, Brychett murdered his jailer. He was soon executed by normal legal processes, although an outraged Elizabeth wanted a commission issued to execute him by martial law. Hawkins was severely but not fatally wounded.

Sir Thomas Smith wrote to Lord Burghley on October 15 that "It is said here that divers within this fortnight, both by words and writings Mr. Hatton has been admonished to take heed to himself, for his life was laid in wait for."[33] Hatton had probably been reared as a Catholic and certainly the first school he went to, St. Mary's College at Oxford, was Catholic at the time, being headed by William Allen. Allen as a Cardinal in exile,

would be castigated as England's most villainous traitor by
Hatton in 1589. Whatever his private religious convictions the
sheer compulsion of events forced Hatton to take action against
both Catholics and Puritans as he remained loyal to the Queen's
policies in the difficult years ahead.

As the Queen's right-hand man not only in politics and
religious policy, but also as a courtier, Hatton had acquired
many offices. In his various positions as Gentleman Pensioner,
Captain of the Guard, and finally as Vice-Chamberlain, Hatton
usually accompanied Elizabeth on her annual progresses around
the country. In the summer of 1573 the progress went to
Canterbury where the Queen and her retinue were rather
reluctantly entertained by Archbishop Matthew Parker, who
wrote to Burghley that he would be able to find places for him
and the Earls of Leicester, Sussex, and Hatton, only if they
brought their own furnishings.

In August, 1574, Hatton accompanied the Queen to Bristol.
A full description of the entertainment there was published in
1575 by Thomas Churchyard, one of the writers of the many
speeches given there before the Queen. The book, called *The
First Part of Churchyard's Chips*, was dedicated to Hatton. Churchyard was an ex-soldier trying to make a living by writing verses
early in the year, Hatton had put him to work on the entertainment for the Bristol visit. Later works of Churchyard were also
dedicated to Hatton, and in the 1580s the writer acted as Hatton's information agent in Scotland.

Other writers befriended by Hatton were Barnabe Riche
and Dr. John Dee. A soldier as well as writer, Riche had served
in the Netherlands and Ireland, where he was Hatton's agent.
He dedicated three books to Hatton: *Alarm to England* in 1578
which described the state of affairs in Ireland; *The Strange and
Wonderful Adventures of Don Simonides, A Gentleman Spaniard*, in 1580;
and *The Second Tome of the Travels and Adventures of Don Simonides*, in
1584. Riche also provided one of the best descriptions of
Hatton's house at Holdenby, which he visited in 1581.

Dr. John Dee, better known than Churchyard or Riche,
dedicated one of his works to Hatton. As an astrologer, chemist,

mathematician, cartographer, and writer on naval affairs, Dee shared Hatton's interest in the Atlantic voyages of Francis Drake and other seamen. In August, 1576, Dee dedicated to Hatton his book on *British Monarchy* or *Hexameron Brytannicum:*

If private wealth be leaf and deere
To any wight on British soil
Ought public weale have any peers?
To that is due all wealth and toil.

Whereof such lore as I of late
Have learned, and for security,
By godly means to guard this state,
To you I now send carefully.[34]

Hatton remained an influential patron of Dee and invested in Drake's many voyages as well as enterprises of other adventurous seamen.

Dee and Hatton were involved in a task of a different sort in April, 1578. The Queen had a painful toothache and those around her were much concerned as to how to deal with it. No one wanted to tell her that the tooth must come out; the physicians refused to carry such an unpleasant message to the Queen. Burghley wrote to Hatton on April 21 concerning the matter, "If my coming hither might either diminish her pain, or be thought convenient, I would not be absent," but he is sure that ". . . you are careful by the physicians to provide the remedy, which is said to be only the withdrawing of some one tooth. . . ."[35] Dr. Dee was then called in and at the Queen's command he conferred with her physicians. Their decision was for Dr. Dee to travel to Europe to consult with other doctors as to the proper remedy. He was allowed one hundred days for this journey, but long before he returned, Elizabeth had finally submitted to the removal of the offending tooth. She followed the heroic example of Bishop John Aylmer of London who allowed one of his teeth to be removed to show the Queen how simple it was.

As Hatton rose in fame and fortune he required better housing in keeping with his status. In 1575 he began to pressure Bishop Cox of Ely for a lease of his London house, Ely Place. The bishop made a strong defense of the property, which belonged to the bishopric rather than to him personally. Part of Elizabethan lore is the Queen's supposed answer to this bishop when he demurred in fulfilling her favorite's wishes:

> Proud Prelate! I understand you are backward in complying with your agreement, but I would have you know, that I who made you what you are can unmake you; and if you do not forthwith fulfill your engagement, by God I will immediately unfrock you.[36]

The authenticity of the letter is in doubt due to many versions of it to be found, but that royal pressure was being used in this case seems to be demonstrated by a letter from Lord North to this same Bishop Cox in November, 1575. North was himself trying to get some of Cox's land at this time. North pointed out to Cox that the Queen was very displeased with him and still remembered that he had refused her a lease on some desired land in that summer. The Queen had recommended Mr. Hatton ". . . to be the keeper of your house in Holborn, a man much favored of her Highness, and much esteemed of the best and honest sort of England."[37] The Queen had put her request for his house very reasonably, so reasonably that:

> . . . it is more than marvellous to know with what face you could deny her. Well! this last denial being added to her former demands, has moved her Highness to so great disliking as she purposes presently to send for you, and to hear what account you can render for this strange dealing toward your gracious sovereign.[38]

North continued with a description of all the Queen had done for Cox coupled with the bishop's obvious ingratitude. As he wrote on, the threat became clear:

. . . My Lord, it will be no pleasure for you to have her Majesty
and the Council know how wretchedly you live within and without your house, how extremely covetous, how great a grazier,
how marvellous a dairyman, how rich a farmer, how great an
owner. It will not like you that the world know of your decayed
houses, or the lead and brick that you sell from them, of the
leases that you pull violently from many, of the free land which
you wrongfully possess, of all the copyholds that you lawlessly
enter into, of the tolls and impost which you raise of God's good
ministers which you ceaselessly displace. You suffer no man to
live longer under you than you like him. And to be flat, you
nourish the ill and discourage the good.[39]

This strong indication of the problems facing him if he continued in his obstreperous way left Cox with no alternative but
to accede to the Queen's wishes. In March, 1576, Hatton got a
twenty-one year lease of the bishop's palace at Holborn in
London. His lease included the large gatehouse, the first court-
yard, the stables, the long gallery with the rooms above and be-
low it, fourteen acres of land, and the keeping of the garden and
orchards. Hatton's rent for these portions of the bishopric's
lands was one red rose, ten loads of hay and ten pounds a year.
Hatton was to repair the gate house, making it into a dwelling.
The bishop retained access through the gatehouse, privileges of
walking in the gardens, and gathering each year twenty bush-
els of roses. Hatton was not satisfied with a short-term lease on
this establishment and almost immediately agitated to acquire
the freehold, which he soon achieved. Hatton was to live at Ely
Place, known as Hatton House, the rest of his life, to entertain
the Queen there, and to die there. Even today the area is known
as Hatton Gardens although the only remaining building of that
period is the tiny chapel of St. Etheldreda.

Hatton was in residence at Ely Place by June, 1577. When
the bishop died in 1581 the see remained vacant for eighteen
years. The Queen took the revenues and Hatton continued to
hold the land and dwellings until his death in 1591. After that a
long legal battle ensued over the rights of his heirs and those of

the Crown and diocese. The disputes were not settled until
1697. The palace then remained with the bishops of Ely until
1772 when it was sold to the Crown.

Hatton was deep in debt at this time, as were most courtiers. Hatton was aided to the extent of fifty pounds by the
Queen's orders to Burghley to apply this sum to his debts.[40] In
January, 1576, Hatton had further grants of land made to him
by the Queen, with more being granted in August. In December
Elizabeth settled 400 pounds a year upon him for life. In the following years he was also granted more lands and made Keeper
of Corfe Castle in Dorset.

This latter property endowed Hatton with many rights and
perquisites. As Corfe Castle is situated on the peninsula called
the Isle of Purbeck, Hatton acquired the titles of Lord Lieutenant and Vice-Admiral of the Isle with this grant. He had rights
to "wreck of the sea," right to hold courts, and right of hunting
red deer. That Hatton prized these privileges is shown by his
suit in 1583 against men he accused of poaching his deer.[41]

In 1576 Hatton also acquired the position of Keeper of the
Castle of Brancksea to the north of the Isle of Purbeck, in the
middle of the Poole Harbor. He also apparently kept aware of
affairs in the united towns of Weymouth and Melcombe Regis
nearby. A letter to William Pitt, mayor of Weymouth, from
Lord Thomas Howard, a younger son of Norfolk, showed
Hatton's great influence with Elizabeth. Concerning a bill which
he wished to back in Parliament, Howard stated his belief that
nothing could be done due to the fact that he expected ". . . that
Sir Christopher Hatton's countenance and credit would work
much against it, and surely would overthrow it when it should
come to her Majesty's hands. . ."[42]

Although Hatton was in debt, his rise to status and power
required the ownership of a country house in which to entertain the Queen. In 1577 Hatton bought the recently completed country house of Kirby in Northamptonshire from the
heirs of Sir Humphrey Stafford. He admitted at the time that he
already owed 10,000 pounds. Not satisfied with this new house,
he almost immediately began plans to build another at his an-

cestral manor of Holdenby, a house on a grand scale worthy of his position and of receiving the Queen. A letter to Sir Thomas Smith demonstrated how Hatton saw these mansions in relationship to Elizabeth. He wrote, "I am going to view my house of Kirby, which I never yet surveyed; leaving my other shrine, I mean Holdenby, still unseen, until that holy Saint may sit in it, to whom it is dedicated. . . "[43]

Holdenby was one of the greatest of Tudor houses to be built. If we except Wolsey's Hampton Court, it was to be exceeded in size only by Audley End, built thirty years later. It was truly magnificent on a scale unprecedented up to that time. Kenilworth, though possessing a better view, was old and inconvenient, whereas Holdenby was all new and the last word in modern planning and decoration.[44]

So vast was the Holdenby estate that Hatton had a license to empark 300 acres of level land, 200 acres of meadow land, and 70 acres of pasture. The house was situated on a hill overlooking the landscape of trees, ponds, deer park, and gardens.

The house itself was probably designed by John Thorpe and the plans still survive in the Soane Museum, London.[45] The facade was especially fine and on a scale not before attempted; it was 220 feet long. There were many courtyards opening off from one another, giving a long vista of plantings and statuary. A hint of some of the grand furnishings can be gained from the survival of the tapestries on the theme of Gideon. Lady Elizabeth Shrewsbury purchased these tapestries after Hatton's death in 1591 for her new house of Hardwick Hall. She paid about 326 pounds for them from Hatton's heir, receiving a rebate of five pounds to cover the cost of replacing the arms of Hatton with her own. Hatton's golden hind was easily converted into a Shrewsbury stag by adding antlers and the new arms were then painted on cloth and sewn over Hatton's.[46] These great Elizabethan treasures are now on display in the long gallery at Hardwick Hall, although they have faded. The tapestries, woven in Brussels for Hatton, are all that remain of the splendid furnishings which decorated the shrine to Elizabeth erected by Hatton in Northamptonshire.

Burghley had created his house of Theobalds for reasons similar to Hatton's. A former generation had lavished money on churches or castles to flaunt their success and to create memorials for future generations. The Elizabethans, in contrast, built great houses. These dwellings were shrines not only to their owners' status but to the glory of Elizabeth as well. Thus Hatton wished to leave his magnificent Holdenby unseen, uncontaminated, until the Queen should grace it with her presence. To her courtiers Elizabeth was indeed the Faerie Queen, the center of their world.[47]

Hatton was anxious for Burghley's opinion of his masterpiece. Burghley visited the still unfinished house in August, 1578, and complimented Hatton on its magnificence and symmetry. He especially mentioned the spectacular new feature, a grand staircase leading to the great chamber above the ground level.

Another friend and fellow courtier, Sir Thomas Heneage, reported to Hatton after visiting Holdenby: "If the praise of a house consists in the seat, beauty, and use, both within and without, Holdenby shall hold the preeminence of all the modern houses I have known or heard of in England."[48] Holdenby was finished by 1579 and Barnabe Riche, visiting it in 1581, wrote:

> . . . for the bravery of the buildings, for the stateliness of the chambers, for the rich furnishings of the lodgings . . . and for all other necessaries apertinent to a palace of pleasure, it is thought by those who have judgment, to be incomparable and to have no fellow in England that is out of her Majesty's hands.[49]

The very grandeur of Holdenby and Theobalds actually led to their disappearance. So obviously fit for royalty, they appealed to Elizabeth's successor, James I, who acquired them by various trades and payments. They were still favorite royal residences at the beginning of the civil war in 1642. In 1647 Charles I was held for a time at Holdenby as a prisoner. In 1650 Holdenby was sold to Adam Baynes of Yorkshire. Unable to maintain the status of such a great estate, Baynes pulled down all but a small portion of the house and sold the materials to builders. The magnificence of the Elizabethans did not adapt easily to habitation by lesser men. One great arch of Holdenby remains standing in the fields near Gretton, Northamptonshire.

In addition to his great interest in building Hatton personified the ideals of Renaissance men in other areas as well. He was especially interested in music. As early as 1576 he was able to provide an envoy from the Spanish Viceroy in the Netherlands, the Sieur de Champagny, with an exceptional entertainment including ". . . a concert of music so excellent and sweet as cannot be expressed."[50] The concert was given at the Queen's manor of Eltham which was in Hatton's keeping. On another occasion he entertained ambassadors at his house with solemn music while he provided gambling for the underlings. His love of music may have stemmed from his famous love of and skill in dancing.

William Byrd, the famous musician, dedicated to Hatton his "Psalms, Sonnets, and Songs of Sadness and Piety" in 1588. In the dedication Byrd mentioned Hatton's love of music and Byrd hoped that " . . . these poor songs of mine might happily yield some sweetness, repose and recreation unto your Lordship's mind, after your daily pains and cares taken in the high affairs of the Commonwealth."[51] In the next year Byrd claimed that ". . . since the publishing in print of my last labors in music, divers persons of great honor and worship have more esteemed and delighted in the exercises of that art than before."[52] Byrd's works were printed by Henry Bynneman, a protege of Hatton's and carried Hatton's cognizance. Hatton and Byrd may have met much earlier when *Tancred and Gismund* was acted in 1567 at the Inner Temple, for Hatton wrote the fourth act of that play and Byrd composed for it the song "Come Tread the Path."

Often alluded to as a "lover of learned men," Hatton was a patron of many writers, some of whom have been mentioned. One of the great Elizabethan poets, Edmund Spenser, honored

Hatton in the first dedicatory sonnet prefacing the *Faerie Queen*:

> Those prudent heads that, with their counsels wise,
> Whilom the pillars of the earth did sustain,
> And taught ambitious Rome to tyrannize,
> And on the neck of all the world to reign,
> Oft from those grave affairs were wont to abstain.
> With the sweet lady muses for to play,
> So Emnius, the elder Africain,
> So Maro often did Caesar's cares allay,
> So you, great Lord! that with your counsel sway
> The burden of this kingdom mightily,
> With like delights sometimes may eke delay
> The rugged brow of careful policy
> And to these idle rhymes lend little space
> Which, for their title's sake, may find more grace.[53]

As Vice-Chamberlain Hatton also had a part in support of drama. He helped the Lord Chamberlain in the production of the many masques and spectacles which were so much a part of court life. The Lord Chamberlain was patron of a company of actors. Hatton and this official defended the players against the Corporation of London which was dominated by Puritans. One of the chief arguments used by the Puritans against the play-houses was the ever present danger of plague spreading among crowds of people. In 1584 the Corporation gained permission from the Privy Council to close two theatres despite the opposition of Hatton and the Lord Chamberlain. All the Privy Council, ". . . saving my Lord Chamberlain and Mr. Vice-Chamberlain . . . "[54] agreed to the pulling down of the two theatres, the *Theatre* and the *Curtain*.

Hatton also patronized the well-known artist of the day, Cornelius Ketel. A portrait of Hatton owned by one of his present-day descendants was probably painted by Ketel.

Hatton played to the full the role of an exalted personage in the Elizabethan age. He was an amateur author himself and a patron of writers and musicians and geographers. He carried to extreme lengths the contemporary fashion for building great country houses much beyond his ability to pay for them. He also took part in and planned the elaborate ceremonials of jousting, tournaments, and progresses which were such an important part of the Elizabethan highlife.

chapter four

A Leader Emerges: The Parliament of 1576

It was fortunate for Mary Stuart that Parliament had been prorogued on June 30, 1572. Had it been in session when the news reached England of the massacre of the French Protestants on St. Bartholomew's Day, it would have been very difficult for Elizabeth to resist national pressure to execute Mary. This French action only served to reinforce the fears and worries of the Puritans concerning the "monstrous and huge dragon"[1] still alive in their midst. Even though Parliament was not sitting there were still complaints against the Queen of Scots.

Burghley wrote to Mary's custodian that "all men now cry out of your prisoner," describing her as "that dangerous traitress and pestilence of Christendom."[2] Under this pressure Elizabeth agreed to a plan to send Mary back to Scotland with the understanding that she would be quickly executed by the Protestant Lords of the Congregation. This plan collapsed and Elizabeth was able to continue her policy of delay when after two months no calamity had befallen her or the kingdom. She continued to prorogue Parliament through the years until the bill against Mary had died of inertia.

41

A similar peace had fallen on the other controversial topic of the 1572 Parliament, reform of the Anglican Church. John Whitgift, then Master of Trinity College in Cambridge, and Thomas Cartwright, a Puritan leader, joined literary battle with well-worded tracts for several months. A "Second Admonition to Parliament" was published after Whitgift had responded to the first "Admonition." Cartwright then answered this tract. It was at this time that the unbalanced Puritan Peter Brychett stabbed John Hawkins, mistaking him for Hatton. This action, following Brychett's attendance at a Puritan lecture, infuriated the Queen and discredited the Puritans. The government was not slow to seize this handy opportunity to enforce religious conformity.

Puritanism had found a stalwart leader in Thomas Cartwright, who was convinced that the structure of Anglican Church government, as well as that of the Catholic Church, was in contradiction with that of the early Christian church. He contended that archbishops should be removed and bishops return to teaching and preaching. Ministers he believed should be elected by the congregations.

It was obvious to the Anglican establishment and the government that Cartwright was dangerous to the religious settlement as it stood. Accordingly Cartwright lost his Lady Margaret professorship of divinity at Cambridge University in 1570, and his fellowship in 1571. In 1573, following his critical writings, the government took the opportunity to urge the ecclesiastical commission to issue a warrant for his arrest. Cartwright then fled abroad, although the Presbyterian prophesyings went on. No further action on the part of the government was taken until after the 1575 Parliament and the topic, although not absent from the debates of that session, was somewhat muted due to Cartwright's flight.

The session of Parliament convened on February 8, 1576 with no formal opening, as it was being held on prorogation. The members got to work at once. Hatton played a much more active and important role in this Parliament. He was now one of the Queen's principal representatives. Apparently he was also able to find seats for such followers as Francis Hawley, his deputy Admiral of Corfe Castle, and Francis Flower, who was residing in Hatton's house at Ely Place. It was Flower who in 1591 would compose the long epitaph for Hatton's tomb in St. Paul's. Hatton's secretary Samual Cox also sat in this Parliament as did Richard Swale, a friend of Hatton who was to be invaluable to him when he became Lord Chancellor. Swale sat for Hatton's first seat, the borough of Higham Ferrars, Northamptonshire.

The very first speaker, Peter Wentworth, began a long narration of the dangers he saw threatening the liberty of speech in the House of Commons. One of his major criticisms was that when members were debating controversial topics messages were often brought into the house prohibiting the members from free discussion. He declared that when the members heard rumors that the Queen disliked a certain bill, they were prevented from having a truly free debate. Hatton was certainly one of the most frequent bearers of messages from the Queen, a role he continued to play while he sat in Commons.

Wentworth was allowed to continue his speech until he directly criticized the Queen's treatment of bills concerning Mary Stuart. Then he was stopped and sent out of the chamber. A committee including all the Privy Councillors and other officials of the house was appointed to interrogate Wentworth that same afternoon. The decision of the committee was reported the following day by Sir Francis Knollys who read to the members the list of "violent and wicked words"[3] used about the Queen. He advised that Wentworth be committed to the Tower. After some debate this was done following Wentworth's censure by the house at the bar. He was put in charge of the Lieutenant of the Tower to be kept a close prisoner.

Wentworth remained a prisoner for just over a month. On March 12, two days before the end of the session, Hatton brought a message from the Queen to the house expressing to them her "great good acceptation" of their "temperate usage" of Wentworth. Hatton reported that the Queen was sending Wentworth back to the house, being "absolutely persuaded that his speech proceeded of abundance of zeal towards her"[4] Hatton reported that the Queen had "not only forgiven but also forgotten the inconsiderateness of the same, and did accept him to be as good grace and favor as ever she did before."[5] Then Hatton spoke on his own to describe the great blessings they had all received from the Queen. He suggested and "it was agreed, that the Speaker in all our names should render her Majesty thanks for the same."[6]

Following a long moralizing speech by Sir Walter Mildmay, Chancellor of the Exchequer and Privy Councillor, Wentworth was again brought to the bar of the house, where he acknowledged his faults, begged the Queen's pardon, and was received into the house again. But Wentworth had been forced to miss nearly the entire session of Parliament.

With Wentworth removed from the first day of the session the necessary business could begin. On February 10, Sir Walter Mildmay made the opening speech on the major topic of money. To introduce his subsidy bill he made a speech concerning Elizabeth's stewardship — how she had found the realm, and how she had restored and preserved it, and how it stood now. He mentioned many government expenditures and gave some account of how the money was spent, although he pointed out that the Queen did not have to render such account. He ended with an appeal to the house to give aid to the Queen. Mildmay got a subsidy and a tax on towns and counties speedily granted.

Elizabethan finance was continually strained. In essence the Crown was to subsist on ordinary revenue from customs and Crown lands. In the first twelve years of the reign this source provided about 200,000 pounds a year, increasing to about 300,000 pounds in the last decade. The Queen was expected to support herself, her Court, and the government from this source. War and fortifications were to be funded from extraordinary revenues which Parliament was to provide by tax bills. Taxation was still regarded as abnormal for the country as a whole. Over the whole reign parliamentary taxation averaged less than 80,000 pounds a year and for the first thirty years it only averaged 50,000 pounds per year. Therefore Elizabeth's total average income until 1588 was not more than 250,000 pounds a year.

Despite the fate of Wentworth religion was not shunned in this session. A petition was introduced and accepted by Commons asking for reforms and order in the Church. The petition specified that abuses had developed, such as blaspheming of the Lord's name, licentious living, an increase in the number of heretics, schismatics, and atheists, and the increase of Papists. This petition was read in the House of Commons on March 2 and presented to the Queen by six Privy Councillors. The Queen regarded the petition as the proper form for subjects to use in requesting action from their sovereign and she accepted this one and acted upon it.

The house also listened to a speech by John Croke, who hoped the Speaker, while thanking the Queen for her goodness, would present their wish for her speedy marriage to safeguard the realm. A committee was formed at once to consider how the Speaker should phrase this request. On March 14 Speaker Bell did include a petition to the Queen to marry saying that he "desired her Majesty to consider in what case we should be left if her Majesty should die without issue; to remember that she was mortal."[7] He described how happy the country was to be governed by her line, that she was the last one, and he hoped she would "as shortly as conveniently might be, to incline herself to marriage."[8] He concluded with a presentation of the subsidy.

In an unusual move Elizabeth adjourned the completion of the proceedings to the next day, perhaps to compose an answer. On the following day Lord Keeper Bacon replied to the Speaker. He stated that the Queen "takes your proceedings in the Parliament, both in the beginning and in the midst and in the ending, so graciously and in so thankful part . . . I am sure I were not able to set forth this point according to her Highness' desire nor to the worthiness of it."[9] The Queen regarded the petition for marriage as coming from "their inward affections and benevolent minds."[10] The Speaker included in his oration the

Queen's understanding of the need for marriage and her gratitude for the willingly given subsidy.

Following the royal assent to the bills, Parliament was
prorogued and the members had begun to leave when Elizabeth began to speak. She made a reflective and involuted speech
considering her good fortune in having such subjects and giving
credit to God for the country's safety. On turning to the topic of
marriage and the succession she said, "I know I am but mortal,"
but advised her listeners to consider the present situation and
"good heed be taken that, in reaching too far after future good,
you peril not the present. . ."[11] She concluded, "I trust God will
not in such haste cut off my days, but that, according to your
own desert and my desire, I may provide some good way for
your full security."[12] With this promise, Parliament was dissolved, not to reconvene for five years.

In the latter part of 1576 Hatton seems to have been depressed and not in the best of health. On August 26 he wrote
from Northamptonshire to Burghley:

> I will love and honor you as your virtue binds me . . . I have
> scarcely had health, Sir, since my coming to this country . . . I
> most humbly thank your Lordship for your loving and grave
> counsel. I will return to my bounden and dutiful service ever so
> soon as possibly I can; your honorable wish for the stay of my
> poor house is that I pray to God for, but yet it does not so please
> Him that it may come to pass. . .[13]

Hatton took the occasion to write of his pleasure in having
Burghley's eldest son Sir Thomas Cecil with him, saying, "I take
great comfort. He is faithful, good, and honest. I pray God you
may live long to joy in him and his."[14]

Whatever the reason for Hatton's malaise he was back at
court in his usual favored position for New Year's events and
received from the Queen "in gilt plate, 400 oz.,"[15] while the
other favorite, Leicester, received only a bowl of silver gilt
weighing 100 ounces. The gifts did not flow in one direction.
Hatton usually gave Elizabeth elaborate jeweled creations
which were undoubtedly extremely costly. His first gift in 1561

Portrait of Elizabeth with a feather fan, c. 1575, said to be her favorite portrait. National Portrait Gallery, London.

A miniature of Sir Christopher Hatton as Lord Chancellor by Nicholas Hilliard. Victoria and Albert Museum, London.

Mary, Queen of Scots. National Portrait Gallery, London.

Sir Christopher Hatton as Chancellor of Oxford University, c. 1588.
National Portrait Gallery, London.

A miniature of Sir Christopher Hatton framed by the symbols of the
zodiac. Northampton Museums and Art Gallery, Northampton,
England.

On the reverse side of the miniature
is a representation of Time and Fate.

Redrawn by J. A. Gotch, printed in his *Old English Houses,* London, 1925, by permission of Methuen & Co. Ltd., Publishers, London. Original plans in manuscript of John Thorpe in the Soane Museum, London.

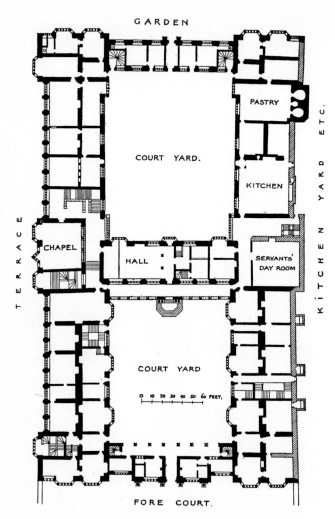

PLAN OF HOLDENBY HOUSE, NORTHAMPTONSHIRE

had been ten pounds in angels (coins) in a red silk purse.[16] As Hatton's career soared, so did the fantasy of his jeweled concoctions given to delight the Queen. In 1571 he gave her a "fairy jewel . . . fully garnished with rubies and diamonds, and flowers set with rubies with one pearl pendant and another in the top. . ."[17] In 1572 he presented ". . . one flower of gold, containing a great emerald, fully garnished with diamonds, rubies, and three pearls pendant, the one bigger than the rest."[18] The description of one more creation will suffice to demonstrate the intricacy of these gifts which were presented to Elizabeth each year by Hatton:

> a carcanet and a border of gold; the same carcanet containing seven red roses of gold, in every of them very small diamonds and in the top a garnet and eight troches of mean pearls, four in every troche, and fourteen pearls pendant, being loose; and the said border containing twenty-four red roses of rubies garnished with a very small diamond in every of them a garnet and pearl pendant. . .[19]

This elaborate creation, difficult to visualize, was given in 1578.

In 1577 honors and favors came to Hatton in abundance. He was appointed Vice-Chamberlain of the Queen's Household, given a seat on the important Privy Council,[20] and knighted by the Queen at Windsor. From the year 1577 Hatton took an increasingly important part in government affairs. His primary role was that of Queen's spokesman in the House of Commons, and secondly he was in charge of implementing the Queen's religious policy of moderation. One of his first acts in religious matters was to become the patron of John Aylmer, who was Archdeacon of Lincoln in 1577. Hatton was responsible for Aylmer's appointment as the Bishop of London. It was probably expected that the Archdeacon would assist in controlling the Puritans in the vital diocese of the capital, although Aylmer himself seemed to have planned action against Puritans and Catholics alike. Due to these actions Aylmer was to earn severe criticism from Hatton.

There is some evidence for Hatton being Catholic at this time or at least being very sympathetic towards Catholics. This may well have been a reflection of the Queen's leniency in that regard. It is apparent that some Puritans regarded Hatton as their enemy. Certainly Peter Brychett had that opinion of Hatton. There is a document in the state papers reporting a conversation between Zachary Jones of Cambridge and an unknown Gifford who had information about some recently imprisoned Catholics. Gifford's opinion was that although some Catholics were in prison, there were more important people who favored Catholics whom he described as "almost second in the realm," and among them Sir Christopher Hatton. He stated that Hatton had made Aylmer Bishop of London in order to quell the Puritans.[21] This may well have been what the Queen expected.

Aylmer's actions taken on his own initiative got him into trouble with both the Queen and Hatton as his letter of May 28, 1578, demonstrated. Aylmer thanked Hatton for his "mild and calm manner of expostulation which you used with me in our last conference."[22] Aylmer had been ill for six days and wished to apologize for his actions. He again mentioned Hatton's consistently mild manner and stated that many petitioners remarked on his unusual amiability. Aylmer wrote,

> I will not forget to commend both to God in my prayers and to all men in speech, that rare conquest that by great wisdom you have had over your affections, which by the motions of flesh and blood most needs have been set on fire marvellously against me, had not a natural instinct of heavenly and Christian philosophy and wisdom quenched the flame thereof. . .[23]

Aylmer asked Hatton's advice on his future actions. His own opinion is stated in his question,

> whether it were not the safest and profitablest way to cut off (even as her Majesty termed it) and to correct offenders on both sides which swerve from the right path of obedience, which I set up as the mark to aim at, purposing to discipline both the Papist and the Puritan in anything wherein . . . they be indifferently touched.[24]

Hatton's supervisory powers were indicated by Aylmer's remark that "It was her Majesty's pleasure that I should understand her mind by you in these things."[25] He asked for Hatton's advice on future actions, and "then you shall see that I shall so guide the helm as the ship shall keep the best and safest course."[26]

The inference that Aylmer had angered Hatton by action against Catholics, possibly friends of Hatton, is confirmed in the next letter from the bishop to Hatton. The Queen was also furious with him and Aylmer wrote a very sycophantic letter. Aylmer begged to have word from Hatton that "your displeasure is appeased"[27] and that "I might have some little inkling that her Majesty stands my gracious Lady."[28] Without these assurances the bishop wrote that he could have no joy in himself, no courage to do his duties, which are "more than the burthen of Atlas."[29] He mentioned his devoted service and the tract he had written in 1559 favoring government of women—an answer to John Knox's "First blast of the trumpet against the monstrous regiment of women," as deserving of recognition. Aylmer's state of mind is evidenced by his sad description of himself. "I study with my eyes on my book, and my mind is in Court," and "I eat without stomach, I sleep without rest, I company without comfort, and live as one dead."[30] Hatton's part in gaining Aylmer his position is alluded to as Aylmer pointed out that Hatton aided other bishops daily, and "will you throw down him whom you have set up yourself?"[31] The bishop concluded with pleas to Hatton to "forget and forgive me" and with promises of ever more gratitude.

On the 17th of June, 1578, Aylmer found himself again explaining his actions to Hatton. A certain John Roper had had his house searched by the bishop's authority and some vestments were found in it. Roper was probably a relative of William Roper who lived at Eltham Park where Hatton was keeper of the Royal Park and had married the daughter of Sir Thomas More.[32] Roper had complained to the council. Aylmer denied that he had any part in this affair and stated that "I was so free from the rifling of his house, that upon the receipt of your letters, I despatched a pursuivant at midnight to call them back."[33]

Aylmer was grieved by this matter as "I was blamed in the hottest time of the paroxysm between you and me."[34]

It is not surprising to find that Aylmer was petitioning Hatton in 1582 for support in gaining a bishopric rather less volatile and dangerous than that of London. The marginal note on Aylmer's letter to Hatton indicates that it was the bishopric of Ely that Aylmer had in mind. The bishop indicated that some bargain had been struck between them, "The time draws nigh for you to remember your honorable promise to me, that I may likewise perform mine to you."[35] He added a point of argument that Hatton could use, "the crookedness of the old tired father"[36] who needs release from his service. Aylmer's rather unpleasant personality came through with his plea for advancement when he wrote:

> Sir, if you will have her Majesty well served, your own creature somewhat in life preserved, and your credit uncracked for commending me first, and now retaining me still in state of reputation by this increase of advancement, put to your hand resolutely.[37]

In spite of his bargain with Hatton, Aylmer did not gain the See of Ely. The Queen kept it vacant for eighteen years following the death of its bishop, Richard Cox, who, had been forced to cede his house to Hatton.

In the summer of 1578 Elizabeth took her Court with her on a long perambulation of the countryside. She traveled from Lord Compton's house at Tottenham to Burghley's mansion at Theobalds and finally went to Leicester's manor at Wanstead. Leicester was absent taking the waters at Buxton spa for his health. On July 9 he wrote to Hatton from Buxton of his improving health and sent his regrets that Elizabeth did not find him there to receive her. "I hope now, ere long, to be with you [Hatton], to enjoy that blessed sight which I have been so long kept from. A few of these days seem many years. . ."[38]

Elizabeth had been well-received at Wanstead by Sir Philip Sidney, who had written a dramatic entertainment for presentation to her. It was called "A Contention between a Forester and a Shepherd for the May-Lady," and was printed at the end of Sidney's *Arcadia*.[39]

On this progress Elizabeth also visited Cambridge University. Burghley was the Chancellor of the university and had been asked by the presiding Vice-Chancellor how he should receive the many noblemen and gentlemen traveling with the Queen. Burghley advised him to provide gloves with a few verses to accompany them for the courtiers. He named the Earls of Leicester and Oxford and the Lord Chamberlain as those to whom gifts should be given, adding that "for himself he could spare·them, so that if Mr. Vice-Chamberlain might have a pair with some verses, it should do well to conciliate his good-will, being a lover of learned men."[40] The gloves were duly presented to those nobles when the university delegation visited the Queen at Audley End on July 26. Gabriel Harvey, a scholar and poet, wrote a volume of Latin verses for the occasion. He divided the fourth book into three sections, dedicating the first part to the Earl of Oxford, the second to Hatton, and the third to Sir Philip Sidney.[41]

That Hatton was in touch with the most important workings of government is evident by the frequent letters to him from Francis Walsingham, Secretary to the Queen. On June 3, 1578, Walsingham wrote concerning the threat of an adventurer, Thomas Stukeley, who with the backing of the Pope had landed in Ireland with several hundred Italians in an attempt to raise a rebellion there.

Walsingham was confident that "so weak an instrument as Stukeley" would not be able to prevail "against a Prince of her Majesty's power, armed with the goodwill of her subjects in that Realm. . ."[42] This expedition had been disastrous from its inception and was destroyed at Smerwick by the English forces led by Lord Grey de Wilton, a distant relative of Hatton.

In the summer of 1578 Walsingham was sent with Lord Cobham to the Netherlands in an attempt to negotiate the end of hostilities there. This mission was a failure and the English soon returned. On his way to the Netherlands Walsingham

wrote on June 16, 1578, to Hatton concerning Scottish affairs.
With the Regent Morton recently overthrown, the government had been placed in the hands of the young King James VI,
who had sent an emissary to London to acknowledge "with
most grateful remembrance, Queen Elizabeth's benefits towards him."[43] This new circumstance led Walsingham to believe that a firm alliance could be made with Scotland. From
Gravesend Walsingham wrote to Hatton urging him to advise
the Queen:

> to further a straiter knot of amity between this crown and Scot-
> land. I find her Majesty in that point, to rest upon some nice
> terms; which I hope, by your good persuasion, will be removed.
> Surely, Sir, if her Majesty let slip this opportunity, I fear we
> shall estrange Scotland from us unrecoverably; and how peri-
> lous that will be, I leave to your good consideration.[44]

But affairs were not moving the way Walsingham wished
and on June 17 he wrote to Hatton concerning his fears that
"the matter (by letting slip the opportunity of time, which over-
throws all good causes), is so far out of frame, as I can hardly
conceive any hope of good issue. . ."[45] On June 23 he expressed his despondency concerning Elizabeth's attitude towards Scotland and himself:

> . . . .Sorry I am to see by your letters her Majesty's indisposi-
> tion to deal effectually in the Scottish causes. If the parties
> presently repaired thither be sent away with evil satisfaction,
> farewell the quietness and good days of England. If I stood (as I
> hear I do not) in her Majesty's good graces . . . I would then dis-
> charge my duty plainly to her. . .[46]

In this letter Walsingham was also depressed about the
situation in the Low Countries and Elizabeth's dilatory policy
there. From Antwerp he wrote, "I am greatly grieved, considering the perilous state this country stands in, to find her
Majesty so strangely affected as she is."[47] He feared that if the
Queen withdrew her support from the Low Countries, the

French would be masters there. "Seeing the peril so great, and knowing how careful you are of her Majesty's honor and safety, I do assure myself that you will take the matter in such sort to heart as the cause imports."[48]

Walsingham had been using Thomas Heneage as a messenger to deliver these letters and to explain more details to Hatton. On June 27 Walsingham wrote to Hatton concerning the Scottish diplomacy since "I perceived the message sent you by Mr. Heneage . . . seemed somewhat dark unto you. . ."[49] Hatton was advised to procure letters sent from the English negotiator in Scotland for study. Walsingham deplored the Queen's hesitation to enter into an alliance with Scotland while Mary Stuart lived. Walsingham reviewed the many reasons why Elizabeth should have no such scruples, including the rebellion Mary had inspired in England. "There is no cause why her Majesty should now make a conscience to strengthen herself with the amity of Scotland. Such scruples of conscience are rather superstitious than religious."[50]

Walsingham believed that Scotland was the "postern-gate to any mischief or peril that may befall to this Realm,"[51] and it behooved the Queen to guard it. He viewed the Scots as a proud people who once their friendship had been refused would not offer it again. He concluded the discussion of the Scottish policy saying, "I am afraid I am too troublesome to you in this matter of Scotland; and, though the country be cold, I can neither think nor speak of it but in heat."[52]

Although Elizabeth continued to maintain her flexible informal policy towards Scotland, James VI was never to become an enemy. He was too concerned with keeping his place in the succession to the English throne to jeopardize it by offending the English Queen.

The situation in the Low Countries continued to be a threat to the security and peace of England. Despite the dire warnings of what would happen if she refused to send assistance to the Protestant rebels there, Elizabeth continued to temporize. She was determined to avoid commitments that would hamper her freedom of action. Watchfulness and flexibility were her strengths. She was a master diplomat, realist, and opportunist, willing to procrastinate rather than to commit her government to irrevocable actions. This policy was the despair of her ministers such as Walsingham and William Davison, both of whom wrote frequently to Hatton on this topic in the hope he could have some influence on the royal policy.

The Queen's policy was nonintervention while at the same time she hoped to influence events favorable to England. This eventually led to the appearance in the Low Countries of the French Duke of Anjou, ostensibly to aid the rebels against Spain. Anjou's plan was to wrest the Netherlands from Spain, unite them with England by marriage with the Queen, and create a Protestant federation to counterbalance the power of Spain. Elizabeth had no doubt contributed to this situation by her dilatory tactics and refusal to send aid to the Netherlanders, who were hard pressed by Spanish forces.

Hatton was much involved with these serious problems of the Low Countries and he constantly received lengthy letters from the delegation sent there with hopes of fending off the French presence. Davison was most concerned on July 22 about the presence of the Duke of Anjou at Mons. He reported that Anjou had written to many towns and states declaring that his sole reason for being there was to aid them.

> The Duke, to blear the eyes of this people, has already put himself in action . . . he gives out that he does nothing but with the liking and knowledge of her Majesty, whose name and credit he uses as a cloak to color his ambitious and deceitful pretext.[53]

Walsingham wrote to Hatton on July 23. He sent a detailed oral report by the bearer of the letter as well. He discussed the intentions of William, the Prince of Orange and leader of the Netherlands, who most naturally was quoted as "that, though he gave out to the contrary, he had rather enjoy the country himself, than either French, Spaniard, English, or Almayne."[54] Walsingham was sure that the Queen would have acquainted Hatton with the material from his letter to her and asked Hatton to burn the letter.

Sir Amias Paulet, the English ambassador in Paris, also wrote to Hatton concerning the impact of Anjou's presence in the Netherlands. He too feared the true intention of the Duke. "If you in England can bridle the French ambition, all will be well; many here being of opinion that your own means will make you able, and that the necessity of the time will constrain others to yield to your counsel."[55]

Walsingham's actions and attitude concerning the Low Countries brought him the Queen's disapproval. He wrote to Hatton most frankly, vindicating his own conduct. He thanked Hatton for letting him know the causes of the Queen's displeasure and hoped that he could explain to her at his return.

> . . . yet in the mean time it is an intolerable grief unto me to receive so hard measure at her Majesty's hands, as if I were some notorious offender. Surely, Sir, it stands not with her Majesty's safety to deal so unkindly with those that serve her faithfully. . . . If there has lacked in us either care, faithfulness, or diligence, then were we worthy of blame. Thus, Sir, you see, as my good friend, I am bound to open unto you my grief . . . And so, with most hearty thanks for your faithful, friendly dealing towards me, I commit you to God's good keeping. Written with a weary hand and a wounded mind.[56]

It was not surprising to Walsingham or Davison that on August 13 a treaty was signed between Anjou and the Dutch states giving the Duke a joint share in the military command. Walsingham undoubtedly did not put much stock in the Duke's assurance that he would do nothing without the Queen's consent. His own problems with the Queen continued and he wrote to Hatton on August 16 thanking him for his support at Court:

> Sir, Your most friendly standing in my defence where it might do me most good, and your comfortable letters written to my poor, comfortless wife, do minister unto me just cause to acknowledge myself greatly beholden unto you, praying you to make account of me as of a most constant and assured friend in all fortunes.[57]

Concerning the intentions of Anjou in the Netherlands there is a letter in the Hatton collection from the Earl of Sussex to Elizabeth written on August 28, 1578. Sussex had been approached by one of Anjou's agents with a detailed set of proposals. One part dealt with marriage, ". . . it rested in your Majesty to dispose of him therein as should please yourself."[58] The other part assured the Queen that he would be guided by her wishes in all actions in the Low Countries.

Sussex explained the motives and plans of Anjou. The Duke was determined to become great either by marriage or possession of the Netherlands, or both, and that in order to have him out of France his mother Catherine de Medici and his brother Henry III would help him in his ambitions. If he were thwarted in both of these means to glory he would then turn his troops over to Don John of Austria, also fighting for possession of the Netherlands, and seek martial glory on the opposite side. Sussex concluded:

> This foundation being thus laid, it is fit to consider the commodities and incommodities of every of them; that is to say, of the marriage, of the alienating of the Low Countries, and of the French assisting Don John.[59]

After a discussion of the advantages to be gained from such a marriage, the personal side of which he politely left to Elizabeth and God, Sussex summarized the situation:

> . . . by your marriage you shall give law to France, Spain, and the Low Countries, England, Scotland, and, in effect, to all Christendom; you shall settle your state surely at home; you shall be strongly defended abroad; you shall be in estimation over all the world; you shall have a husband as a servant and defender of all your causes present; you shall be like a serpent in the sight of evil, and like a dove in the sight of the good; you shall be the peacemaker to all Christendom; your fame shall exceed all other Princes that were ever in Europe; and God will bless you as His own chosen vessel both in this world and in the world to come.[60]

Surely never were so many happy conclusions expected from any marriage! Sussex did admit there might be some adverse points to this proposal though which might "be fittest to be left to your Majesty . . . as you may best judge of them . . . and be such as my heart trembles to think of them, and I pray God never live to see them."[61]

Sussex did face up to recognizing them, however. First there was the problem that Elizabeth might not like the idea of marriage, which would lead to a discontented life. Eight other detailed points were devoted to the perpetual problems which might arise if Elizabeth married a foreign prince. Problems of politics, religion, and trade were reviewed. He feared the effect on England if the husband should become king of his own country, the problems of dividing a possible child's inheritance, the danger to Elizabeth herself if her husband were deceitful, and always the problem of the difference in religion between husband and wife.

Walsingham meanwhile continued to write to Hatton and deplored the fact that the Queen could not be persuaded to actively aid the Protestants in the Netherlands. He understood that "no man could treat more effectively than yourself."[62] Walsingham's conclusion was that when dutiful councillors cannot prevail with a Prince, "it is a sign that God has closed up her heart from seeing."[63]

The situation did appear desperate in the Netherlands. There were four armies encamped there. In addition to the armies of William of Orange and the Spanish, John Casimir (son of the Elector Palatinate, supported by English money) was present, and lastly Anjou's forces. As the financial support of these groups weakened, chaos ensued, and the soldiers began to live off the land. Plague added a further grim touch to the scene. In September Walsingham and the delegation were ordered back to England.

But Elizabeth's luck held. Events did not turn out so disastrously for England as Walsingham had predicted. Philip of Spain had become tired of pouring money into the country. Early in 1578 Philip had sent Bernadino de Mendoza to England to reopen the embassy, which had been closed since the expulsion of the last ambassador in January, 1572, for complicity in the Ridolfi Plot. Don John of Austria, appointed to lead the Spanish forces in the Netherlands by his half-brother Philip, was having no success. After a military defeat in August, 1578, Don John died of a fever in October. Walsingham's comment at this fortuitous turn of events was, "God deals most lovingly with her Majesty in taking away her enemies."[64] Elizabeth had begun a new tactic, the weaving of a second web of courtship diplomacy around Anjou in order to divert him from causing trouble elsewhere.

Sir William Cecil, Lord Burghley, holding his staff of office as Lord Treasurer. Portrait attributed to Marcus Gheeraerts the Younger, 1585. National Portrait Gallery, London.

The Armada Portrait of Elizabeth, painted by George Gower, c. 1588. National Portrait Gallery, London.

Sir Christopher Hatton, Lord High Chancellor of England, 1589.
National Portrait Gallery, London.

The "Phoenix" portrait of Elizabeth, c. 1575-80, probably painted by Nicholas Lilliard, and so named because of the jewel on her bodice. National Portrait Gallery, London.

Hilliard miniature of Queen Elizabeth. Victoria and Albert Museum, London.

Detail of a full length portrait of Elizabeth, painted to commemorate her visit to the home of Sir Henry Lee at Ditchley, Oxfordshire. National Portrait Gallery, London.

chapter five

Marriage Diplomacy

While Walsingham was predicting calamitous results from the Queen's diplomatic policies, she was coming around to a new course. Being a female ruler did have certain advantages and Elizabeth made excellent use of them. At this critical time she revived the marriage negotiations with the Duke of Anjou. At first the object of this renewed courtship was to draw off the ambitious Duke from meddling in the Netherlands, but as the wooing became more intense a seriousness developed which was entirely missing from earlier such maneuvers.

This courtship policy had been used intermittently since 1570 when the first Duke of Anjou had been proposed as a husband for Elizabeth. He had been too ardently a Catholic to accede to the requirements of an English consort and eventually his brother, then the Duke of Alençon, had been suggested. It was this Alençon who had succeeded to the title of Anjou who was now the suitor. Since most sources continue to designate this younger man as Alençon, the practice will be continued here.

For practical reasons then, the second French courtship of

Alençon began. The first episode had dragged on for several years and finally faded out in 1576. Walsingham, on hearing of the new policy, expressed his disgust to Hatton, "I would to God her Majesty would forbear the entertaining any longer the marriage matter. No one thing has prcured her so much hatred abroad as these wooing matters, for that it is conceived she dallies therein.."[1] Walsingham was no doubt correct in his view of the Queen's dallying tactics, but this policy had many potential advantages—blunting Alençon's ambitions in the Netherlands, possible provision of an heir to end the succession problem and that of Mary Stuart, strengthening the Anglo-French Alliance, and perhaps affecting Philip's actions in the Low Countires. If a bit of dallying could achieve these diplomatic successes the Queen would thereby secure both domestic and foreign peace.

The chief obstacles to this marriage were the Queen's age and Alençon's religion, but neither seemed insurmountable. Elizabeth was forty-five at this time, and the Duke twenty years younger. This disparity of ages added an element of risk to the proposed marriage. In the matter of religion the Duke was no zealot and had been willing to support the Huguenots in France and the Protestants in the Netherlands.

The courtship began with the arrival of Alençon's agent Jean de Simier in January, 1579. He was a favorite of Alençon's and was described as "a most choice courtier, exquisitely skilled in lovetoys, pleasant conceits, and court-dalliances."[2] Simier was as good as reputed and carried on a gallant flirtation so necessary to the Queen's vanity. Simier's gifts which he judiciously distributed at Court also won him some adherents. Simier so delighted the Queen that she bestowed a royal nickname upon him. He became her "monkey" and Alençon her "frog." Simier gallantly raided the Queen's bedroom to steal her nightcap to send as a love token to Alençon. The gallantry, masques, and wooing went on all winter with the Queen becoming more fond of Simier and the prospect of marriage. Once she even visited Simier in his bedchamber before he was completely dressed. She obviously reveled in this love game and thoroughly enjoyed the attentions from Simier as well as the disgruntlement of her own courtiers.

While the courtship by proxy proceeded Burghley was dealing with the business side of the proposed marriage, where problems were to develop. The articles of marriage included these provisions: Alençon would be crowned king immediately after marriage; he would share jointly with the queen the authority to grant all benefices, offices, and lands; and he would have an annual income of 60,000 pounds during marriage, and during the minority of any child.

These articles were the subject of much heated discussion in the council of March and April of 1579. Two factions developed, Walsingham leading those in opposition, and Burghley and Sussex those who approved. Walsingham's group brought up the subject of the Queen's age. To have a first child at forty-six he argued would be extremely dangerous. Much discussion followed. On July 8 Simier was given permission to arrange for the Duke's visit.

At the news that Elizabeth had signed the passport for Alençon's visit Leicester sulked off to his manor at Wanstead, feigning illness. Elizabeth was never able to ignore her favorites when they might really be ill, so she visited him there. While Leicester was away Simier was fired upon in the palace gardens. Three weeks earlier Simier had been riding in the royal barge with Elizabeth, Hatton, and Leicester when a shooting had occurred and most people assumed that Simier was the intended victim. After the second shooting Simier concluded that Leicester was behind the actions because of his dislike of the marriage plans.

Simier was in possession of the greatest secret at Court which he now disclosed to the Queen in retaliation. He had discovered that Leicester had been secretly married in September, 1578, to Lettice Knollys, the widow of the Earl of Essex and daughter of Sir Francis Knollys. This infuriated Elizabeth. For while Leicester had been moping around as a forlorn widower, counselling the Queen against marriage to anyone but himself, he had contracted a marriage with the lovely Lettice.

In her initial fury Elizabeth ordered Leicester to the Tower, but Sussex intervened to spare her own dignity, despite his dislike of Leicester. Leicester was instead sent to a tower in Greenwich Park and was said to be taking a physic and not able to see anyone. He was allowed to retire to Wanstead after a few days. Lettice, whom the Queen hated and called the she-wolf, was ordered never to appear at Court.

There is a remarkable letter from Hatton to Leicester which indicates the news of Leicester's marriage might not have been entirely a surprise to Elizabeth. Hatton wrote it on June 18, 1578, from Hampton Court. Hatton described the Queen as being in continual and great melancholy, "the cause therof I can but guess at, notwithstanding that I bear and suffer the whole brunt of her mislike in generality."[3] He reported that she "dreams of marriage that might seem injurious to her; making myself to be either the man or a pattern of the matter."[4] Hatton tried to reassure her that since she had made no commitment to marry anyone therefore, "by any man's marriage she can receive no wrong."[5] Hatton concluded, "I am not the man that should thus suddenly marry, for God knows I never meant it. By my next I think you shall hear more of this matter; I fear it will be found some evil practice."[6]

The marriage mentioned is unlikely to be Elizabeth's as the proposals for the French negotiations were not begun until August. It was believed by many that Leicester and Lettice had secretly married many months before the announced official date in September. It is possible that Elizabeth had heard some rumors of Leicester's intentions. Elizabeth was certainly taxing Hatton with her suspicions and insinuating that he was no better. There had indeed been some rumors written by Mary Stuart to her representative in Paris that Hatton was secretly married.

When Elizabeth's "frog," Alençon, presented himself at Greenwich on August 17 she was favorably impressed. He was an accomplished courtier and wooed her in a suitably romantic manner. She no longer worried about his pockmarked face or unimpressive height. He was in England for twelve days, a period which the romantic couple spent alone, as Alençon was supposedly there in secret. When Alençon left he was convinced that he had won Elizabeth's heart and sent her a flower of gold with a frog on it. Simier remained to finish the contractual arrangements.

But the council and the English people were not so pleased with events and it soon became apparent to Elizabeth that she faced stiff opposition to what was perhaps her only real chance for a marriage. It is impossible to know if she really did wish to marry Alençon. In those seemingly happy courtship days her attitude fluctuated daily. In any event it became clear that the opinion of the people in England would make such a marriage an untenable choice.

In August the Puritan John Stubbs expressed the fears of many Englishmen in a forceful tract entitled "The Discovery of a Gaping Gulf Whereunto England is like to be swallowed by another French Marriage if the Lord forbid not the Bans by letting her Majesty see the sin and Punishment thereof." Stubbs pointed out the danger of the marriage both to the Protestant religion and the person of the Queen. He maintained that the Queen was too old for marriage and at a very dangerous age for childbearing, which certainly was not flattering for the Queen to read! Stubbs described the French courtier as not only a debauched person but "the old serpent himself in the form of a man come a second time to seduce the English Eve and to ruin the English paradise."[7] He described Alençon as "an imp of the crown of France" trying to "marry with the crowned nymph of England" and his wooing as "unmanlike, unprincelike."[8]

Elizabeth was predictably furious. Not only had she personally been insulted but a foreign power had been slandered. Without consulting anyone, Elizabeth had Stubbs, together with his printer and publisher, arrested, tried, and condemned to lose their right hands and be imprisoned. Elizabeth ordered a long proclamation to be read to the City companies and the clergy. A preacher was sent to read a speech at St. Paul's Cross, praising the government and the Queen's steadfast religion. The people applauded his praise of the Queen but did not like to hear his criticisms of Stubbs. The printer of Stubbs' tract was pardoned but the other two had to suffer.

Stubbs endured the barbarous punishment most stoically and when his right hand was severed he lifted his hat with his left, cried "God Save the Queen," and fainted. There was a deep silence from the large crowd of spectators. Stubbs was taken to prison where he later appealed to Hatton, who had taken an active part in his prosecution. Stubbs described the

> . . . round dealing which your Honor used at my first examination, and your severe shifting out of that fault which bred me all my woe, doth not, for all that, affray me from coming to your Honor with some hope of pitying me, now fallen into the extremity of affliction.[9]

Stubbs maintained that although his imprisonment had been long and his small estate almost wiped out, "yet is the continuance of her Highness's indignation more to my heart's grief, and pinches me more nearly than all the rest."[10] He reminded Hatton that he had been loyal to the Queen even at the execution of the sentence and that he had been an obedient subject. He begged Hatton's mediation for the sake of his wife and child. Elizabeth eventually realized that she had overreacted. Stubbs was released and later received at Court. In 1581 he became a member of Parliament.

Even after this severe example denunciations continued to resound from many pulpits against the unpopular marriage. Hatton worked with the Bishop of London to influence a pro-government speech of a minister. The Bishop wrote to Hatton on September 28 regarding the outcome.

> I thank God your travail and mine with the preacher hath taken good effect; and the instructions which you ministered unto him were very zealously . . . and profitably remembered . . . that it hath much stayed the heady, confirmed the good and the wise in the great good opinion conceived generally of her Majesty, and somewhat quenched the sparks of murmuring, misliking, and misconstruing of matters of State, wherewith the seditious libeller had kindled many of the busier sort.[11]

The Bishop gave the details of the preacher's remarks about Stubbs, who was accused of meddling in matters "both above his reach, and that did not belong to him." It was an evil conceit that caused Stubbs to distrust the care of the Queen in religious matters "which she had both carefully and happily maintained ever since her entry into her most gracious reign." These remarks about the Queen seem well received but "they utterly bent their brows at the sharp and bitter speeches which he gave against the author of the book."[12]

Bishop Aylmer concluded that anyone who spoke against a foreign prince was considered a patriot by the English, and that they were so dazzled by Elizabeth that when they looked at another they considered him a monster. Aylmer reported that he was aware of discontent in the countryside and had called many into account and would call more but that he feared the effect upon his own diocese of London if they were aware of the widespread disaffection. The Bishop ended by apologizing for the length of time it had taken him to "gather any liklihood of the people's and preachers' humors."[13]

Parliament was to have met on October 20 but the Queen prorogued it, as the last thing that she wished was to have the members of Commons enter into an organized debate on the marriage plans.

In early October Elizabeth asked the Privy Council to give her their advice concerning the marriage. They conferred and debated for several days, on one day not stirring from the room from eight a.m. until seven p.m. Walsingham was absent but it was well known what his vote would have been. Of the twelve present seven, including Leicester and Hatton, were against the marriage and five, under Burghley's leadership, were for it. They decided to question the Queen as to her wishes. Their lack of instant support and approval for the marriage infuriated Elizabeth. She had convinced herself of the wisdom of the contract, possibly aided by her hurt pride over Leicester's marriage. But she wished to act with the support of the Council which would share the responsibility for the decisive move. She had also expected Burghley to carry the day in the Council.

Later the Council did word an appropriate statement giving

their unanimous approval "if so it shall please her." This was
not sufficient support given the continuing outcry in the country against the foreign Catholic match. And so although the discussions with Simier continued about terms Elizabeth declared
a moratorium on the conclusion of the contract. By the end of
the two months she had apparently decided to let the matter
fade away. Leicester was back in favor and with Hatton's added
presence Elizabeth began to lose interest in Alençon and Simier.
But the correspondence continued to some extent and the
project could always be revived if the Catholic menace appeared
perilous.

Although enjoying renewed security in his serving of the
unmarried queen, Hatton's life was very busy. He required ever
more sources of revenue to support his standard of living. In
late 1578 he had incurred the disapproval of Burghley regarding a royal grant and wrote to the latter explaining the
situation:

> . . . My poor case hath no defence; I ask, because I want; my
> reward is made less . . . I do my service with diligence and
> travail . . . and therefore in charitable goodness I should not in
> any reasonable cause be so contemptuously rejected . . . I seek a
> debt which grew to me through her Majesty's reward; but your
> Lordship's direction will lead me to further charge, without any
> comfort of her Majesty's care and goodness in the gift she made
> to relieve me. . .[14]

Hatton had served Elizabeth well. He particularly earned
her approval and concern for his personal safety in helping to
quell a riot in Hertfordshire. In April, 1579, there was a distur-
bance in the village of Northam Mins apparently concerning the
enclosure of a common. Hatton was in the area with Privy
Councillor Sir Ralph Sadler and the two of them were successful in ending the riot. Leicester wrote to congratulate Hatton on
his success and report the Queen's approval:

> . . . in how gracious part she takes this your careful and
> diligent service done for the dispersing and quieting of these re-
> bellious and tumultuous persons . . . Her Highness hath been

informed of the great pains you have taken, of the wise and
discreet orders which you have prescribed, as well for the es-
tablishing of good and assured ways to prevent any further in-
convenience by these lewd people. . . [15]

Leicester conveyed to Hatton Elizabeth's wish that he rest
before returning to Court.

Francis Walsingham also wrote to Hatton about the riot.
Hatton's other nickname of "mutton" is used in this letter as
Walsingham quoted the Queen, "she willed me to let you understand, that, upon report made unto her of an outrage committed upon certain of Sir John Brockett's sheep, she feared greatly
her Mutton, lest he should take some harm amongst those
disordered people."[16]

In his influential position both as Councillor and as a royal
favorite, Hatton was approached by a wide variety of people for
aid and intercession with the Queen. Edmund Grindal, the
Archbishop of Canterbury, had been sequestered by royal orders for countenancing certain prophesyings of which Elizabeth disapproved. Grindal wrote to Hatton on May 22, 1579,
petitioning his mediation and asking for

> . . . your intercession to her Majesty for my restitution to
> her favor and execution of mine office. I trust that the remem-
> brance of my two years' restraint of liberty in this my old and
> sickly age will move her Majesty to some consideration over me,
> . . . by your honorable and good mediation.[17]

But even Hatton could not change Elizabeth's views about
Grindal. The Archbishop remained sequestered until very near
the end of his life.

As mediator Hatton was called upon in the argument
between the often troublesome Earl of Oxford and Sir Philip
Sidney. This socially disruptive dispute arose over the bad
manners of Oxford, who ordered Sidney off a royal tennis
court. When Sidney refused to leave abusive words were flung
back and forth and Sidney eventually challenged Oxford. The
Queen remonstrated with Sidney for acting in such a manner to
such a high personage. Feeling he had the right of the matter,

Sidney refused to submit and withdrew from Court to Wilton House in Wiltshire, the home of his sister, the Countess of Pembroke.

Sidney wrote to Hatton on August 28 thanking him for his efforts to heal the rift but maintaining ". . . howsoever I might have forgiven him, I should never have forgiven myself if I had lain under so proud an injury as he would have laid upon me . . . let him therefore, as he will digest it . . . let me crave still the continuance of my happiness in your favor and friendship. . ."[18]

Hatton was also sought as a mediator by Dr. Laurence Humfrey, Dean of Gloucester, the Queen's Professor of Divinity and President of Magdalen College. He wrote to Hatton on November 13 to complain of an infringement of his privileges. The Mayor of Gloucester had arrested a gentleman of Leicester's household within Humfrey's precinct, had beaten and imprisoned the servants who were trying to prevent the arrest, and had commited various other outrages, all violations of Humfrey's privileges within his college grounds. "And because I know your Honor of yourself well inclined to the preservation of right, and have of your goodness accepted the patronage of our Church, I beseech you let the matter be examined, either by your Honor or by the ecclesiastical commission. . ."[19]

Hatton's nephew William Newport, son of his only sister, was a student at Magdalen. Dean Himfrey also wrote to Hatton of Newport's progress and thanked Hatton for his promise of preferment:

> . . . which as it is before desert of my part, and of small acquaintance with me or my qualities, so must I account the more of your goodness; hoping, for the one, you shall not find me unmindful, and touching the other, upon further knowledge and experience you shall have no cause to repent for any good word or deed bestowed upon me. . .[20]

The promotion mentioned may be Humfrey's appointment in October, 1580, as Dean of Winchester.

Hatton's reputation for fairness was demonstrated by a letter from Henry Howard, the younger brother of the executed Duke of Norfolk. Disparaging remarks had been made concerning an action by Howard which he denied. He states:

> . . . it grieved me not a little to perceive by your most courteous and honorable lines that any man could deal so hardly and unjustly with me as to report unto a person of your quality how forward I had been in preferring discourtesy so near a place . . . so can I not esteem this as the least of many of your most friendly favors towards me, that you, whom I desire to satisfy in any doubt, vouchsafe to call me to mine answer before you yield to your unjust reports. . .[21]

Henry Howard and his nephews were implicated in later plots revolving around Mary Stuart and while in prison they wrote to Hatton.

Not all of the letters to Hatton were those of appeal or praise. The Lord Mayor of London, Sir Nicholas Woodroffe, wrote on February 11, 1580, a rather curt letter refusing to grant the freedom of the City for a Hatton dependant, Richard Bateman. It seems the courtiers had been overusing this privilege, much to the detriment of the citizens of the City. The Mayor had just recently granted this privilege for Hatton's use and was now expressing reluctance to repeat it:

> . . . the rather that we lately granted one in like sort at your request, and, upon our letters signifying the hardness of those grants to our Citizens, you were contented so to esteem the matter, and to promise forbearing to press us with the like; it may please you to to take in good part that in our consideration we have not thought convenient for the City to increase the number of freemen with admitting Bateman into that number.[22]

Hatton's compassion and willingness to intercede for those in the Queen's bad graces is shown by his aid to Margaret Countess of Derby. She was first cousin once removed to the Queen and, as almost all blood relatives of the Tudors, had a difficult time. She had married Henry Stanley, fourth Earl of

Derby, by whom she had four sons. She wrote to Hatton because she said he was the only person at Court who had shown
any sympathy for her plight.

The Countess had apparently been imprisoned and wrote
to Hatton thanking him for her release:

> . . . Your Honorable dealing hath bound me so much unto
> you as it is impossible you should make a gentlewoman more be-
> holding unto you than I am; for the liberty which I have at-
> tained . . . I do freely acknowledge to have only proceeded . . .
> by your honorable mediation. You are the sole person in Court
> that hath taken compassion on me. . .[23]

She continued to describe her ill health and financial problems
as well as her depression at Elizabeth's displeasure: "as I am
now, I live dying, and death were much better welcome unto me
than life, if I must be still in her Highness' misliking. . ."[24]

Hatton in his turn had to sue for favors from such as Lord
Burghley to whom he wrote on July 22, 1580, asking for
support for the renewal of his wine import monopoly. This
grant was due to expire in the next year. Hatton wrote:

> , , , I have therefore humbly moved her Majesty for the re-
> newing of my lease; in the which I earnestly beseech you of your
> good favor towards me . . . I humbly pray your Lordship that
> you will advertise me your good pleasure herein, and give me
> leave to go on with the suit. . .[25]

Burghley had apparently aided Hatton substantially in his
serious financial matters, ". . . I do acknowledge with all thank-
fulness the recovery of my poor estate, in effect all entirely
ruined, to have grown out of your great goodness and favor towards me. . ."[26]

Away from Court and reporting about a sick servant,
Hatton once wrote to the Queen another of his respectfully
intimate letters. In September, 1580, he wrote that his servant
who had been "more than half-dead" was recovering "through
your most princely love of his poor Master, and holy charitable
care, without respect of your own danger. . ."[27] He told her

that an "unpleasant and forward a countenance is grown in me through my absence from your most amiable and royal presence." He vowed to "live and die in pure and unspotted faith towards you for EveR."[28] Hatton remained firmly committed to "an ideal of womanhood, harboring a strange passion that could not be reciprocated."[29]

Kept away from Elizabeth by fears of infection from his ailing servant, Hatton wrote to his old friend and confidant Thomas Heneage on September 11, 1580. He sent his message and the gift of a ring for Elizabeth, to be delivered by a healthy bearer. He wrote most frankly of his feelings:

> . . . that I may daily know . . . the true state of our Mistress, whom through choice I love no less than he that by the greatness of a kingly birth and fortune is most fit to have her. I am likewise bold to commend my most humble duty by this letter and ring, which hath the virtue to expel infectious airs, and is, as is told to me, to be wearen betwixt the sweet dugs,— the chaste nest of most pure constancy.[30]

He continued with the news that the illness was feared to be smallpox and that he was moving on to his house of Kirby, "leaving my other shrine, I mean Holdenby, still unseen until that holy saint may sit in it, to whom it is dedicated."[31]

On September 19 Hatton replied to a letter from Elizabeth in even more courtly prose.

> The gracious assurance which your Highness's grave letters do most liberally give me of your singular favor and inestimable goodness, I have received on my knees with such reverence as becomes your most obliged bondman; . . . and I do offer in God's presence myself, my life, and all that I am or is me, to be disposed to the end, and my death to do your service, in inviolable faith and sincerity.[32]

He complimented Elizabeth on her writing style, but the subject was even more to his liking; "Your words are sweet, your heart is full of rare and royal faith; the writing of your fair hand, directed by your constant and sacred heart, do raise in me joy unspeakable."[33] He asked her pardon for his presumption in giving some extraordinary advice concerning her marital state:

> Against love and ambition your Highness hath holden a long war; they are the violent affections that encumber the hearts of men; but now, my most dear Sovereign, it is more than time to yield, or else this love will leave you in war and disquietness of yourself and estate, and the ambition of the world will be most maliciously bent to encumber your sweet quiet, and the happy peace of this most blessed Realm. . . And so your Highness' most humble Lydds, a thousand times more happy in that you vouchsafe them yours, than in that they cover and conserve the poor eyes, most lowly do leave you in your kingly seat in God's most holy protection. . . Your Majesty's sheep and most bound vassel.[34]

Elizabeth's "sheep" was back in London by September 26, in residence at Hatton House. He wrote to Walsingham to give his opinion of the problems in Ireland. A second papal expedition had reached Ireland in July, 1579, led by an Irish noble and equipped with a papal banner and agent. This was actually a very small group but with great potential for causing further risings. In September, 1579, reinforcements arrived. There were about six hundred men along with a supply of weapons for the Irish. Philip II had permitted this group to be organized in Spain and there were a few Spaniards among them. This was obviously no small problem and Hatton described his thoughts:

> My zealous care over her Majesty's safety, now fearfully stirred up with this evil news of the affairs of Ireland, . . . doth give me occasion . . . to write some little of my simple opinion.[35]

Hatton's advice was to "resist the beginning" before other enemies could join the Irish revolt. He referred to the fact that Portugal had just come into Philip's possession and with that success the Spanish king might well join with the Pope and turn on England. Hatton recognized that in "Ireland and Scotland the entries and ways to our destruction most aptly be found."[36]

In a discussion of the Scottish situation, Hatton assessed "the malice of France" which is "there ever made up against us." His advice was that some wise man might be sent to Scotland to buy support and especially to forestall any attempt to send for aid from the King of France. "With the disposition of France, which lies now in her Majesty's arbitrament, I dare not meddle, for she only knows what shall become thereof."[37] Hatton was fearful of a coalition of the Pope, Spain, and even France, which would win the Low Countries, Ireland, and Scotland. "I cannot but mourn in my heart to see us beset on all sides with so great and apparent dangers."[38] If Elizabeth's courtship diplomacy was to be used at the end Hatton wondered "if her Highness mean to marry, I wonder she so delays it."[39]

Though the latest Spanish expedition to Ireland was almost completely wiped out, problems there continued. A cousin of Hatton's, Arthur Lord Grey of Wilton, had been appointed Lord Deputy of Ireland in 1579. He wrote to Hatton on March 14, 1581, reporting new revolts there and the arrival of Scots. He pleaded with Hatton to "help forward, through your honorable solicitation to her Majesty, with more forces, and to hasten them hither with all possible expedition. . ."[40]

Many dangers were coalescing on the English horizon. Philip II was undoubtedly disturbed when he learned that Drake had passed successfully through the Straits of Magellan. An interesting ceremony took place after this safe passage. Drake renamed his flagship, formerly the *Pelican*, calling it the *Golden Hind*. The Golden Hind was a part of Hatton's coat of arms and Hatton was a heavy investor in Drake's voyage. So was Elizabeth. She deflated Spanish Ambassador Bernadino de Mendoza when he came to complain of Drake's piracy by demanding an explanation from Mendoza of the presence of Spaniards in Ireland. Even in this dangerous period she would not sacrifice Drake to placate Philip. In fact Elizabeth used the occasion of visiting Drake on his arrival in Deptford as public evidence of an Anglo-French alliance. She allowed the French agent of Alençon to knight Drake for her and the agent was permitted to carry off a purple and gold garter to be given to the Duke of Alençon.

Two weeks later the commissioners arrived from France with the hope of arranging a marriage treaty. Nothing was spared to make this meeting a glorious affair. Tilts, triumphs, dances, and fetes of all kinds were produced with great splendor. A special banqueting house was built in the gardens of Whitehall. There were two months of this routine of splendid dinners and rich pageantry. The probable intention of Elizabeth at this time was to achieve a political alliance without a marriage, an arrangement which Walsingham had been trying to accomplish in France for some frustrating months. But the King of France, Henry III, and Catherine de Medici would settle for nothing less than first, a marriage, and second, an alliance.

Elizabeth appointed a commission to discuss marriage details. She could now be sure that the six members would not agree. Of the group only Sussex was totally in favor of the marriage, while Leicester, Hatton, and Walsingham were opposed to it, and Burghley and Bedford were neutral. As the discussions went on Elizabeth wrote fondly to Alençon. She encouraged his hopes by sending him 30,000 pounds to help pay his troops in the Netherlands. But this large sum was not enough and he could get no help from his brother, Henry III, so at the end of October he arrived in England to woo the Queen once more.

The Court was at Richmond and Alençon was lodged in a house near the palace where he was looked after by Lord Henry Howard and Howard's nephew Philip, Earl of Arundel. Days passed filled with business negotiations and a somewhat ridiculous courtship. It is probable that Elizabeth wished to prolong the discussions until she could achieve her purpose without conceding too much. Alençon wanted her financial support for his adventures in the Netherlands. She made a qualified agreement to provide this support if Alençon's brother also helped, and coupled with this was a clause binding Alençon to support the Huguenot cause in France. This move would effectively prevent the French King from aiding any enemy of Elizabeth's and to put Alençon in a political situation in France analogous to that of Mary Stuart in England.

Although she no longer considered marrying Alençon Elizabeth felt it would not do to send him off disgruntled or without hope. On November 17 while walking in the gallery at Whitehall Elizabeth astounded her courtiers by declaring that the Duke should be her husband; taking a ring from her hand, she kissed him and gave it to him as a pledge. Alençon gave her a ring in return and was overjoyed. Burghley was grateful that she had finally arrived at a decision but Leicester sulked and Hatton was in tears. This was most probably a premeditated piece of Elizabethan acting. She did not now want this marriage, and she had set the terms in such a way that the King of France would probably never agree to the marriage. Her charade not only saved face for Alençon but also raised his credit with the bankers, a factor which would allow him to return to the Netherlands more quickly.

Elizabeth maintained that her ladies had kept her awake all night wailing and talking of the dangers of marriage so that she was forced to sacrifice her own happiness for the sake of her people. This wailing could have been distressing but hardly would have been a decisive factor. The effective pressure was the earlier opposition she had seen in her Council. So Alençon was told to wait still longer and he did stay on for another three months, fighting a battle of wits.

Eventually Elizabeth promised him a loan of 60,000 pounds, half to be paid fifteen days after his departure and the remainder within fifty days. Still he lingered. At the end of December he was paid 10,000 pounds. But Elizabeth was not rid of him until February 1. She accompanied him to Canterbury where she wept "diplomatic tears" and ordered Leicester, Lord Hunsdon, and other peers to escort him to Antwerp.

No doubt Elizabeth felt real regret at the departure of this last suitor. Although correspondence continued between the two, she was now faced with acceptance of the role of old maid. Alençon as often pressed for the rest of his money as for marriage. He made a great blunder when in January, 1583, he tried to take the town of Antwerp from his allies, failed, and fled. Elizabeth was trying to patch up the situation when on June 10, 1584, Alençon died of fever. Elizabeth wept again, perhaps for herself.

chapter six

Catholic Conspiracies and Parliament of 1581

Over a period of several years indications of growing threats to the safety of England had become all too apparent. In 1579 there had been the landing of papal-backed forces in Ireland, in 1580 came the expansion of Spain by the absorption of Portugal, and still more threatening was the development of clandestine Jesuit missions to England itself. The Enterprise, the holy war of Catholicism against England, seemed imminent. The year of 1580 was to be the beginning of a special Jesuit mission into England led by two distinguished men, Edmund Campion and Robert Parsons. In the threat these men and their followers posed to the English state there is little to distinguish them from twentieth-century groups known as fifth columnists. Although the motivation was spiritual there was no way in the sixteenth century to divide spiritual from political actions. Until this time Elizabeth had turned a blind eye to the existence of the English Catholics as long as they remained quiet and discreet. With the arrival of Campion and Parsons this policy of "benign neglect" became untenable.

That the Jesuits brought real danger to England with the

prospect of assassination of its Queen is demonstrated by the reply of the papal secretary in December, 1580, to a question put by certain English Jesuits:

> Since that guilty woman of England rules over two such noble kingdoms of Christendom and is the cause of so much injury of the Catholic faith and loss of so many million souls, there is no doubt that whosoever sends her out of the world with the pious intention of doing God service, not only does not sin but gains merit.[1]

Since any attempt to invade England always relied upon English Catholics to rise and join the foreign troops in overthrowing Elizabeth, the missionaries were undoubtedly involved in the destruction of the Queen and her government.

The work of the priests, necessarily carried on in secret, was surprisingly successful. They went about the country in disguise, hiding in various houses, inspiring Catholics with their own determination, and recalling them to church discipline. Their success was fatal to Elizabeth's hope of eventually absorbing the English Catholics into the Anglican Church. It also inflamed the Puritans to greater acts of intolerance. It was inevitable that much of the work of the Parliament of 1581 would deal with this menace in a spirit of hatred and vengeance. Members were extremely nationalistic in their reactions to this threat to their religion and to their Queen. She was described as a "Princess known by long experience to be a principal patron of the Gospel, virtuous, wise, faithful, just, unspotted in word and deed, merciful; . . . a Queen, besides, of this noble realm, our native country, renowned of the world."[2]

As these controversies gained momentum in 1580, Hatton, finding many of his Catholic friends in serious trouble, became deeply involved. When Parsons arrived in England in June, 1580, he went to visit Thomas Pound who had been in the Marshalsea Prison for some years because of his religious beliefs and actions. Pound was a nephew of the Earl of Southampton and had been an acquaintance of Hatton's both at the Court and the Inns of Court. Pound helped to persuade Parsons and Campion to announce their intentions openly and to ask for a public debate. Some idea of the looseness of supervision of the prisoners can be gained by the fact that Pound was able to take Parsons to his room. Parsons ate with the prisoners and was able to visit the Catholic Club, an association founded by George Gilbert. Priests and Catholic gentlemen were able to meet at the club unmolested by paying the owner of the house well.

Parsons had arrived on June 11 and when Campion came two weeks later the two men decided to take their mission to the country. Just before they left the London area, Pound arrived, having been able to absent himself from prison. He urged them to publicize the fact that their mission was religious only and to disclaim any political intentions. Campion wrote a tract named the "Brag" or "Challenge" in response to Pound's advice. He denied any political involvement, begged permission to debate religious doctrine before the Privy Council, and challenged the men of the universities to debate with him in the presence of the Queen. In his conclusion he professed his faith and readiness for martyrdom.

Pound took the declaration to London, read it to the prisoners, and in his enthusiasm challenged two Puritan ministers who were visiting the prison to a debate. He also rashly wrote petitions to the Council and to the Bishop of London asking for a public debate. Ten days later he learned just how unwise his actions had been. He was taken from his loose prison to the Bishop's manor at Bishop's Stortford where he was placed in irons and lodged in solitary confinement. In this grave situation Pound wrote to Hatton, reminding him of their earlier acquaintanceship and asking permission to allow one of Pound's men to supply food and other necessities to him.

Hatton had apparently already written to Aylmer in an attempt to alleviate Pound's position. The letter began, "Your noble courtesy towards me, already showed in writing so ex-

ceeding friendly to my Lord of London as you did. . ."[3] The
Bishop had had the temerity to refuse Hatton's request this
time. Pound described his miserable situation:

> Oh, God, Sir Christopher, I would you saw the spectacle of
> it, what a place I am brought into; here is nothing but a huge,
> vast room, cold water, bare walls, no windows but loopholes too
> high to look out at; nor bed, nor bedstead, nor place very fit for
> any, nor chimney, nor table, nor light, . . . in the midst of the
> house a huge pair of stocks; and nothing else but chains.[4]

These conditions were such partly because the manor was a
half-ruined castle. Pound reminded Hatton of his appearance in
entertainments at Kenilworth Castle before the Queen and
begged Hatton to "try once more what stead you can stand me
in."[5] In this instance as in others, Hatton showed compassion
for Catholics as well as all others who petitioned him. As a
powerful man at Court he naturally received petitions of all
kinds, but there is testimony of his genuine sympathy in letters
from such different men as the Duke of Norfolk, Thomas
Pound, and Charles Arundel, who were Catholic, and John
Stubbs and Thomas Norton, who were Protestant.

Quite naturally the government feared political repercus-
sions from the successes of the Jesuits. Campion was taken,
racked, and after a public disputation with members of the
Anglican Church, was executed. Thomas Norton, a fervid
Puritan, was one of the commission that caused Campion to be
racked and he was later called to account for it. He admitted the
charge against him, that he had said if Campion would not for
his duty to God and the Queen tell the truth, "he should be
made a foot longer than God had made him."[6] Norton was imprisoned for a time and was released in April, 1582. Hatton and
Burghley had stood by him and on April 10 he wrote to thank
Hatton:

> My heart always assured me that your honor did bear me a
> charitable mind, for so you ever made appearance; and I am well

acquainted with the nobleness of your nature not to seem other than you are; . . . yet how much and in what sort particularly in my late wretchedness I have been bound to you I had no mean to understand by the closeness of my restraint . . . I have attained to hear some part of your great pity towards me, beside the comfort that my poor wife received of your gracious speeches in her heavy extremity.[7]

It was becoming increasingly difficult to differentiate between the religious and political aspects of Catholicism. Most Catholic Englishmen, while remaining loyal to the Queen, were fined or briefly imprisoned in their homes. Yet as the dangers from foreign Catholics grew in the 1580s, the government felt forced to take a more repressive attitude.

The Tresham family also had occasion at this time to appeal to Hatton for aid, finding themselves in trouble because of their religion. Sir Thomas Tresham was a neighbor of Hatton's in Northamptonshire who although reared as a Protestant had been converted to Catholicism in 1580 by Robert Parsons. The timing of Tresham's conversion was unfortunate. The leniency with which the Act of Uniformity, which required Anglican Church attendance, had been enforced was being reversed under pressure of events. Tresham had given shelter to Parsons and Campion, an act which brought him into the Star Chamber on a charge of contempt, for he had refused to swear that he had not given Campion shelter.

The sentence given Tresham was not a light one. He was committed to the Fleet Prison for seven years following his trial. Tresham not only had his own actions to account for but wrote Hatton concerning the problem of his brother William. Hatton was a good friend to William, having earlier engineered his release from imprisonment, restored him to the Queen's favor, and obtained a place in the Gentlemen-Pensioners for him. The ungrateful William had recently left England without permission, which not only blighted his reputation but also that of the remaining brother.

William, in letters to Hatton and the Privy Council, maintained that he fled because of the ill feeling towards him held by

Leicester. William's letter to Hatton is extraordinary. He claimed to be ". . . fraught with woe and full of heaviness"[8] due to the rejection of the friendliness he offered to Hatton. The friendship had been of long duration, he claimed, dating from the period before Hatton was a councillor, and never ceased . . . until I was so strangely rejected,"[9] most undeservedly, according to Tresham. He claimed that his rejection was due to pressure on the part of Leicester:

> How may it be thought that ever you would have rejected me, your devoted poor friend, for the sole pleasure of the Earl of Leicester, without any occasion or small suspicion given on my part to yourself, knowing especially, as you do, that he affects you only to serve his own turn?[10]

William Tresham warned Hatton to "take heed of him in time!" He begged Hatton to "with the eyes of wisdom look into him thoroughly"[11] and not to be overconfident. Tresham knew that his words would count little in exile but begged Hatton to consider the plight of his imprisoned brother. He concluded with an unusual blunt warning which offended Hatton:

> I pray you, Sir, remember that the bee gathers honey of every flower, and of many travails frames a sweet and comfortable being for herself and young ones all the cold winter; but the grasshopper all the summertime enjoys with gallantry in the pleasant meadows, and dies commonly with the cold dew of Bartholomew. You know that the high cedar-trees on the tops of huge mountains are most subject to the danger of storms, and therefore have most need of many and sure roots. We are all in God's hands, to be raised or pulled down as it shall please Him; and there is none so high now, but may one day, through affliction, stand in as great need of comfort as now my poor brother and your dear friend does. . .The day may come that you find either him, or his, better able than now they are to acknowledge in all good sort, and thankfully to requite your kindness.[12]

This highly offensive letter, barely concealing what seems very much like a threat of eventual retaliation, sent Hatton's secretary (Samuel Cox) to visit Thomas Tresham in prison. Cox began by describing William's flight as a grievous error, but an even graver fault was the tone of his letters. Hatton was upset by the words and "much wonders to be threatened with that family which he always has loved."[13] According to Cox Hatton had promised that if adversity came to him he would be ". . . no such fainting thing"[14] as a grasshopper. Hatton yet promised to help restore Thomas to the royal favor and urged William to return to England. However, William did not come back until 1603. In 1583 Thomas wrote to Hatton again from Fleet Prison. He had paid his fines, had served in prison, and he begged Hatton to intercede for him with the Queen. Shortly following that letter Tresham was released to live in his own house.

Charles Arundell, who was often under suspicion of pro-Catholic plots, was another who appealed to Hatton in several letters in these unsettled time. Arundell was a member of the Catholic Association formed to aid Campion and Parsons on their arrival in England. He was often in trouble with the government.

In 1581 the Earl of Oxford confessed to the Queen that he had been converted to Catholicism with Henry Howard, Francis Southwell, and Charles Arundell. Having recanted, Oxford accused his friends of conspiracy against the Queen. Although Oxford was not able to provide evidence as to the men's guilt of conspiracy, they were restrained for a time and Howard was given into the custody of Hatton. Arundell was sent to Surrey, where he wrote to Hatton on May 23, 1581, that ". . . I crave no more . . . but that your virtue may in this time of distress both plead and promise for your poor friend, that wants means, not will, to make his faith more evident."[15] On July 20 he wrote to ask Hatton for a speedy trial:

> for then shall my enemies sink with shame, and I depart out of the field with honor; and whatsoever either malice has unjustly built, or a fool devised upon a false ground, must play castle-come-down, and dissolve to nothing.[16]

Arundell promised also to confirm his good faith by formal depositions and oaths of witnesses. In a further letter to Hatton in

which he mentioned having been imprisoned for eight months
Arundell mentioned the hope he had apparently received from
Hatton:

> I have received such comfort of your last message . . . as I
> am emboldened thereby most humbly to crave your goodness,
> either to procure my trial, that I am sure will acquit me, or to re-
> lease me of my bands, with free enlargement, that would greatly
> ease and relieve me.[17]

Arundell claimed that he had been "lightly suspected, nothing
faulty, and never offending her [the Queen] so much as in
thought."[18]

In a later letter Arundell again proclaimed his innocence to
Hatton and deplored his living, "which is much harder I assure
you than I complain of."[19] Later he wrote of having "most
plainly unfolded before you my knowledge in all points, not concealing anything to excuse myself, nor adding more than is
truth to harm others. "[20] This point would indicate that Hatton
had taken his customary role in the examination of religious offenders. Still later Arundel wrote:

> I account it not my least good hap that you shall have the
> hearing of my cause. As I have already most plainly and sincere-
> ly betrayed my knowledge in all points of my examination, so I
> beseech you with all humility to be the means to restore me to
> my former liberty, and to her Majesty's good favor, without the
> which I desire not life.[21]

Arundell was released but did not prove his good faith.
With the discovery of the Throckmorton plot in 1582 he fled to
the continent where he became part of a Catholic group
involved in several subsequent conspiracies. He eventually
became a pensioner of Philip II and had no further contact with
Hatton.

In 1582 the English government was anxiously watching
Scottish affairs, suspecting conspiracies against England led by
the French agents of the Duc de Guise. James VI was only too
ready to play upon Elizabeth's fears by fraternizing with her

enemies. Walsingham was sent with a delegation to remonstrate with James and attempt to restore English influence, but with no success. The eyes of the government turned to a new direction when a Spanish-Guise plot was uncovered. Walsingham had learned from one of his spies in the French embassy of the suspicious movements of a Francis Throckmorton. This young Englishman had been drawn into a conspiracy by Mary Stuart's agent Thomas Morgan and had become the intermediary through which Morgan, Mary, and the Spanish ambassador communicated. In November, 1583, Throckmorton was arrested and on the rack he confessed his full activities. He was executed, several others arrested, and the Spanish ambassador, Don Bernardino de Mendoza, was ordered from the country within fifteen days. It was at this time that other Catholics who had appealed to Hatton for aid either fled the country as did Charles Arundell, or like the Earl of Northumberland stayed at home and were imprisoned.

The Earl's name had been on a list of English noblemen found in Throckmorton's papers who were said to be favorable to Mary Stuart. Henry Percy was the eighth earl of Northumberland, the successor to a brother who had been executed for his part in the Northern Rebellion. Henry, although loyal to Elizabeth at that time, soon became involved with attempts to free Mary Stuart. He had been arrested in 1571, sent to the Tower, and released with a fine which was never paid. In December, 1583, because his name was found on the list belonging to Throckmorton, he was again arrested and committed to the Tower.

Hatton was involved in this case as in others involving conspiracy. He was sent by the Queen to interview the Earl before Percy was sent to the Tower. Hatton reminded Northumberland of the earlier royal clemency and advised him to tell the truth either in letter to the Queen or to him. If the Earl would tell the truth Hatton promised that he would not be sent to the Tower and would again receive all leniency possible. Northumberland, however, believed that the government had no evidence against him and remained silent.

While the Earl was in the Tower he tried to communicate

with others involved in his case and when that tactic was discovered the keeper was changed. Thomas Bailiff, one of Hatton's men, was put in charge of the Earl at this time. Northumberland managed to get information from his servant in the
Tower that the servant was going to confess because he could
not face the rack. This man had witnessed the Earl's meeting
with Mary's agents and their discussion of a projected invasion
of England. When Northumberland learned this he had a pistol
smuggled into the prison and bolting his cell door, shot himself.

This was the reconstruction of the event as produced by a
court of inquiry which took place two days after Northumberland's death on June 21, 1585. The court consisted of the Lord
Chancellor, Attorney-General, Soliciter-General, Lord Chief
Baron, and Hatton. Bromley, the Lord Chancellor, remarked
that the inquiry had been held on the orders of the Privy
Council in case "through the sinister means of such persons as
be evil-affected to the present estate of her Majesty's government, some bad and untrue conceits might be had, as well as of
the Earl's detainment as of the manner of his death."[22] After
defining the Earl's treasonous conduct it was emphasized that
the Earl committed suicide behind the locked door in order to
forestall his certain attainder.[23]

Although there are those who have charged Hatton with
implication in the Earl's death,[24] it is unlikely that he or the
government ordered the shooting. Hatton stood to gain nothing
by the Earl's death and the government by the suicide certainly
lost the right to confiscate the Earl's estate.

Lord Henry Howard, who was taken into custody for his
religious deviations as described earlier, was released rather
quickly but was back in prison in 1584 on other charges of
treason. He also wrote to Hatton remembering his ready aid in
Howard's former problems. He complained of being in prison
for six months and protested he only spoke to Throckmorton
once on innocent matters. He had been accused of receiving a
ring from Mary Stuart and the government feared that he
would repeat the attempts of the Duke of Norfolk to marry the
Queen of Scots and supplant Elizabeth. He denied ever receiv-

ing any such ring. He had been ill. "This long and close endur-
ance has already brought me to that extremity of the stone, as, I
protest to God, I had rather yield my life in the favor of
Almighty God to any sudden stroke of Fortune whatsoever,
than languish in this endless maze of pain and misery. . ." He
begged Hatton ". . . first for charity, and then for the pity and
compassion which is engrafted in your honorable mind,"[25] to aid
him.

A month later Howard wrote to assure Hatton of his
friendship, having heard that others had questioned it. "God
can witness mine upright conceit of yourself, and of your plain
and honorable dealing. . ."[26] He complained of having been
seven months in prison without any offense given to his Prince
or country. ". . . I rest yours, and so will do, in spite of those
that labor to imprint another fancy in your favorable judgment."[27] Howard was not taken back into the Queen's favor
until near the end of her life, but he lived on to an improved
state in the reign of James I, who made him the Earl of
Northampton.

Another Howard, Philip, Earl of Arundel, was also implicated in the Throckmorton Plot and sent to the Tower. He had
been released and had tried to flee to the continent but was cap-
tured on the way. He was committed again to the Tower and
wrote to Hatton on May 5, 1585. Walsingham had written to
Hatton on May 1 that Arundel was too unafraid and that "his
courage is to be abated, and no advantage to be lost until he be
drawn to use some other language, seasoned with more humility."[28] Walsingham evidently believed Arundel was being encouraged by some comfort "and that not from mean persons."
He was concerned about the trustworthiness of the Lieutenant
of the Tower, Sir Owen Hopton, and suggested that the Queen
might be wise to choose another. Arundel had been put in
charge of Henry MacWilliam and Walsingham asked Hatton to
advise MacWilliam to guard him closely. Walsingham believed
that the Tower was ". . . the corruptest prison in England."[29]

From Arundel's letter to Hatton it is evident that Hatton
had again been Arundel's examiner. Arundel tried to remem-

ber anything he may have forgotten to confess to Hatton. He
admitted he was slipping but had not fallen. He admitted that he
had been confessed in the Catholic religion and had written to
Dr. William Allen, an action which he recognized offended the
Queen, but ". . . I do utterly deny and disavow, that ever I was
privy to any plot or practice laid or made against her Majesty, or
her state."[30] He begged for mercy which he eventually received
when he was finally brought to trial in 1589. He was sentenced
to death but reprieved and fined 10,000 pounds and imprisoned
during the Queen's pleasure. He died in 1595.

These letters illustrate how closely Hatton was involved
with and in charge of the religious conspirators who were a
great cause of government concern during the 1580s. He generally examined the accused and they were often at least temporarily in his charge. Elizabeth recognized the environment his
work created in a message sent him about a Catholic priest who
was in Hatton's house at the time. "Her Highness thinks your
house will shortly be like [a] Gravesend barge, never without a
knave, a priest or a thief. . ."[31]

There was no denying the fact that the peaceful days of
Elizabeth's reign were rapidly vanishing; the Puritan members
of Parliament would be difficult to control in the upcoming
session.

The Parliament that met in January, 1581, had been prorogued twenty-six times since its last meeting. The delicate
marriage negotiations with Alençon and the steady flow of con-
tinental seminarians had changed both foreign and domestic sit-
uations. But even in the heated atmosphere of foreign dangers
Elizabeth was not to be pressured to acts of repression which
were against her wishes. She had vetoed an act for compulsory
church attendance in 1571 and Parliament had failed to succeed
in its passage in 1572 and again in 1576. She was to maintain
her position even in this threatening year of 1581. As well as
fending off external dangers by diplomatic means as long as
possible, Elizabeth was determined to maintain her sovereignty
against the Puritan danger which she instinctively grasped as
being equally crucial. When Archbishop Grindal refused to obey

her command to decrease the number of preachers and to suppress all prophesying he was deprived of the duties of his office. However, despite the Queen's feelings, the topic of religion would be introduced into this next Parliamentary session.

When the Commons assembled on January 16, 1581, their first problem was to choose a new Speaker. Robert Bell, the previous Speaker, had been made a judge. John Popham was chosen as the Speaker. The head of the upper house was likewise new this session. Sir Nicholas Bacon had died and Sir Thomas Bromley was appointed as Lord Chancellor.

In his opening speech on the afternoon of January 20 in the Queen's presence, Bromley emphasized the limits of free speech to be observed by the members of Commons. He answered the Speaker's petition for freedom of speech in this manner:

> Concerning freedom of speech, her Majesty grants it as liberally as it has at any time heretofore granted; not-withstanding, would have them know that it is always tied within limits, namely, not to deal with her state—which he showed to be intended as well touching her prerogative as also in religion.[32]

With this special admonition in mind Commons could have no illusions concerning their prescribed limits.

Commons met on January 21 to begin work and after a decorous beginning they were immediately shaken by a speech by Paul Wentworth. Puritan Wentworth made a motion for a public fast to gain God's blessing and he also proposed that a sermon be preached in the house each morning.

This seemingly innocent petition had great political implications. Fasting was a special characteristic of Puritanism and the clergy of the Church of England felt it was used much too often. The attitude of the Anglican clergy can be understood by the chastisement given by the Archbishop of York to one of his bishops on the subject, "My Lord, you are noted to yield too much to general fastings . . . There lurks matter under that pretended piety. The devil is craft; and the young ministers of these our times grow mad."[33]

Wentworth had also acted insubordinately by directly interfering with the royal authority over all acts of public worship. Coming immediately after Bromley's injunctions about not meddling in religious matters, this could only be seen as an act of defiance. There was an immediate and heated debate. The majority favored the proposal. Opponents tried to add an amendment making the fast a private matter. The vote on this point was 115 for a public fast and 100 for a private one.[34]

The Queen was quick to react to the issues raised. On the following morning the Speaker arrived late at the house and when he appeared he only read the prayer and adjourned the Commons. The next day, January 23, the assembled members heard Elizabeth's message. Speaker Popham relayed to them the Queen's "misliking" of their action and advised them to apologize to her and warned them that in the future they should deal only with matters within the bounds of their authority.

As the Queen's personal representative, Hatton took charge of the situation. Bringing a message from the Queen he:

> . . . showed to them her great admiration of the rashness of this House in committing such an apparent contempt against her Majesty's express commandment . . . as to attempt and put in execution such an innovation as the same fast without her Majesty's privity and pleasure first known; blaming first the whole House and then Mr. Speaker. . .[35]

After reproving the members Hatton declared that the Queen had recognized the zeal, duty, and fidelity of the house and its concern with religion, her safety, and the state of the Commonwealth. Hatton stated further that:

> nevertheless of her inestimable and princely good love and disposition, and of her Highness' most gracious clemency construes the said offense and contempt to be rash, unadvised, and an inconsiderate error . . . proceeding of zeal and not of the wilful or malicious intent of this House. . .[36]

Hatton reported that the Queen attributed Wentworth's action partly to her leniency with his brother Peter. She had also considered the religious matter raised and would present her proposals to the house in due course. Hatton advised that someone from the house be sent to the Queen to make their humble submission. Mildmay and other officials spoke in the same vein. Accordingly the Speaker put the question and it was resolved that Hatton present to the Queen "the most humble submission of this whole House with their said error and contempt."[37] When one member tried to speak for the liberty of the house he was not given the time to do so.

On January 25 Hatton reported to the house on his mission to the Queen. Elizabeth had accepted their submission most graciously and was pleased to remit their offense. She expressed confidence that their future actions would be discreet and assured them through Hatton that it was not the matter she had objected to, but the manner. It was "tending to innovation, presuming to indict a form of public fast without order and without her Majesty's privity, intruding upon her Highness' authority ecclesiastical."[38]

By her prompt and decisive action Elizabeth blunted this Puritan attack in the Commons in 1581 as she had done in 1576. But it did not entirely end the debate on religious issues in this Parliament.

When the divisive topic of religion was momentarily quiet and while the members were basking in the Queen's graceful words, Mildmay took the opportunity to make the government speech for supply. The speech was well-prepared and dealt with a broad range of policy as well as finance. Mildmay spoke of "the present state we be in; of the dangers that we may justly be in doubt of; what provision ought to be made in time to prevent or resist them."[39] He concluded his long patriotic speech proclaiming that "for such a Queen and such a country, and for the defence of the honor and surety of them both, nothing ought to be so dear unto us that with most willing hearts we should not spend and adventure freely."[40]

Thomas Norton followed with a motion to appoint a committee to frame the required legislation which in essence took some of the initiative from the government members. A

large committee was formed including all Privy Councillors in
the house and fifty-seven others. A smaller group of four
lawyers was delegated to draw up particulars for necessary legislation. Two bills were reported out of this committee—one for
the subsidy and one called the "Bill for Religion." The latter bill
was to be passed as "Act to Retain the Queen's Majesty's
Subjects to their due Obedience," and it was a severely anti-
Catholic piece of legislation.

The original religious bill, which was much harsher than
the one finally passed, was presented on February 7. Hatton
reported to Commons that the Lords were considering a similar
measure and he suggested a conference, which was agreed to.
The bill being considered in the Lords was much milder than the
one in the Commons for it dealt mainly with increasing the
penalties for nonattendance at church. After many joint conferences a second bill agreeable to both houses was produced
which mainly followed the lines of the original Commons bill.
Following the first reading of the bill on February 18, there was
a request from the Lords for further conferences and as a result
of these meetings a third bill was introduced on March 4. This
measure was rapidly passed in both houses.

The third bill contained notably milder clauses and Sir John
Neale surmised that in the intervening days the Queen had
again stepped in to moderate the punitive wishes of the Puritans.[41] One section of this act provided for severe penalties
against missionaries who attempted to convert Englishmen and
to withdraw them from their obedience to the Queen. Such
men were to be considered traitors.

Included in this bill were heavy fines imposed for nonattendance at church. A series of clauses from the second bill
aimed at removing convicted professionals such as lawyers and
teachers from their positions of influence and a requirement of
a loyalty oath from law students were dropped. Neale credits
the Queen with keeping her head even in times of stress:

> . . . by an exercise of royal authority she resisted the great
> advisory bodies of the realm; Council, Lords and Commons. We

have only to consider what would have happpened if she had been prepared to give her assent to that second bill, to realize how much the English liberal tradition owes to her sanity.[42]

Francis Bacon, eight or nine years later, wrote that the Queen based her religious policy on two points: first, "that consciences are not to be forced"; and second, that "causes of conscience, when they exceed their bounds and grow to be matter of faction, lose their nature."[43] Bacon remarked that:

> Her Majesty, not liking to make windows into men's hearts and secret thoughts, except the abundance of them overflow into overt and express acts or affirmations, tempers her law so as it restrains only manifest disobedience, in impugning and impeaching advisedly and maliciously her Majesty's supreme power, and maintaining and extolling a foreign jurisdiction.[44]

Hatton apparently agreed with and wholeheartedly implemented the Queen's unusually moderate policies. As evidence has shown, Hatton showed compassion to Catholic and Puritan alike when they failed to maintain their balance between loyalty to the state and religious conscience. Camden wrote of Hatton that his attitude was that "neither searing or cutting was to be used" in matters of religion.[45] Great stress would be put upon the Queen's and Hatton's delicate balancing act as the external threat from Spain and the internal pressures of the Puritans increased in the late 1580s.

A further concern of the Parliament of 1581 was the rewriting of a slander bill or an "Act against Seditious Words and Rumors uttered against the Queen's most excellent Majesty." This act was an extension of a previous bill passed in Mary's reign and it began in the Lords. Hatton brought messages to the Commons from the Lords to ascertain whether the lower house would be content to leave in force the penalty for slander of the Queen. In this new bill the option of inflicting the penalty vanished and the term of imprisonment was raised from three months to three years. Had this act applied only to Catholics it would have been welcome, but this was the very bill

under which the Puritan John Stubbs had been found guilty and
it undoubtedly spelled great dangers for Puritans. Accordingly
the Puritans developed several amendments and word changes
which were designed to eliminate the threat against the Puritans. Lords refused this change and sent the bill back to the
House of Commons. It was stalemated until Hatton spoke in his
persuasive manner reminding the members of the Commons of
"the great benefits and blessings of God upon this realm in the
godly, most loving, and careful government and ministry of her
Majesty."[46] and their appreciation of her care and their obedience to her. He discussed the problems presented by the act and
arranged for the appointment of a committee to rewrite it.

The work of the committee produced a milder bill with
reduced penalties and with "malicious intent" having to be
proved in an effort to save any future Puritan victims. Norton's
severe addition to the effect that it was seditious to say that the
religious doctrines of the Church of England were heretical or
schismatical was omitted. This bill was finally passed by both
houses at the very end of the session.

On March 3 there were several motions and arguments
made concerning reforms in religion. It was announced that
Hatton, Walsingham, Wilson, and Mildmay had already spoken
to the bishops on these reforms. It was resolved by the house
that these four men should ask the clergy to continue their
efforts for reform. They also asked that this request be considered to be from the whole house, not just the four men pre-
senting the request.[47] Additionally they asked for redress of
other "griefs" which had been contained in their earlier petition.
In order that this discussion would not offend the Queen, they
ended with the argument that:

> . . . All the said speeches, motions, and arguments should
> by the whole House be deemed in every man to proceed of good
> and godly zeal, without any evil intent or meaning at all.[48]

This had been an orderly discussion, ably led by Hatton.

On March 7 Mildmay reported to the Commons on the
Councillors' mission. Many members of the Lords, including the

bishops, had proven willing to join with the Commons in a suit to the Queen for religious reforms, and they had received a positive reply from her. The reforms in question concerned the great number of unlearned and unable ministers, abuse of excommunication for small offenses, the commutation of penance, and the growing practice of having one man hold several religious offices at the same time. The Queen had responded to their petition saying that she had ordered these reforms during the last session of Parliament, "of her own good consideration and before any petition or suit thereof made by this House."[49] She had commanded the clergy to such actions and they had not achieved the reforms as yet. The Queen promised to see that members of the clergy did so. Mildmay advised the house to be satisfied with the Queen's answer and to send their formal thanks to her. After some argument he was able to persude them to commission the Speaker to thank the Queen in his closing speech.

Elizabeth did take action and carried out her promise to the members of Parliament. She commissioned Archbishop Sandys of York to work out the procedure with the assistance of three or four bishops of his choosing. These men put down their conclusions as to what could be done and delivered the articles to Elizabeth. Sandys reported being pressed by Hatton and others to give them an answer. On applying to the Queen as to how to answer them, Sandys reported that the Queen had authority herself to deal with clerical matters and that Parliament should not meddle, an answer not wholly approved of in the Commons. The dissatisfied members held the bishops responsible for the lack of zeal in reforms of this nature. In fierce arguments some members tried to impute at least a part of the blame to the Queen, but Thomas Norton strongly defended her and put all the onus onto the bishops. In spite of this defense of the royal honor Norton soon found himself in the Tower for his unrestrained criticism of the Alençon marriage negotiations. Norton was soon released but kept under restraint in his lodgings until April, 1582, when Hatton and Burghley were able to secure his pardon.

One further bill on religion was introduced into this session of Parliament by the government. It was backed by Convocation and was against Protestant sectaries. The government wished to have proscribed a mystical sect called the Family of Love which had its origins in the Netherlands. The Queen, suspecting their loyalty, had issued a proclamation against them the previous October. The bill, debated long and volubly in the second reading, was recommitted, and a new third bill read. This too was sent to a committee where it remained. This Parliament could apparently not decide on any religious point without long and tedious arguments. Hatton was interested in getting the session concluded and with no further action likely in the immediate future, this session of Parliament was prorogued on Saturday, March 18, 1581. Elizabeth came to end the session. The Speaker in conclusion reminded the Queen of her promise to reform religion as requested by the members and thanked her for her gracious answer to them.

Concerning her personal safety, the Speaker begged the Queen to:

> have a vigilant and provident care of the safety of her own most royal person, against the malicious attempts of some mighty foreign enemies abroad and the traitorous practices of most unnatural, disobedient subjects both abroad and at home, envying the blessed, most happy, quiet government of this realm under her Highness, upon the thread of whose life only, next to God, depended the life and whole state and stay of every her good and dutiful subjects.[50]

The Lord Chancellor replied for the Queen, thanking them for their care and work, but excluding those members who "have this session dealt more rashly in some things than was fit for them to do."[51] The Chancellor mentioned that the point concerning reforms did not have to be repeated and that they should have been satisfied with the Queen's previous answer. He concluded by thanking them for the subsidy in the Queen's name. The titles of the bills passed were read, the Queen vetoing only one act, an unimportant one concerning hops.

Parliament was then prorogued until April 24, but a whole series of prorogations was to follow until this group was dissolved on April 19, 1583.

Before the next Parliament would meet, John Whitgift would be Archbishop of Canterbury and aided by Hatton would be prepared for the decisive battle with the Puritans. Mary Stuart's situation would also be in its final chapter. William of Orange would be assassinated and Elizabeth's procrastinating policy in the Netherlands replaced by active intervention. And time itself would mark finish to any marriage negotiations by Elizabeth. Hatton would play an ever larger role in these problems, continuing his supervision of the activities of Catholics and Puritans. This would bring him into the final conviction of a series of conspirators and of Mary Stuart herself.

chapter seven
Parliament of 1584–1585

As the decade of the 1580s progressed threats to the English government increased dangerously. Plans to attack the country and murder Elizabeth were being organized on the continent and in England itself. The French leader of the Catholic League, the Duke of Guise, hoped to have Elizabeth assassinated and was plotting to take over Scotland. Within England in the autumn of 1583 a young man named Somerville left his home in Warwickshire to kill the Queen. He was probably unbalanced and he foolishly talked about his plan and was caught. These repeated dangers to the Queen's life convinced the government that the time for tolerance was over. But they could not get Elizabeth to agree. In this dangerous and unstable atmosphere the men of Parliament met to consider what could be done to safeguard their reluctant Queen.

Domestically the devoted councillors and courtiers of the Queen faced the difficult problem of safeguarding her from the machinations of the Counter-Reformation. Foreign attack appeared much closer after diplomatic relations were severed with Spain following the discovery of the Spanish ambassa-

dor's part in the Throckmorton plot. The assassination of
William the Silent, the Protestant hero, in the Netherlands in
July, 1584, was seen as another indication of what could soon
happen in England. This murder gave the English Protestants a
severe shock which seemed to call for action on their part. With
Parliament still prorogued no legislation could provide for
Elizabeth's defense. If the Queen were killed with no Parliament
in session chaos would certainly follow. All royal officials would
automatically lose their positions. There would be no Privy
Council, as all authority derived from the Queen's commission
would have lapsed. This situation would provide an open road
to the throne for Mary Stuart.

Given these circumstances the Privy Councillors decided to
take action on their own. A document called the Bond of
Association was drawn up, probably by Walsingham and Burghley. This Bond formed its signatories into a group of vigilantes.
The first clause was general and simply bound them to obey the
Queen and to defend her against all enemies. The second clause
was more specific, being directed towards any person claiming
title to the Crown of England who attempted to have the Queen
removed. Any person who derived any claim to the throne from
the guilty person was also to be resisted. The obvious reference
is to Mary Stuart and James VI. On reading these clauses over it
became clear to the Councillors that this attempt to deny the
conspirators the throne if they were successful in murdering
Elizabeth would be very ineffective. If Elizabeth were dead not
only the Catholics but others motivated by prudence and
ambition would flock to support Mary as the only remaining
claimant.

Therefore the second clause was rewritten to incorporate
essentially a lynch law. The signatories were to promise on oath
never to accept "any such pretended successor by whom or for
whom any such detestable act shall be attempted or committed,
or any that may claim by or from that individual."[1] Such
persons were to be prosecuted to the death and the signers were
"to take the uttermost revenge on them . . . by any possible
means . . . for their utter overthrow and extirpation."[2] Thus

any further conspiracy on behalf of Mary would lead to her death at once and James would be included in this proscription as well.

Copies of this Bond were circulated throughout the country from October to November, 1584, while the elections were being held for a new Parliament. Thousands of patriotic men's signatures were obtained. Although later the Queen was to deny any knowledge of this Bond, it is doubtful that the Council could have done all this in absolute secrecy. She may well not have been aware of the change in the second clause which made it so punitive. It is obvious that the passions aroused in the Puritans by the Catholic dangers would seek an outlet in legislation when Parliament convened.

At the same time that the Privy Council was taking action against the Catholic threat, the Anglican clergy was attempting to protect the religious establishment against the inroads of the Puritans. As the activities of each Parliament have shown, there was a determined core of Protestants who were dissatisfied with the Church establishment and wished to reform it in accordance with their views. They planned to purge the church of any symbol of the Catholic origins of the Anglican Church, thus the heated arguments over the use of vestments and the wording of the *Book of Common Prayer*. This group had adopted a Presbyterian plan for the Church which they hoped to install when they had eradicated the ecclesiastical hierarchy of archbishops and bishops whom they clearly saw as their enemies.

The religious governmental structure these Protestants envisaged consisted first of ministers and elders on the lowest level for each church, second a conference or *classes* composed of representatives from twelve churches who would meet about every six weeks, third a provincial synod representing twenty-four *classes* who would meet twice a year, and fourth, at the top, the national synod.

This organization provided an ideal framework for revolutionary action with local participation and national unity. In many ways this organization threatened the established order of both Church and State in England even more than Catholi-

cism, which was seen to have treasonous foreign ties. Yet inter-
nally Catholicism lacked the strong hierarchy the Puritans had
developed.

Being quite aware of the dangers of this organization, the
Queen had, in vain, repeatedly ordered the bishops to repress
the prophesyings or meetings of these groups. Instead of the
movement declining, it grew in strength and by 1582 had made
plans to infiltrate the Anglican Church. The first national synod
was held in July, 1582. With the death of Archbishop Grindal
who had refused to take action against the prophesyings in
1583, the Queen was at last able to appoint an archbishop after
her own heart. This was John Whitgift, critic of Thomas
Cartwright, the leader of English Presbyterianism.

Whitgift, a friend of Hatton's, began work at once, by
requiring all clergy to accept three articles. The first one
required acceptance of the royal supremacy and caused no
complaints. The second article was the inflammatory one. This
required affirmation that the *Book of Common Prayer* contained
nothing contrary to God's word. All clergy were ordered to use
no other book. This was something the Puritans would not do.
The third article required obedience to all Articles of Religion
despite the fact that a statute had been passed in 1571 requiring conformity to only the doctrinal one.

This action of Whitgift's seemed certain to get reaction, and
it did. John Field, the secretary of the Puritan movement, wrote
to a clerical friend, "The peace of the Church is at an end if he be
not curbed."[3] The Puritans also complained to Burghley and
members of the Council, who alarmed at this repression of de-
fenders against Catholicism, wrote to Whitgift. Burghley especially disliked the *ex officio* oath used by the Court of High Commission. In questioning of suspected clergymen this device
allowed the examiners to have the defendant incriminate himself. If the defendant refused to take the oath he could then be
cited for contempt. Burghley wrote to Whitgift that "this kind
of proceeding is too much savoring of the Romish Inquisition,
and is rather a device to seek for offenders than to reform
any."[4] Burghley advised suspected ministers to refuse to answer

under these rules. Obviously Whitgift had aroused some mighty opposition, but he continued in his work strongly supported by the Queen. Hatton of course was also involved in the implementation of these policies.

Clearly the Parliament which assembled on November 23, 1584, would have some momentous topics for discussion. This Parliament had an unusual number of new members, only 97 of the 460 having sat before. The newcomers included many courtiers such as Francis Bacon, Robert Cecil, Francis Drake, and Walter Raleigh. Sir Richard Knightley, a Puritan friend and neighbor of Hatton's in Northamptonshire who was later to be prosecuted by Hatton, joined this house. Sir Francis Knollys, Walsingham, Mildmay, and Hatton represented the government in the Commons.

The traditional ceremony of opening the session took place with John Puckering being chosen the Speaker and Lord Chancellor Bromley once again granting the members freedom of speech from the Queen. The Queen once again had her Lord Chancellor reply that "her Highness willingly condescended thereunto, only she restrained the cause of religion to be spoken of among them."[5] The reaction of the members was quick and took a new form of looking to the past for precedents to support their involvement in religion. Mention was made of the work done in the Reformation, most acts of that period having originated in the House of Commons. The medieval acts of *Provisors* and *Praemunire* were brought into service in the defense of their claim to free speech in religious affairs. The first prohibited the Pope from appointing English clerics; the second prohibited English subjects from appealing cases tried in English courts to the papal court. It was hardly likely that this reaction of a group of new members of the Commons was totally unrelated to the fact that the national synod of the Puritans was meeting in London at this time.

The government's main business of this session was to provide for the Queen's safety following the informal Bond of Association. Mildmay and Hatton spoke on this topic on the first day of business. These two speakers were very effective in focusing the attention of the members on this topic. It was said, "I never heard in Parliament the like matters uttered, and especially the things contained in the latter speech [Hatton's]. They were *magnalia regni* [great matters of state]."[6]

Mildmay's speech lasted over an hour and touched on the benefits of the English situation under the rule of Elizabeth and the dangers to England from the Catholics. Hatton's speech lasted over two hours, but only a resume of one section has survived. Hatton in his most eloquent fashion took his audience through a history of Anglo-Spanish relations ending with the expulsion of the last Spanish ambassador.

What seem likely to be Hatton's notes for his speech on this bill for the Queen's safety are included in *The Bardon Papers*. In Hatton's handwriting are a series of points seemingly made for a speech concerning Elizabeth's safety. The first points made concern the dignity, virtues, and great cares which the Queen takes for her people's peace and safety. These notes describe the people's duty "To seek to preserve her with the services of our bodies, lives, and goods; to resist all perils and dangers towards her person so far as the wit of men and force can reach."[7]

Since Hatton is known to have made similar lists for other speeches concerning Mary Stuart and the dangers she represented, these points could well be those he made in the now lost earlier portion of his speech.

Following these two orations a committee was formed to consider what action should be taken. Mildmay laid before the members the three dangers they needed to provide remedies for—invasion, rebellion, and violence to the Queen. Immediately the subject on all minds was raised. It was said that "No way could be invented so perfect for her Majesty's safety as to take away that person in respect of whom all the mischiefs had been heretofore wrought."[8] The death of Mary Stuart was their aim. The government members of the committee repressed this kind of talk at once, since the Queen was at the time negotiating with the Scots for the return of Mary. The official members were then appointed to draft a bill for the Queen's safety which did not include Mary's execution.

This new bill was based partly on the Bond of Association, which was directed against any claimant to the throne, and heirs of the claimant if they were found guilty by a commission of Councillors, Lords, clergy, and judges of conspiring against the Queen. A major difference was the lessening of this bill's effect on the heirs of a claimant, who were not included in the lynch law clause of this act, as they had been in the Bond of Association. This discrepancy between act and Bond led to a great debate in the house. The critics pointed to a major flaw. If the Queen were dead and all authority lapsed, how could the actions provided for in the bill actually take place? Those who had signed the Bond which required them to pursue James to the death found it hard to reconcile the two documents, having given their solemn oath to uphold the first. But with the Scottish policy of the government now favoring James, the members could not be allowed to take such a punitive action against him.

With this action denied them the members came the following day with another motion: "That if any successor should combine himself in league with the Pope, allowing and receiving his religion, he should for that fact be disabled for ever to claim the Crown."[9] This action, which Parliament would not be able to enforce until 1689, caused more consternation on the government bench. This was meddling with the succession, "a thing most disliking to her Majesty and utterly forbidden us to deal with."[10] By legislating specifically against Mary Parliament might incur war. Diplomatic effects could be expected on the future of Henry of Navarre, the Protestant successor to the King of France, who might likewise be set aside. Elizabeth expected much from Henry's accession to the French throne and had already secretly aided him and the French Huguenots. And lastly it was brought up that if Mary Tudor had acted thus with Elizabeth they would not have her blessed rule at the time. These arguments won the day and the motion was handed back, "and no more speech had of it."[11]

This bill was read in the house on December 14 and had its second reading the following morning. Little debate ensued and it was sent for its engrossment. Many were not satisfied with it but no doubt found themselves reluctant to oppose the government's obvious wishes.

On December 18 Hatton rose in the house to interject the Queen's views. She wanted to know the points of the bill for her safety. She thanked them for their care of her, which "her Majesty said (but he might not say) was more than her merit."[12] She did not want anyone punished for the crime of another, "nor that anything should pass in that Act that should be repugnant to the Law of God or the Law of Nature, or grievous to the conscience of any of her good subjects, or that should not abide the view of the world, as well as enemies as friends."[13] Learning that the clause concerning James VI led to much argument, she "would have it clean dashed out."[14] Elizabeth wanted no one disabled by this Act without his being tried and she especially did not want the crime imputed also to the heir, unless he was also found guilty.

This royal view was very well received and Hatton made a motion to refer the bill to the committee, which was done. Then they met opposition from one member who found he had problems of conscience. He found it difficult to have taken the Oath of Association to do one thing, which now was found by law not proper to do. This block allowed the Queen to equivocate. The Councillors were ordered to take the bill no further and it was set aside for the Christmas recess.

Considering the Queen's safety against another danger, the committee had also been working on a bill to prevent Jesuit missionaries from coming into the country. Any Englishman who had become a Catholic priest since 1559 was to leave the country within forty days. If he remained he would be charged with treason. Neale makes a strong point for the necessity of this harsh act given the dangers which threatened English society. He wrote,

> In fact it was a humane and reasonable attempt to resolve the dilemma of a state exposed by ideological warfare to insidious and deadly peril. If a society has the right to defend its existence,

the individual can hardly claim a conflicting right to remain within the community while acknowledging an external allegiance that threatens to destroy it.[15]

The second clause of the bill made it treason to knowingly aid Jesuits or priests. In the House of Lords the penalty was reduced to that of a felony, but an attempt to require the aid to be attested to by two witnesses was unsuccessful. Other clauses included one requiring English Catholics to return from the continent within a time limit, imposing charges of *praemunire* on anyone sending aid to priests abroad, and forbidding the sending of English children abroad without a special licence from the Queen.

While the bill was having its third reading the procedure was interrupted by an outburst from one of the members, Dr. William Parry. He denounced the bill as a whole, calling it "full of blood, danger, despair and terror to the English subjects of this realm."[16] He was certain that the bill would pass both houses, but he hoped that the Queen would not sign it. He said he would "reserve his reasons of his negative voice against the bill, then to be discovered by him only unto her Majesty."[17]

The members of the house were outraged that Parry would accuse them of writing such a bill and especially that he would not give any reason for his charge. He was immediately sent out of the chamber in the custody of the Sergeant. In his absence discussion of his actions took place and the opinion was that custom allowed each member to speak freely on the bills being discussed. Parry was then brought back to the house and asked to give his reasons for such a speech. He said he had meant no offense to the members of the house, stating that he was servant of the Queen, and again refused to give any reasons for his attitude towards the bill except to the Queen. Following more debate and more words with Parry, the house again sent him out in custody of the Sergeant.

Parry's role is somewhat fuzzy. He had recently returned from the continent where he had acted as a spy for Burghley among Catholics there. He apparently was also planning with his Catholic acquaintances there to assassinate Elizabeth. Whether he was a double agent or an *agent provocateur* is not clear. Although apparently Catholic he had found no problem in taking the Oath of Supremacy in order to sit in Parliament. It is possible that he hoped that his dramatic protest in the House of Commons might persuade the Queen to be more lenient towards Catholics.

Obviously the attention now directed upon one of the government agents could become embarrassing, and Parry was examined by the councillors before the Commons met again. When it did meet, Hatton conveyed the Queen's thanks for the lenient action taken by the members and assured them that she was fairly well satisfied with Parry's explanation to her. The Queen suggested that once he apologized to the house he should be pardoned. Her wishes were carried out but this was not to be the last the house heard from Parry.

By now little had been accomplished in this session and it was long past its planned duration. On Saturday, December 19, the Queen sent Hatton to announce the coming adjournment for the Christmas season. The members were pleased by the gracious wording of the Queen's good wishes for their holiday. The Speaker proposed that the councillors in the house should express their "most humble, loyal and dutiful thanks for her good opinion of them."[18]

Elizabeth did not miss this opportunity to enhance the good relations between the members and herself. On the following Monday Hatton made an eloquent speech giving the Queen's response. Using his recognized oratorical powers Hatton expressed the Queen's "most princely, gracious and kind acceptation of their thanks,"[19] although she denied that she deserved them. She returned them thanks, "yea and that in redoubling to them their thanks ten-thousand fold."[20] In a typically convoluted sentence Hatton expressed the Queen's belief that the blessings and benefits which the country enjoyed came first from God and secondly from the merits of "so religious, godly and obedient subjects."[21]

Later that same day the message came that the Queen had

adjourned Parliament until February 4. Hatton concluded this session in the same eloquent vein with another speech. He reminded them of the recent fond words from the Queen and suggested that they join in prayer "for the long continuance of the most prosperous preservation of her Majesty."[22] He then produced a prayer which he said was written by "an honest, godly, and learned man,"[23] and he offered to read it for the members to repeat after him. This they did on their knees.

During the Christmas adjournment Burghley busied himself with further details of the bill for the Queen's safety. He was concerned with the inevitable chaos which would follow an assassination of Elizabeth and wrote a proposal for a most unusual plan. In essence his plan was to put the Crown into a commission of councillors who would immediately recall the last Parliament which would then be sovereign. The entire plan was unacceptable to the Queen. The mere idea of Parliament being supreme in any circumstances ran counter to all of her governmental policies. Still there was always the risk of an assassin being successful. There is an indication that she was very troubled about this situation. In a letter from Hatton to Burghley on January 26, 1585, Hatton wrote that the Queen required his presence with the Lord Chancellor and the Lord Steward "about the matter of Parliament."[24] Burghley was "to advertise these Lords, that they fail not to be here; at which time I shall attend you. . ."[25]

In any case Elizabeth continued to take her chances, hoping that time would solve the entangled problems of the succession, religion, and the security of the country. That her gamble succeeded does not make it any the less risky at the time and the government and Parliament were to find further immediate evidence of the danger they feared.

Very shortly after Parliament reassembled in early February, 1585, the news burst upon them of yet another plot to kill the Queen, this time by their own member, Dr. Parry. Parry's plot was revealed to the government by his acquaintance, Edmund Neville, whom Parry had tried to gain as a partner in the act. Parry was immediately arrested and questioned by

Walsingham, who gave him a chance to claim his role was only that of an *agent provocateur,* and in that part he had spoken of the murder of the Queen. Parry missed his chance to clear himself and denied he had said any such words. When told there was a witness against him Parry continued to deny that he had ever spoken of such a plan. Later he was questioned by Leicester and Hatton in addition to Walsingham, and on maintaining his denial was sent to the Tower. On February 11 he was again examined by Walsingham, Hatton, and Lord Hunsdon. At that time he made a confession.

On February 24 Hatton gave the members of the house a complete account of Parry's plot. He explained that Parry had made plans to kill the Queen when she was at St. James' or to attack her with a group of five or six men with pistols. Hatton concluded his explanation with a detailed account of Parry's career.

Even before Hatton had formally given the members of the house the details of the plot they had voted to unseat Parry from his place in the house. And on February 23 it was moved that as Parry had plotted as a member of the house a petition should be made to the Queen to devise a punishment fitting "his so extraordinary and most horrible kind of treason."[26] Hatton and Knollys were asked to take this request to the Queen.

The following day Hatton returned with Elizabeth's answer. She thanked them for their concern but would only allow the ordinary course of law to be used. Hatton followed this message with further details of Parry's life. One member of the house, George Ireland, emotionally burst out, "It makes my heart leap for joy to think we have such a jewel. It makes all my joints to tremble for fear when I consider the loss of such a jewel."[27] Hatton answered that the Queen "takes it in most gracious and kind part your great care of her; that you esteem her to be such a jewel. She saith herself—though I may not, nor will not say it—that your care is far above her worthiness."[28]

It was quite natural for Parliament to take up again the problem of Mary Stuart, the beneficiary of any successful attempt on Elizabeth's life. In a letter to Mary on March 22 Elizabeth wrote that a motion had been made in Parliament to revive the act against the Queen of Scots. Elizabeth pointed out that the bill had been passed by both houses of Parliament and that she had stopped this bill as she had an earlier one, and not without great disapproval of the members.[29]

While Parliament turned back with increased urgency to the work on a bill for the Queen's safety, Hatton was busy as the leading government commissioner in Parry's trial. The other commissioners were Henry, Lord Hunsdon, Sir Francis Knollys, Sir James Crofts, and Sir John Popham. When Parry had been charged Hatton spoke:

> These matters contained in this indictment and confessed by this man, are of great importance; they touch the person of the Queen . . ., the very state and well-being of the whole Commonwealth, and the truth of God's word established in these her Majesty's dominions, and the open demonstration of that capital envy of the Man of Rome . . . Wherefore I pray you, for the satisfaction of this great multitude, let the whole matter appear, that everyone may see that the matter of itself is as bad as the indictment imports, and as he has confessed. . . .[30]

It was agreed that certain letters of Parry's and his confession should be read. Parry offered to read them but the clerk was ordered to do so after Hatton allowed Parry to verify them. Hatton then asked Parry if what he had confessed was true and if he confessed it willingly or if any coercion had been used to extort it. Parry responded that he made the confession without constraint and that it was true. When the incriminating letters had been read Parry asked to speak and Hatton responded:

> If you will say anything for the better opening to the world of those your foul and horrible facts, speak on; that which you have confessed, which else would have been and do stand proved against you, for my part, will not sit to hear you.[31]

Attorney-General Popham declared that all had been done but the judgment. Parry begged them to hear him and Hatton replied, "Parry, then do your duty according to conscience, and utter all that you can say concerning those your most wicked facts."[32] Parry began by claiming that he had never meant to kill the Queen, at which Hatton broke in:

> This is absurd; you have not only confessed generally that you were guilty, according to the indictment, which . . . in express words, does contain, that you had traitorously compassed and intended the death and destruction of her Majesty; but you also said particularly that you were guilty of every of the treasons contained therein.[33]

Hatton continued to press Parry. He pointed out that Parry had given his motives to be "mislike of the state" and "mislike of her Majesty" and that he had joined the "wicked Papists." This group, he said, held the Queen not to be the lawful ruler, no Christian, and they believed it was a meritorious deed to kill her. Hatton accused Parry of writing his intentions to murder the Queen to the Pope and having received letters approving his proposal.

> All this you have plainly confessed; and I protest before this great assembly, you have confessed it more plainly and in better sort than my memory will serve me to utter; and say you now, that you never meant it?[34]

Parry now claimed that his confession had been extorted, to which Hunsdon and Hatton both replied that there had been no torture or threatening words used. Parry said that if he had not confessed he would have been tortured. Hatton insisted no such threats had been made, "but I will tell you what we said."

> I spoke these words: "If you will willingly utter the truth of yourself, it may do you good, I wish you to do so, if you will not, we must then proceed in the ordinary course to take your examination. Whereunto you answered, that you would tell the truth of yourself." Was not this the truth?[35]

To this Parry yielded, not really having a choice. Hatton continued exclaiming on Elizabeth's magnanimity considering the fact that they had found on Parry two Scottish daggers which he had intended to use to kill the Queen.

In Hatton's speech on Elizabeth's clemency he mentioned that the Queen had had so little fear that she had kept to herself the knowledge of Parry's plot which had been related to her in their secret talks. Hatton remarked that the Queen had not even told the Privy Council of it. This remark has been interpreted to mean that the government did not believe that Parry meant to kill the Queen and this was Hatton's attempt to explain why he was now being convicted for the same actions for which he had formerly been rewarded. Parry was either being sacrificed to the Puritan anger or the pressures of the Puritan councillors. In Parry's last words there was evidence that he believed Leicester was the cause of his downfall.

It was true that Parry had used the bait of assassinating the Queen in his talks with Catholics in his role as *agent provocateur*. Did he mean it finally or not? How could the government decide when he stopped playing his agent's role and began acting on his own? It is possible, as Brooks suggests,[36] that it was decided to make a distinction between what the Queen knew and what the Privy Council knew. The Queen thus remained magnanimous while the Council dealt with the danger as they saw fit. This method was similar to that taken by the Council in dealing with Mary Stuart in 1587.

Hatton reminded Parry of his statement concerning his meeting Elizabeth at Hampton Court and being struck with her likeness to Henry VIII. Parry had testified that he had then turned away and wept bitterly. But still, according to Hatton, Parry said to himself "that there was no remedy but to do it."[37] "Did you not confess this?"[38] asked Hatton. Parry acknowledged this and then fell into a rage saying again that he had never meant to kill the Queen but that he saw that he must die because" he was not settled."[39] Hatton asked him what he meant by that statement and Parry told him to look in his study

and in his new books and that he would find what he meant.
Hatton protested that he did not know what he meant but, "you
do not well to use such dark speeches, unless you would plainly
utter what you do mean thereby."[40]

Brooks theorizes that by use of the word "unsettled" Parry
was referring to the code of the Leicester Puritan party, and
that this was used in the recently published *Leycester's Commonwealth*.[41] This group was in support of the claim to the throne of
the Protestant Earl of Huntingdon, a relative of the Earl of
Leicester.

The concern of this group was whether one was settled (in
religion) or not. If the answer was yes then the person was
known to be of that faction. Parry evidently believed, as
Hunsdon accused, that he was condemned because of his
religion rather than for treason. He was certainly technically
guilty of having spoken of killing the Queen, whether he meant
it, was boasting, or was perhaps a little mad. There was never
any doubt about the verdict and he was pronounced guilty and
sentenced to the full rigors of the traitor's death. Parry cried
out, "I here summon Queen Elizabeth to answer for my blood
before God."[42] He was executed March 2, 1585, protesting his
innocence to the end.

A joint parliamentary committee from Lords and Commons
had been meeting during the time of the trial in an effort to
write an acceptable bill for the Queen's safety. One was finally
concluded which Hatton introduced into the Commons on
March 3. This bill reflected Queen Elizabeth's insistence that
only the guilty should suffer by providing for an investigation
and judgment to be necessary procedures before any act of
violence. It would bar from succession only the one who was
really shown to have been involved in any assassination plot.
Under the terms of this act Mary's trial would be held and James
VI's rights to the English throne maintained. In spite of some
criticisms in the Commons the bill was passed and ready for the
royal assent by March 13.

After rapidly passing a bill against Jesuit priests as well as a
subsidy bill Commons began to consider a bill which was des-

tined to arouse royal displeasure. This act concerned conduct and permissible activities on Sunday. It began as a rather mild set of prohibitions but as it emerged from committee many pleasurable pursuits were banned, such as hunting, hawking, and attending markets and fairs. After some arguments about amendments the two houses agreed on this being a "good and godly law."[43] Despite this assessment, the Queen vetoed it.

This did not deter the Puritan members of the Commons who on December 14 produced several petitions for a reformation of the Church of England. They were particularly concerned about what they thought were unacceptable clergy in the country. Despite the royal prohibition at the beginning of this Parliament barring discussion of religion, Commons proceeded to hear three petitions on that subject. Encouraged by this development one member spoke up for a "bill and book" which he handed to the Speaker. This was a bill for a complete change of church organization to one on the Presbyterian lines that included adoption of the *Genevan Prayer Book.*

This was indeed stepping onto dangerous ground. After Knollys had ineffectually spoken, Hatton took charge. He "so pressed and moved the House"[44] that the members decided not to hear the "bill and book" and to trust the Queen to act on the reforms mentioned in the petitions. Hatton had headed off a potentially dangerous situation. This bill was to be introduced again in the next Parliament with Hatton again effectively intervening.

The petitions were debated further. They were eventually answered by Archbishop Whitgift in the House of Lords, clause by clause. In his arrogant way Whitgift only succeeded in antagonizing all of his listeners. Later Robert Beale, secretary of the Privy Council and a Puritan, wrote that "In all the histories and records of time past, never prince or subject gave such an insufficient and opprobrious answer."[45] And naturally "the House was nothing satisfied."[46]

In debate on the subsidy one member mentioned the use of the old strategy of linking supply with grievances, as he said "the opportunity very fit, the rather for that Her Majesty, expecting a benevolence from them, would the sooner yield to their lawful and necessary petitions".[47]

Little did this anonymous member know the Queen's attitude expressed in her gracious reception of the clerical subsidy, saying that "she did accept of it thankfully, and the rather that it came voluntarily and frankly, whereas the laity must be entreated and moved thereunto."[48] When Burghley responded with a note of the fact that the bishop's money was but a mite compared with the parliamentary sums, the Queen answered, "I esteem more of their mites than of your pounds, for that they came of themselves, not moved, but you tarry till you be urged thereunto."[49]

Elizabeth then expressed her concern and displeasure that some members of the Commons had spoken disrespectfully of the clergy "which we will not suffer".[50] She also understood that some of her Council had countenanced the meddling action of the members and "we will redress or else uncouncil some of them."[51] No doubt Mildmay and Knollys were under criticism here, certainly not Hatton.

Burghley still interjected his views when Elizabeth bade Whitgift repress conventicles and appoint only proper clergy. Burghley accused the Bishop of Lichfield of making ministers for pay of men who were not worthy to keep horses. The Archbishop's rejoinder was that it was not possible to have learned men in each of the thirteen thousand parishes in England. Elizabeth responded to this,

> Jesus! Thirteen thousand! It is not to be looked for. . . My meaning is not [that] you should make choice of learned ministers only, for they are not to be found, but of honest, sober and wise men and such as can read the scriptures and homilies well unto the people.[52]

After commanding the clergy to require conformity and unity among the ministers, she dismissed them.

Still the committee of the House of Commons worked on a statement which answered Whitgift point by point as he had dealt with their petition. But the work of the committee never got to the house. The Queen roused the Speaker out of his sickbed to appear at Greenwich, having apparently heard of this further action of the house members. On the next morning, March 2, Puckering reported on the Queen's words to the house. He spoke from two sets of notes, one prepared with the aid of Hatton, one with that of Walsingham. The Queen's message dealt with their meddling with religion despite the prohibition and she blamed the Speaker for allowing it. She reminded them that she was the Supreme Governor of the Church of England next under God and although she agreed there was some need for redress she could not "choose but marvel" at their method of proceeding. She saw dangers in this method, "as the Papists will think the Church of England did not have sufficient laws," or that the Queen was not trusted. She regretted having to chastise them and was

> greatly grieved that she has occasion to cause this thus to be delivered unto you, whom she does know and affirms to be as loving subjects as any prince in the world has. And therefore, of her great and tender favor, she could not choose but as a mother over her children eftsoons to warn you to forbear any further proceedings in this course: the rather for that . . . it pertains least unto them, being the lowest of the three estates.[53]

The message on religion concluded with her firm statement that "she will receive no motion of innovation, nor alter nor change any law whereby the religion or church of England stands established at this day."[54]

She also took the opportunity to reprimand the members for neglecting their attendance at the house, leaving before the conclusion of the day's session, and discussing their business at ordinaries or taverns, which was undignified.

The members of the house did not take this strong message from the Queen quietly. Undaunted at this firm statement of royal prerogative, members responded with proposals to depose the Speaker for going to the Queen without their permission and a plan to reject a command from the Queen. These ideas, even spoken of without action, were indeed revolutionary. The house then went on to draft a bill requiring the upper clergy to take their oath in chancery and forbade an oath of obedience from bishops to archbishops. A second bill was an attempt to scale down excessive fees levied in ecclesiastical courts by setting down a list of fees.

The out-of-control members continued to write a bill ostensibly to add force to an earlier act to fine those who tried to attain a benefice without being qualified. In fact, this was an unusual use of secular power to attain one of the clauses in their pet'.ion to Whitgift. Despite some members who were reminded of the Queen's prohibition, the bill was read and passed. In the House of Lords Leicester attacked Whitgift, who called for support from the Queen and mentioned the rebellious acts of the members of the lower house. He begged the Queen to "continue your gracious goodness towards us."[55]

At last peremptory action was necessary. The Queen sent a command to the Commons not to meet on Saturday, March 27, and on the following Monday Parliament was prorogued. Two bills on religion had passed both houses and the Queen vetoed them.

The formal closing of this session found the members of Commons being chastised by the Lord Chancellor for the Queen and by the Queen herself. After thanking the members for their concern for her safety and for the subsidy, the Queen said:

> Yet one matter touches me so near, as I may not overskip: religion, the ground on which all other matters ought to take root, and being corrupted, may mar all the tree; and that there be some fault-finders with the order of the clergy, which so may make a slander to myself and the Church, whose over-ruler God has made me, whose negligence cannot be excused if any schisms or errors heretical were suffered.[56]

Elizabeth admitted there were matters which needed

improvement but insisted they could be amended "without heedless or open exclamation."[57] She mentioned the religious learning she herself had and that religion was of prime importance to her as "I know of no creature that breathes whose life stands hourly in more peril for it than mine."[58] She continued in her reprimand:

> And so you see that you wrong me too much, if any such there be as doubt my coldness in that behalf. For, if I were not persuaded that mine were the true way of God's will, God forbid I should live to prescribe it to you.[59]

Elizabeth deplored the presumption of the Puritans which was "so great, as I may not suffer it," yet she did not mean to animate the Catholics by this attitude nor to "tolerate newfangledness."[60] Again the Queen expressed her determination to "guide them both by God's holy true rule" and saw that in "both parts be peril."[61] The "newfangledness" was a definite threat to kingly rule in her opinion. The Queen concluded by thanking them for the subsidy which she assured them would be employed to their common good. This was a fine example of an Elizabethan speech, marked with firmness and her strong sense of her royal prerogative, but also full of affection and devotion to her subjects which went far towards soothing the situation between the Crown and Parliament.

At the conclusion of the speeches Parliament was prorogued until the following May. No doubt the Queen would have been happy to dissolve this contentious group, but with the everpresent dangers she found it expedient to keep them on call.

Hatton's work continued to be that of supervision of religious matters. He was concerned about safeguarding the ports from the entry of seminarians following this Parliament's actions against them. Walsingham wrote on May 1, 1585:

> I will give present order, throughout the ports for the stay of the party, according to the description contained in your letter. It

may please you to give some charge to your servant Pyne, to look well to the port of London, for that most of the profession do pass that way.[62].

Hatton continued to have accused men lodged in his house as Heneage indicated to him from the Court at Croydon on May 2:

> her Highness's pleasure is . . . that she would have Isaac Higgins, now in your custody yet detained three or four days, . . . that he should be again better examined; and that Mr. Secretary should be sent to, and likewise Mr. Topcliffe with those in that commission, to know if the name of this man be in any of their rules, which they keep of such bad fellows as carry and recarry books and letters into this Realm, and out of it, which being certainly known, that he be kept or let go, as shall be thought best by you for her Majesty's service.[63]

It was in this letter that Heneage enclosed a quip of the Queen's to the effect that Hatton's house "will shortly be like a Gravesend barge, never without a knave, a priest, or a thief."[64]

In December, 1585, the government was faced with a worsening situation in the Netherlands which finally forced the Queen to agree to send an army there under the leadership of Leicester. As a commander Leicester was to perform much as his stepson Essex would later behave in France. Leicester was not a great general nor a wise administrator and immediately disobeyed the Queen's instructions. He accepted the title from the government of the Netherlands of "His excellency the Governor and Captain-General" which infuriated the Queen. In her anger she refused to listen to anyone until Burghley threatened to resign and the Netherlands petitioned her to allow Leicester to keep the title for the time being. It was at this time that Hatton played his customary role as mediator, advising Leicester "to bestow some two or three hundred crowns in some rare thing for a token to her Majesty."[65]

Leicester's conduct contributed much to the failure of this expedition. He did not obey orders, did nothing to end corruption among the captains, and in fact even increased their pay as well as his own. He was recalled in November, 1586, only to be sent back again seven months later at which time he scored another resounding failure. A major port, Sluys, fell into the hands of the Spanish largely through his lack of organization and he was again recalled. Nothing could weaken his position at court and although he had achieved nothing militarily, he was nevertheless given the command of the English forces assembled at Tilbury to meet the Armada in 1588. Leicester and Hatton were durable figures at Elizabeth's court. With war now threatening England in 1586 it was even more essential to watch for conspiracies. Hatton's next major work in that area was to take charge of the trials of those caught in the Babington conspiracy, which ensnared Mary Stuart at last.

chapter eight

Concerns of a Courtier

One of Hatton's major lifelong problems once he had a foot on the road to success was how to finance his role at Elizabeth's Court. He had no family wealth and no doubt had been sent to London to make his own way in life. This he certainly did in the larger sense, but he lived constantly in debt due to the glorious style he had to maintain. Aspirants at Court were not noticed if they did not dress as gentlemen.

As a courtier and official he was required to live at Court, displaying himself in apparel proper to his status there. No Elizabethan officials were paid a living wage and Hatton was no exception. The fees pertaining to the office of Vice-Chamberlain, which he held from 1577 to 1587, were never more than 66 pounds, 13 shillings, 4 pence a year. This was completely inadequate to maintain Hatton's establishment. He added to his financial needs by the extensive building in which he indulged, which was not unusual for men of his rank at Court.

As previously cited, the Queen had made various grants of land and keeperships to Hatton; for example, she made him the Keeper of Corfe Castle. Such keeperships carried with them various rights and privileges which provided some revenue. Elizabeth had also granted him an annuity of 400 pounds a year. This was unusual and was quite a considerable income for that time. Hatton's customary New Year's gift from the Queen consisted of 400 ounces of silver, which hardly covered the cost of the elaborately designed jewels he gave her each year.

Since the royal coffers had insufficient cash for the purpose, it was the royal custom in Tudor times to supplement incomes of officials by granting them monopolies of certain commodities. This system conferred upon the recipient control of the manufacture, sale, or import of a certain article. Usually the monopoly would be farmed out to another person who paid the owner of the monopoly a set sum. In other cases a government tax would be farmed out for a set figure with the grantee making what profit he could from the collection of the tax. These monopolies were very unpopular with commercial and working classes and were to bring serious political problems to Elizabeth in her later years, as well as to the Stuarts.

Not surprisingly, Hatton was successful in acquiring monopolies. Early in his career he had a license to import a limited amount of yarn from Ireland. This license expired in 1576, apparently without renewal. Hatton also possessed the extremely lucrative customs duties on all types of wines. When this monopoly was about to end in 1580 he wrote to Burghley to ask the latter's support with the Queen for its renewal. Hatton admitted his dependence upon this source of revenue and that his fortunes at that time were "in effect all entirely ruined."[1]

There is evidence that Hatton also supported others in their search for revenues, with the expectation of a percentage of the profit. William Tipper, a merchant of London, was enterprising enough to try to revive a method of controlling foreign merchants called "hosting." This procedure required foreign merchants to live with assigned English landlords or hosts. This custom had long been out of use but was still legally in force. In 1576 Tipper, with Hatton's backing, acquired a grant from the Crown and from the City of London to be host. Although many English merchants and all foreign ones involved resisted the revived rule, the Mayor and Aldermen of London supported it and appealed to Hatton ". . . to deal with her Majesty for the same."[2] Since Tipper was allowed to collect twopence in every pound's worth of goods either bought or sold by the merchants under this law, Hatton no doubt would have had a sizable commission as Tipper's patron.

Unfortunately this likely and inventive source of money ran into difficulties both from Elizabeth's officials and foreign governments who came to the defense of their merchants. An old friend of Hatton's, William Davison, wrote to him from Antwerp in February, 1580, that the Archduke Matthias had sent two representatives to complain of Tipper's patent.[3] This archduke had come to the Netherlands in 1578 at the request of the Catholic party there to head the government. Davison had not known originally that Hatton was concerned in the matter and begged him to withdraw from the dubious enterprise. It seems doubtful that Tipper ever received a large amount from this patent although he held it for several years.

The undaunted Tipper, still backed by Hatton, turned to other paths. He tried to go into the business of investigating faulty titles of land by purchasing a patent from another person. Again he became entangled in the intricacies of several competitive suits and finally became the agent of Edward Dyer, Hatton's old friend, who acquired the titles patent in 1588.

Hatton also searched for a fortune, as did many courtiers and even the Queen herself, by investing in the ocean voyages of Francis Drake. The name the *Golden Hind* that Drake gave to his flagship on his famous circumnavigation of the world is a reminder that Hatton was a promoter and investor.

Hatton was an important member of that circle of energetic, curious, and covetous men who were involved with England's new exploits of the sea. His friend Edward Dyer brought Hatton into contact with Dr. John Dee, who was an astrologer, geographer, and was in favor with the Queen, who often visited him. Dee dedicated to Hatton the first volume of his series on the British Empire, which was named *General and Rare Memorials pertaining to the Perfect Art of Navigation*. There is some evidence that Dee planned Drake's voyage around the world in search of treasure,[4] and that the proposal was contained in the book dedicated to Hatton.

Hatton, in company with many courtiers such as Leicester, Walsingham, the Earl of Lincoln, Sir William Winter, and again the Queen, clearly invested a substantial sum in Drake's voyage, although the exact amount is not known. Two of Hatton's nominees accompanied Drake. One of them, John Thomas, was captain of another of Drake's ships, the *Marigold*. The other Hatton man was John Brewer, Drake's trumpeter. At Court only Burghley set his face against this type of action, which certainly had as part of its mission the raiding of Spanish ships and settlements.

While Drake's journey was in progress the *Marigold*, captained by Thomas, disappeared shortly after passing the Straits of Magellan. Three years later when Drake landed at Plymouth it was Hatton's man, John Brewer the trumpeter, who was sent to the Queen with the news.

Hatton, Leicester, and Walsingham were absent from the council when Burghley called it to decide what to do with the treasure which Drake had acquired. The decision was to put it in the Tower until restitution to Spain could be made. When the document was brought to the absent three councillors they refused to sign it. They were described by the Spanish ambassador, Bernardino de Mendoza, as "the principal owners in the venture."[5] Quite naturally these impenitent three investors took the matter to the Queen who as a coinvestor rescinded the order. Althought the idea of restitution remained to be argued for some time, the treasure melted away, with Drake being allowed 10,000 pounds for himself and more for the crew. The other partners were said to have received a 4700 percent profit upon their investment. Hatton received 2300 pounds.[6]

Hatton also invested in other voyages such as those of Martin Frobisher, who searched for the Northwest passage. Again he had as his representative one of the ship's captains, George Best, who wrote a book of these voyages dedicated to Hatton. Best also named for Hatton the place still known as

Hatton Headland on Resolution Island south of Frobisher Bay. Hatton seems to have invested 50 pounds in these last journeys. In 1581 he invested 250 pounds in the voyages of Edward Fenton to the East Indies. In 1584 he joined with the Queen, Leicester, John Hawkins, Drake, and Raleigh in venturing 1000 pounds in a project to develop an eastern trading company. The last known Hatton investment was that of 1000 pounds in the expedition of Essex and Drake to Cadiz in 1589, while he was Lord Chancellor.

There is an interesting note to the final fate of the famous *Golden Hind*. The steeple of St. Paul's was demolished in a storm in 1581. Hatton and Mildmay were delegated by the Privy Council to repair it. There was suggested the plan of setting up the *Golden Hind* on the tower of St. Paul's. Unfortunately this creative idea was not carried out and the legendary ship was put into a shed at Deptford, where it eventually disintegrated.

In addition to earning fame as well as fortune by his backing of the exploits of Elizabethan seamen, Hatton also looked for revenue from one other normal Elizabethan source—Ireland. Hatton's distant cousin Arthur, Lord Grey of Wilton, was the unwilling Irish Deputy for four years. Several letters to Hatton survive in which Arthur hoped to be reprieved from his duty in that difficult land. Hatton naturally looked for Irish land grants and with the attainder of the Earl of Desmond, a large grant in Munster became his. He gained fifty-three Irish and twenty English tenants, and the post of Constable of the Royal Castle of Dungarvan. Apparently the prospects did not look good in Ireland and Hatton wrote to Burghley concerning repairs for the castle ". . . as it shall please her Majesty," adding that he is "not greedy of advancement in Irish honors."[7]

Thus Hatton prospered on the slippery ladder of favor in Elizabeth's court where competitiveness, flattery, and exhibitionism were the requisite qualities for success. In his letters Hatton demonstrated an acute awareness of the cult of the monarch in his excessive allegorical writings of his love for his queen. He also understood the psychological advantages in Elizabeth's court of remaining unmarried. The Queen seemed to dislike the institution of marriage altogether. All courtiers who married had times of trouble when they were out of the royal favor. Elizabeth meant to keep all attention riveted upon her both as queen and woman, and his letters have indicated that it may have been difficult sometimes for Hatton to know which personification was to be addressed. Spenser in his *Faerie Queene* described Elizabeth as bearing two persons, one of the most royal Queen or Empress, and the other of a virtuous and beautiful lady.

Having acquired by royal pressure a proper home in London from the Bishop of Ely, Hatton bought a country manor of Kirby and built the largest house in the country, Holdenby, in which to entertain the Queen. He and Burghley overspent their fortunes greatly to build their manorial shrines for Elizabeth. Hatton no doubt felt it was essential to have such an establishment both to reflect his own successful status as well as to offer the Queen proper housing.

One last source of concern for Hatton in maintaining his favored position in the Queen's eyes was the sudden climb to popularity of Walter Raleigh. The latter had appeared at court and risen so rapidly to fame that incidents were invented to explain the rise, such as the story of his cloak being thrown in the mud for the Queen to walk upon. Raleigh's first court appearance was in 1581 and he soon enjoyed the lease of Durham House on very favorable terms, though he was not knighted until 1585 and had to wait two more years for office. In comparison with the slow but steady climb of Hatton this success was indeed meteoric and a natural source of concern to Hatton.

Raleigh first appeared at Court to report on his service in Ireland. The Queen immediately took to the tall dark adventurer and had him remain at Court. She naturally went through the rituals of royal flirtations and encouraged Raleigh to think himself in love with her. Raleigh could delight the Queen with his witty brilliant conversation and with Leicester married and Alençon back in Flanders he made the most of his chances. He dressed in extravagant finery, even outshining Hatton. He was given various grants and licenses to help pay for such glamorous accoutrements.

For a short time Raleigh was a potent threat, and Hatton sought reassurance from the Queen. He sent a letter to her accompanied by three tokens. Thomas Heneage was the messenger who reported to Hatton by letter on October 25, 1582, on the Queen's reactions. One of the tokens was a small gold bucket with reference to the current pronunciation of Raleigh's first name as "Water." Heneage wrote that Elizabeth was pleased with both the letter and gifts, saying, "there was never such another."[8] She reportedly blushed as she read the letter and ordered Heneage to write to Hatton that her "sheep" of the field:

> was so dear unto her that she bounded her banks so sure as no water nor floods could be able ever to overthrow them. And, for better assurance unto you that you should fear no drowning, she has sent you a bird . . . that brought the good tidings and the covenant that there should be no more destruction by water . . . that you should remember she was a Shepherd, and then you might think how dear her Sheep was unto her.[9]

Hatton still worried about Raleigh's influence in March, 1585, and again used Heneage as a messenger to the Queen. Hatton sent a letter and a love token, a true lover's knot of gold. Heneage wrote to Hatton from Croydon on April 2 regarding the Queen's reception:

> Sir, your bracelets be embraced according to their worth . . . you have great cause to take most comfort, . . . for seldom in my life have I seen more hearty and noble affection expressed by her Majesty towards you which she showed upon this occasion. . . She thinks you faithfullest and of most worth . . . she thought your absence as long as yourself did, and marvelled that you came not.[10]

The Court was visiting at Croydon and apparently Hatton had been displaced from his proper lodgings by Raleigh. When

Heneage told the Queen of this situation, "she grew very much displeased and would not believe that any should be placed in your lodging."[11] On further investigation it was learned that Raleigh occupied Hatton's rooms, "wherewith she grew more angry with my Lord Chamberlain than I wished she had been, and used bitterness of speech against Raleigh telling me before that she had rather see him hanged than equal him with you, or that the world should think she did so."[12] Heneage also reported that the Queen chided Hatton for sending such an expensive trinket, knowing she would not send it back.

Raleigh had not the temperament to win friends in the court nor to remain forever the meek supplicant of the Queen's love. He was not content to remain unmarried and direct his entire emotional life to worshipping the Queen, as Hatton was. Raleigh was to fall into disgrace with the Queen when he loved and married Elizabeth Throckmorton; he and his wife were banished from Court. Hatton had no further competitors for his role as chief lover of the Queen and he and Leicester jogged amiably along in their accustomed positions at court for the rest of their lives.

chapter nine

A Darkness of Conspiracies

His duties as a government prosecutor kept Hatton very busy in 1586 as yet another plot threatened the life and throne of the Queen. Elizabeth had refused to allow Parliament and the English Protestants to execute Mary Stuart in 1572 following the Queen of Scots' involvement in the Ridolfi Plot. As a new plot unfolded Elizabeth would not be so successful. Hatton took an active role against this final Stuart conspiracy to unseat Elizabeth.

Since 1572 the English had grown ever more fearful for Elizabeth's safety. In October, 1583, John Sommerville betrayed his intention to kill Elizabeth. He was a Warwickshire Catholic who was arrested and quickly executed. In June, 1584, a second attempt on the life of William of Orange was successful. Shortly after that the fears of Parliament took the form of the Bond of Association which thousands of men signed. This Bond, which obliged its signatories to protect the Queen, to prevent anyone with knowledge of a plot from gaining the throne, and to pursue such a person to the death has been described in detail

earlier. Excitement and apprehension grew with knowledge of
Dr. Parry's plan to kill the Queen in January, 1585. At that time
Parliament attempted to revive the proceedings against Mary
Stuart begun in 1572 and was rebuffed by Elizabeth. Thus
matters stood.

The death of William of Orange had left a political vacuum
in the Netherlands which Elizabeth reluctantly agreed must be
filled by English aid if the rebellion in that area were to continue against Spain. A treaty was signed and Elizabeth consented
to the dispatch of English troops to aid the beleaguered provinces. In addition, after much delay she appointed Leicester to
lead the troops, even though she resisted his leaving England. In
effect an undeclared war was now taking place. Philip of Spain
thought again of the Enterprise and was ready to listen to plans
to eliminate Elizabeth.[1] In this atmosphere the watch over the
captive Mary Stuart became more vigilant. She was moved
twice in 1586, from Sheffield to Tutbury and then to Chartley.
Her guardian was now a zealous Puritan, Sir Amias Paulet.
With his help Walsingham began to construct a trap for Mary in
order to gain unassailable evidence, acceptable even to Elizabeth, of Walsingham's long-held suspicions of Mary's complicity in former plots. A supposedly safe channel for letters to
friends outside was opened to Mary through George Gifford,
an English Catholic, who agreed to play the role of double
agent. Gifford had persuasive credentials from Mary's agent
Thomas Morgan and Mary accepted this plan without reserva-
tion. The procedure was simple. Messages were wrapped in
waterproof cases and put into the bunghole of ingoing beer
casks and in returning empty ones. Naturally they were inter-
cepted and copied by Walsingham's secretary.

Walsingham did not have to wait long before very
interesting letters began to arrive. First he learned that an
English Catholic, John Ballard, had arrived in France with news
that the Catholics in England were ready to rise in conjunction
with a foreign invasion. In June Walsingham first began to find
news of another conspiracy called the Babington plot.

Anthony Babington had been a page in Mary's household at

one time and had been caught up in romantic and religious dreams of freeing her. He now offered to murder Elizabeth and free Mary with the aid of five friends. On Gifford's advice Babington wrote the methods of the entire undertaking to Mary on July 6. In addition to the death of Elizabeth and the liberation of Mary this most imprudent letter contained details of an invasion force and the aid expected from English Catholics. This indiscreet youth also asked for assurances that the six men involved would be rewarded if they lived or that their heirs would in the likely event of their deaths.

This dangerous letter with its essentially unrealistic plot was taken personally to Chartley by Walsingham's secretary Thomas Phelippes. Then they waited for Mary to commit herself in writing to the murder of the Queen. They had not long to wait, for on July 17 came Mary's answer and it was as Walsingham expected. The letter contained complete approval of the plan, adding a list of items to be checked, such as the numbers of men involved and the points of landing for the expected invasion. She even asked how the plotters meant to proceed in the murder of Elizabeth. She concluded with advice on setting her free as well. Ominously, Walsingham's secretary drew a sketch of a gallows on the copy of this letter as he hurried it to his master. Walsingham kept this letter in his hands for eleven days, then had a postscript forged on it asking for the names of the six men scheduled to commit the assassination of Elizabeth. Babington received this on July 29.

Two of the men were already known to be Babington himself and John Ballard. The others were readily identified because the group had been seen often together and had foolishly posed for a group portrait. But Walsingham didn't wait for the reply from Babington. On August 4 Ballard was arrested and although Babington fled he was arrested ten days later. At the same time Mary's secretaries were arrested at Chartley and her papers and effects seized.

Babington and his co-conspirators were confined in the Tower, where Babington made his first confession on August 18. The other men arrested were John Ballard, Edward Windsor, John Savage, Robert Barnewall, Chidiock Tichbourne, Thomas Salusbury, Edward Abington, Charles Tilney, Henry Dunne, Robert Gage, and Charnock. These were men of good family and many of them were related to members of the Court or were members themselves. This status made them even more dangerous to the safety of Elizabeth.

The confessions of Ballard, Savage, and Tichbourne were taken on August 8, 10, and 11. Babington was examined at Hatton's house in Holborn near the middle of August by Sir Thomas Bromley, Walsingham, Burghley, and Hatton. There were nine examinations between August 18 and September 8 and after repeated interrogations of these men Hatton left for Holdenby before September 2. Hatton had apparently gone to Holdenby to study the documents taken in the case and had been taken ill. He had been expected back in London by September 12 but wrote to Burghley, "I am come to my poor house, full of a fever, with stitches, spitting of blood, and other bad accidents. I must commit myself to God and the physician for awhile . . . by reason of my sickness I cannot return."[2] Hatton deplored the delay in the trials of the plotters, also writing ". . . God hath mightily defended us. He is all and EveR one. I beseech Him that these our negligences may not tempt Him."[3] Nevertheless by September 12 he had recovered sufficiently to be in London taking an active part in the trials which began on the following day and continued for several days.

The trials of these conspirators took three days. The prisoners were tried in two groups, the first one apparently consisting of those who were prepared to plead guilty. Savage was questioned first and admitted his guilt on the conspiracy charge but he denied that he was guilty of an attempt to kill the queen. It was explained to him that he had to plead to the entire charge and Hatton elaborated:

> . . . to say that you are guilty to that, and not to this, is no plea, for you must either confess it generally, or deny it generally; wherefore delay not the time, but say either guilty, or not; and if you say guilty, then shall you hear further; if not guilty, her Majesty's learned counsel is ready to give evidence against you.[4]

After this admonishment Savage pleaded guilty and his confession was read to the Court. Hatton then put his customary question: "Savage, I must ask you one question; was not all this willingly and voluntarily confessed by yourself, without menacing, without torture, or without offer of any torture?"[5] Savage agreed that no torture had been used. Hatton then had the court adjourned until the next day when Savage would be judged and other cases heard. In these trials Hatton was the principal interrogator and made the decisions concerning procedure even though the Lord Chief Justice, the Lord Chief Justice of Common Pleas, and Lord Chief Baron of the Exchequer were in attendance.

On September 14, the cases of Babington, Tichbourne, Dunne, Barnewall, Salusbury and Ballard were heard. After the indictments were read Ballard tried to plead guilty only to planning the rescue of Mary Stuart and not to conspiracy against the life of Elizabeth. Hatton's reply was, "Ballard, under your own hand are all things confessed; therefore now it is much vanity to stand vaingloriously in denying it."[6] Ballard then admitted his guilt as charged. When Henry Dunne was asked how he pleaded he answered that when he was asked to take part in this plot he prayed to God that what was done would be to His glory. Hatton asked, "Then it was thus, that they said the Queen should be killed, and you said, 'God's will be done.' "[7] When Dunne affirmed this Hatton responded, "Oh, wretch, wretch! Your conscience and own confession show that you are guilty."[8]

The other conspirators also pleaded guilty, Babington blaming Ballard in persuading him to take part in the plot. Hatton admonished Ballard, "O, Ballard, Ballard, what have you done? A sort of brave youths otherwise endued with good gifts, by your inducement have you brought to their utter destruction and ruin."[9] When Ballard spoke to Babington that he wished that his life could save Babington's and that he would say no more, Hatton replied, "Nay, Ballard, you must say more and shall say more, for you must not commit high treasons and then huddle them up; but is this your *Religio Catholica?* Nay rather, it is Diabolica."[10]

When Barnewell also insisted that he had meant no violence to the Queen, Hatton presented contrary evidence:

> O, Barnewall, Barnewall, did you not come to Richmond,
> and when her Majesty walked abroad, did not you there view
> her and all her company, what weapons they had, how she
> walked alone? And . . . make relation to Babington how it was a
> most easy matter to kill her Majesty and what you had seen and
> done. . .?[11]

Hatton continued to review Barnewall's actions, stating that the
Queen had noticed him. Barnewall insisted that what he did was
done for conscience sake and Hatton responded, "You would
have killed the Queen for conscience! Fie on such a conscience."[12]

On the third day of the trials Edward Abington and Charles
Tilney, who had both pleaded not guilty, were heard. They put
up a spirited defense, claiming that under the Elizabethan statute on treason two witnesses were required to verify commission of the crime. They were summarily told that they were
being tried under an act of Edward III which did not require witnesses. Their sentences were predictable. In fact Elizabeth was
so disturbed by these events that she required the full savage
measure of punishment for traitors be carried out, and this was
done with the first seven men executed. Burghley relayed these
instructions to Hatton to inform the judges.[13] She may have felt
especially threatened because several of these conspirators were
men of the Court who had enjoyed easy access to her chambers.
Babington and Tilney had been Gentlemen-Pensioners and
Tichbourne was a follower of Hatton. But after the execution of
the first group in the usual manner of hanging, disemboweling
and quartering, in full view of the audience, the Queen sent
word that the others were to be allowed to hang until dead.

The *Bardon Papers*, a collection of papers for Hatton's use in
these cases and that of Mary Stuart, contain an outline of the
speech which Hatton gave at the end of these trials.

> Then began Sir Christopher Hatton, and made an excellent
> good speech, in opening and setting forth their treasons, and

how they all proceeded from the wicked priests, the ministers of the Pope. And first, he showed how these wicked and devilish youths had conspired to murder the Queen's most excellent Majesty; secondly, to bring in foreign invasion; thirdly, to deliver the Queen of Scots and make her queen; fourthly, to sack the city of London; fifthly, to rob and destroy all the wealthy subjects of this realm; sixthly, to kill divers of the Privy Council, as the Earl of Leicester, the Lord Treasurer, Mr. Secretary, Sir Ralph Sadler, Sir Amias Paulet, seventhly, to set fire on all the Queen's ships; eighthly, to cloy all the great ordnance; ninthly and lastly, to subvert religion and the whole estate of government.[14]

Hatton continued saying that the inventors of these practices did not try to convert the older men but persuaded the younger ones," . . . and of those the most ripe wits, whose high hearts and ambitious minds do carry them headlong to all wickedness."[15]

Nearly all of the prisoners pleaded to have their families taken care of since their estates were forfeit to the crown. Charnock hopelessly appealed to Hatton to get Elizabeth to pardon him. Hatton answered, "Charnock, your offence is too high for me to be an obtainer of your pardon, but I am sorry for you."[16] Hatton did agree to see that a debt of Charnock's would be paid.

Walsingham then turned to the last piece of evidence needed to complete his case against Mary Stuart, whose name had not been allowed to be mentioned in the trials of the young conspirators. Walsingham wanted Mary's secretaries Claude Nau and Gilbert Curle to confess as to the authenticity of Mary's letter to Babington approving of the plot. These two men were in an untenable position, having copies of their letters in the government's hands.

It is not surprising that they confessed rather readily and implicated Mary by doing so. Hatton had been one of the Privy Councillors who examined them, concerning which Burghley wrote to him to September 4:

> . . . that they would yield somewhat to confirm their mistress, if they were persuaded that themselves might escape, and the

blow fall upon their mistress, betwixt her head and shoulders, surely we would have the whole from them.[17]

Although Mary felt betrayed by these confessions, the secretaries had little recourse. The rack was not a pleasant alternative and even had they persisted in denials Walsingham would not have altered his procedures because of them. With the Babington conspirators executed, Nau and Curle in prison, and Mary already guilty under the Act of Association there was obviously little left of Mary's buoyant hopes of freedom which she had enjoyed only a short time before.

The cause of this governmental activity, Mary Stuart, was still totally unaware of the turn of events, being completely out of touch at Chartley. Naturally her spirits and hopes were high and she gaily accepted the offer of Paulet to ride out to a buck hunt on August 11. She was happy at the thought of meeting some of the gentry at the hunt and when she saw some horsemen coming towards her she no doubt could think them the Babington men coming to rescue her. She was soon bereft of that illusion. The leader of the party was Sir Thomas Gorges who had a message from Elizabeth accusing Mary of conspiracy against her and the State. Mary was then taken to Tixall, a country house nearby, while her apartments at Chartley were thoroughly searched and inventoried. Mary remained in her rooms at Tixall for two weeks and then was taken back to Chartley. Nau and Curle were then taken away and sent to London with the results already noted. Mary never saw them again. Nau was returned to France after a few months and Curle was kept in prison a year.

England became filled with rumors that Elizabeth had been killed, that there was civil war in the country accompanied by an invasion by Parma and the French Guise at the same time. Elizabeth herself panicked at the danger which had come so close to her person and crown. The fleet put to sea and coastal areas were ordered to muster their defenses. Paulet, who was still in charge of Mary at Chartley, became nervous and asked for stronger quarters in which to guard his captive. The Council suggested the Tower but Elizabeth would not agree to that. Therefore on September 21 Mary was taken to a place unknown to her. On September 25 the procession reached the castle of Fotheringay in Northamptonshire which Mary would not leave alive. She was put into rather small and mean apartments which at first led her to fear a secret death, which she abhorred. There is reason to believe that Elizabeth also hoped that some gentleman would secretly poison Mary under his oath in the Act of Association. She bitterly questioned the value of such an oath to her when she was resisting the death warrant for Mary later. The opinions of the crowned heads of Europe also seemed to have regarded a secret death as the better way politically.

As Mary learned that the state rooms in Fotheringay were being prepared for a delegation from London she became more cheerful. She ardently desired an open public confrontation with her accusers. The thiry-six commissioners appointed to try Mary met in London and read copies of of the evidence Walsingham had assembled. They agreed that she should be brought to trial under the 1585 Act of Association. This act provided for the trial and punishment with death of anyone claiming the crown of England and attempting to injure the Queen.

Members of this commission arrived at Fotheringay on October 11, Hatton among them; he stayed at Mildmay's home at Apethorpe about five miles distant. Mary was immediately given a copy of their commission to try her. The following day another deputation arrived at the castle to obtain Mary's consent to appear at the trial and the interrogation they planned for her. Mary maintained they had no jurisdiction over her because she was an anointed sovereign. The next day yet another group appeared to affirm that she was subject to England's laws and would be tried *in absentia* if she refused to appear. Mary wept and insisted again she was no subject of England. She repeated her wish to be heard before Parliament. This topic continued to be the subject of argument.

On October 13 Hatton received a chiding letter from Eliza-

beth while he was at Apethorpe. The bearer had apparently had
a ". . . wonderful sore journey," indicating a hastily sent
message. Hatton replied:

> . . . He [the bearer] had from your Majesty a little daunted
> me. I most humbly crave your Majesty's pardon. God and your
> Majesty be praised I have recovered my perfect health; and if
> now for my ease or pleasure I should be found negligent in your
> service, I were much unworthy of that life which many a time
> your Royal Majesty has given me. I might likewise sustain some
> obloquy, whereof I have heard somewhat; but my will and wit,
> and whatever is in me, shall be found assuredly yours, whether I
> be sick or whole, or what EveR become of me deem they what
> pleases them. . .[18]

If it was Elizabeth's intent to goad Hatton on to complete the
work at Fotheringay, she succeeded. Hatton persuaded Mary to
reconsider her claims to immunity and to accept the jurisdiction
of the commission. Hatton's persuasive words solved the
impasse. He told Mary that although she was indeed a queen
". . . in such a crime the royal dignity is not exempt from
answering, neither by the civil nor canon law, nor by the law of
nations nor of nature."[19]

Hatton reasoned with Mary that if such offenses could be
committed without punishment, ". . . all justice would stag-
ger, yea, fall to the ground."[20] He maintained that if Mary were
innocent ". . . she stained her reputation in avoiding a trial."[21]
Hatton advised Mary that although she maintained her innocence Elizabeth had reluctantly been forced to disagree with
her, and he praised the quality of the prudent men the Queen
had sent to determine the truth. Hatton said that Elizabeth
would be overjoyed if Mary could prove her innocence and that
the Queen had ". . . affirmed to me at my coming from her,
that never anything befell her more grievous, than that you
were charged with such a crime."[22] He concluded by advising
Mary to throw aside the useless privilege of royal dignity and to
appear in the trial to prove her innocence, ". . . lest by avoiding
trial, you draw upon yourself suspicion, and lay upon your
reputation an eternal blot and aspersion."[23]

During the days of argument Mary had received a letter from Elizabeth accusing her of having ". . . planned in divers ways and manners to take my life and to ruin my kingdom by the shedding of blood."[24] She ordered Mary to answer the commission as if she herself were present, adding ". . . But answer fully, and you may receive greater favor from us."[25] It is doubtful that Mary could have any hope of a pardon from this letter, or that she was totally persuaded by Hatton's logic, but in any case she agreed to appear at the trial on October 14, saying that she ". . . was persuaded by Hatton's reasons, which she had weighed with advisement."[26] Perhaps his words made it easier for Mary to accede gracefully to an unavoidable action. Perhaps Elizabeth's letters to both Mary and Hatton had motivated his words and her acceptance. A recent biographer of Mary Stuart writes that Mary at this time acquired the serenity and calm of a person well aware she was soon to die. Mary was acting the role of martyr for the wider world of Catholic Europe, a role in which she was highly persuasive.[27]

The trial began in a room above the great hall of Fotheringay on October 15 and was under the direction of Burghley. Hatton was present as indicated in a drawing of the scene but took no further part in the trial. He is depicted sitting with the other five Privy Councillors facing the chair of State set up to represent the Queen of England in the trial scene.

The charges were presented and the letters of Babington read. Mary consistently denied her complicity in wishing the death of Elizabeth, although she did not deny her wish for personal liberation. The letters written by her secretaries were introduced with Mary claiming that some interpolations could have been done by Nau. She insisted that the secretaries should be produced to testify personally. Mary, without counsel or secretarial aid, defended herself very well and was closely questioned by the commissioners. A second day of similar questioning and denials ended this pseudo-trial.

The court would have proceeded to judgment at once but had been called back to London by Elizabeth, who wanted no rapid conclusion. There the matter was debated once more in Star Chamber with unanimous agreement as to Mary's guilt.

Hatton's efforts in this case were now to be directed to the exposition of the government's case against Mary in the House of Commons.

Having had no doubt as to the commissioner's verdict, the Privy Councillors had planned to call a Parliament to support them. Burghley wrote to Walsingham on September 8 that "We stick upon Parliament, which her Majesty mislikes to have, but we all persist, to make the burden better borne and the world abroad better satisfied."[28] The councillors knew well the difficulty to be anticipated in getting Elizabeth's approval for the execution of Mary and wanted support from the whole Parliament. It had been planned for Parliament to convene on October 15, but due to the delay with Mary's trial it had been postponed until October 29. The Queen was tactfully absent from the opening of Parliament, remaining in her palace upriver at Richmond. This distance kept her councillors rushing up and down river, much to Burghley's annoyance at the delays this caused. He suffered from gout and complained at often being up before five in the morning.

The House of Commons went through its usual formal opening with the reelection of Puckering as Speaker. They continued normal business by reading bills on November 3, no doubt waiting for the councillors to initiate the true business, that of Mary Stuart. Hatton then appeared on the floor of the house and stopped debate ". . . having matter of most great importance to deliver to this House from her Majesty."[29] He began one of his major speeches, notes of which are found in the *Bardon Papers*.[30] He declared the cause of Parliament being called, not to make more laws nor for a subsidy, but ". . . to consult for such matters as the like were never erst heard of, nor any Parliament called for in former times that can be found or read of."[31] Hatton then proceeded to ". . . excellently, plainly, and effectually make relation of the horrible and wicked practices . . . of the Queen of Scots so called."[32]

Hatton made known to the members of Commons the entire case against Mary, beginning with the Norfolk plot and continuing through all the series of plots against Elizabeth in favor of Mary. He also gave the members a complete account of Mary's part in the Babington conspiracy and maintained that these attempts and practices of Mary tended to:

> the ruin and overthrow of the true and sincere religion . . ., the invasion of foreign forces . . ., rebellion and civil wars, . . . yea, and withall (which his heart quaked and trembled to utter and think on) the death and destruction of the most sacred person of our most gracious sovereign lady the Queen's Majesty, to the utter desolation and conquest of this most noble realm of England. . .[33]

His concluding sentences concerned his hope that speedy justice should be had ". . . for cutting of her off, by course of justice."[34] He believed that Elizabeth would never be safe without this action. His last dramatic sentence was, "Absalom must perish, lest Israel perish.."[35]

The custom seems to have been established of Hatton and Mildmay speaking in tandem and Mildmay spoke against Mary also. He pointed out that the plot had been directed against Elizabeth, whom he praised highly, in contrast with the iniquitous life of Mary. Here he highlighted the murder of Darnley. He spoke of the honorable treatment Mary had received in England and repeated her role in the Babington conspiracy. Two other Privy Councillors, Sir Ralph Sadler and John Wolley, followed this speech of Mildmay's before debate was adjourned until the following day.

On November 4, following many more speeches in complete agreement on the subject of Mary, a committee was named to confer with a similar committee from Lords with the intention of sending a petition to the Queen for the speedy execution of Mary. Following the joint committee meeting each house heard again the official account of the trial and judgment of the commissioners. Both houses unanimously agreed that the verdict was just and lawful and agreed to press Elizabeth to proceed according to the Act of Association.[36]

Both houses agreed to write a petition to the effect that

Mary must die. Due to the dispersing of the houses the petition was delayed in being presented to the Queen, as this letter from Burghley and Hatton to Secretary William Davison on September 10 demonstrated:

> . . . Whereas I, the Treasurer perceive by the report of me, the Vice-Chamberlain, that her Majesty could be content with the coming of Lords. . . . and the Commons should be rather tomorrow than Saturday. In very truth so would we both have it; but the dispersing of both Houses is such . . . not possible to give the Lords appointed warning to come afore Saturday, and in like sort it will be to-morrow nine o'clock before the Commons assemble; wherefore we both pray this night you to make our excuse to her Majesty. . .[37]

On Friday, November 11, Hatton informed the house that an audience with the Queen would be held at Richmond to include twenty peers and forty members of Commons. This took place on the following day and here the Speaker presented the petition. Elizabeth responded with a long characteristic speech thanking them for their concern for her safety, of her sadness in hearing of Mary's condemnation, and her promise to send them a message of her conclusion.

Hatton also made a motion that the petition would include a reference to the Act of Association which had been omitted in the petition as a basis for Mary's trial. It seems that Elizabeth had seen an advance copy of the petition and noticed this omission. She had written Burghley to have it included but it was not possible in Lords since they had adjourned until the following Tuesday. But Hatton could and did include it in the petition of Commons.[38]

Hatton made a motion that the Speaker ". . . be put in remembrance by this House . . . to urge to her Majesty that matter and necessity of the late Instruments of Association, respecting especially the consciences of a great number of her Highness' good and loyal subjects which cannot be dispensed with by laws. . .[39]

On Monday, November 14, Hatton addressed the assembly

after the Speaker had reported on the committee's meeting with the Queen. He commended the Speaker on his bearing at the audience and then reported a further message from the Queen, which she had forgotten to tell the committee. She was ". . . moved with some commiseration towards the Scottish Queen, in respect of her former dignity . . . her nearness of kindred, . . . also her sex."[40] The Queen would:

> . . . be pleased to forbear the taking of her blood, if by any other means could be devised consonant with the safety of herself and of the kingdom, . . . else not therein leaving them all nevertheless to their own free liberty and dispositions of proceedings . . . at their choices: For as her Majesty would willingly hearken to the device and reasons of any particular member of this House; so Mr. Vice Chamberlain showed they may exhibit their conceits in the case either to any of the Privy Council, being of this House, or else to Mr. Speaker, to be further signified over to her Highness. . .[41]

Hatton also reminded the house that as had been announced at the beginning of this Parliament, no laws should be made. He therefore advised adjournment until Friday at which time they might expect to hear from the Queen concerning their petition. The members agreed and reconvened on Friday only to find no reply from Elizabeth, who was waiting for some alternative solution to come from them. Debate ensued with many members taking part. It was concluded that,

> . . . no other device or means whatsoever could or can possibly be found or imagined that such safety can in any wise at all be had so long as the said Queen of Scots does or shall live, they do withal very earnestly move and persuade the prosecution of the said petition lately delivered jointly by the Lords and this House to her Majesty for the necessity of the speedy executing of the said Queen of Scots, as the one and only mean (as far as man's reason can reach) to provide for the safety of the continuance of true religion, of her Majesty's most royal person, and of the peaceable estate of this realm from the manifest and imminent danger of utter subversion, destruction and desolation.[42]

In this day's debates Hatton spoke last to clarify a possible misunderstanding about the Queen's last message, that ". . . it was a peremptory proposition to them to exclude them from all other courses of proceeding, showed to them again, as he did before, that her Majesty commanded that message to be propounded to them for consultation only, and not for direction, leaving . . . every member . . . to their own free liberty. . ."[43] Hatton agreed with the petition and its prosecution and suggested another consultation with the committee from Lords. This was resolved and the session was adjourned until Monday.

On Monday, November 21, Sir Francis Knollys began the report on the committee's work, but it was ". . . the impressive Hatton—who had quite eclipsed him, and every other Councillor in leadership of the House—who took charge of the business."[44] Hatton explained the discussion in the conference, gave reasons for Mary's execution, and asked if anyone had another solution.[45] No one did. Hatton then moved to continue to uphold their petition for Mary's execution which was resolved by the house. A further committee was also sent to confer with the Lords for united action. On Tuesday, November 22, Lords reported a plan to send members to ask for an audience with Elizabeth. Commons appointed Hatton and John Wolley to represent them. The Lords had further decided to be ready with more reasons why their decision should be adopted by the Queen and Hatton recommended that Commons do the same. Hatton advised that he could not meet in committee nor be in the house before ten o'clock next morning ". . . but of necessity must both attend her Majesty's good pleasure for answer and also lodge at the Court all night."[46]

On November 23 Hatton reported that an audience with the Queen had been arranged for the next afternoon. Hatton warned them that there was to be no debate with the Queen and advised them to put all of their arguments into the speech of the Speaker of the House. The speeches of the Lord Chancellor and the speaker were given before the Queen on November 24, following which they were treated to a long graceful response from Elizabeth.

In this speech the Queen assured them she had not dragged out her decision on Mary for form's sake. Again she expressed the hope that some solution other than death could be devised, saying, ". . . I have just cause to complain that I, who have in my time pardoned so many rebels, winked at so many treasons . . . should now be forced to this proceeding, against such a person."[47] She thanked them for their petition and concern for her and asked them to ". . . take in good part my answer answerless."[48] The representatives of Parliament had to be content with this response. They reported back to their respective houses on Friday, November 25. In Commons the point was raised that the new ambassador from France had arrived and it was feared that he would exert pressure upon the Queen to save Mary. Hatton answered that the joint committee had already thought of this possibility and had warned the Lord Chamberlain and others to be watchful.[49]

Elizabeth had almost exhausted all delaying tactics. The problem of Mary Stuart would not solve itself. There is reason to believe that she even hoped that the jailers of Mary would kill the Scottish Queen themselves under their oath the Act of Association as referred to earlier. This was indignantly refused by Sir Amias Paulet.[50] Elizabeth had tried to get Parliament to devise some other punishment short of death. This too had failed. The crucial problem had to be solved by an action on Elizabeth's part. She had to proclaim the sentence against Mary and sign the warrant for the execution. After much vacillation Elizabeth finally allowed the proclamation of the sentence to be made public on December 4, 1586, after which Parliament was adjourned until February 15. This was only half of what the members wanted, and the Speaker asked the Privy Councillors to plead with the Queen for the remainder of their petition to be granted. The public announcement of the sentence was received by the citizens of London with great joy. They celebrated with bonfires and the singing of psalms. Elizabeth had now to decide in ten and one-half weeks what was to be done with Mary Stuart.

The Privy Councillors were eager to finish the business.

Walsingham drew up the warrant and the Letters Patent to be sent to Paulet at Fotheringay were done by Burghley. They fervently hoped for immediate action on the part of the Queen.

Elizabeth meantime was talking with the French ambassadors from Henry III and with emissaries from James VI, who made protestations in favor of his mother. Initially James had sent a less than diplomatic letter alluding to the stain on Henry VIII's reputation by ". . . the beheading of his bedfellows."[51] James' honor required some show of indignation on his part but his greatest concern was the preservation of his right to the English throne. As the Act of Association had been rewritten on Elizabeth's orders the right of James to succession to the English throne was not tainted by his mother's downfall. Therefore, despite his shocked expressions his views were those expressed in a letter to the Earl of Leicester, "How fond and inconstant I were if I should prefer my mother to the title, let all men judge."[52] Elizabeth received additional Scottish delegates at the end of December. She listened to all their arguments, countered their points, and maintained her right to proceed in the case adamantly. Still, she hesitated while the Court moved to Greenwich for Christmas.

While Elizabeth was pondering Mary's fate a fresh plot was discovered whose aim was to kill Elizabeth. Apparently this idea was fostered by the French embassy. William Stafford, the son of one of Elizabeth's ladies of the bedchamber, was approached by du Trapp, the secretary of the French ambassador.[53] Stafford was promised glory and a great deal of money if he would kill Elizabeth. Stafford refused but did recommend a man named Moody as a possible assassin. The only problem was that Moody was in jail in London. Moody was, however, quite ready to discuss the means of killing the Queen, and suggested poison or a bag of twenty pounds of gunpowder placed under her bed. Before this wildly impractical plot got any further Stafford informed the Council. Du Trapp was seized as he tried to get to France and was questioned by Hatton and Secretary William Davison. Meanwhile, rumors were spread that ". . . the Queen of Scots was broken out of prison; that the City of London was fired; that many thousand Spaniards were landed in Wales; that certain noblemen were fled; and such like . . . The stir and confusion was great: such as I think happened not in England these hundred years past, even from out of the north into these parts, and over all the West as far as Cornwall."[54] It is certainly possible that this faintly ridiculous plot with its concurrent spread of rumors was an invention by some members of the government in order to pressure Elizabeth to act. It would be consistent with the Queen's version of the execution of the warrant against Mary. Elizabeth was heard to say, *"Aut fer, aut feri: ne feriare, feri"*[55] (Suffer or strike, in order not to be struck, strike).

In any case the Privy Councillors Burghley, Leicester, Hatton, and Davison questioned the French ambassador, Michel de Castelnau, Siegneur de la Mauvissière, concerning the matter on January 12. They informed him of their reason for apprehending du Trapp and of the conversations between Stafford, Moody, and du Trapp. When the ambassador angrily denied any knowledge of this plot Stafford was brought in, whereupon both the ambassador and Stafford accused each of initiating the conspiracy. Mauvissière admitted that he had been an accessory to this plot, but denied that he had a duty to inform any but his own ruler. Burghley gravely advised the ambassador to beware of becoming involved in such matters again, and that he did not believe him ". . . acquitted of the guilt of the offence, though he escaped the punishment."[56] Whatever the provenance of this plot, it did somewhat nullify the intercession from the French on Mary's behalf.

This episode and the attendant rumors only served to harden English attitudes towards Mary Stuart and heightened their intention to see her executed. Mary had been shown the sentence but remained steadfast in her protestations of innocence. Perhaps she relied on the obvious hesitation of Elizabeth to order the execution.

But Mary reckoned without the Council. As mentioned earlier Burghley had drawn up the warrant in late December, and it was given to Councillor William Davison to await Elizabeth's signature. Davison had only recently been named to that position and was an old friend of Hatton's. Davison had been assigned for long periods to Antwerp. From there he had often written to Hatton, keeping him fully informed as to conditions there. Hatton was also godfather to one of Davison's sons. Davison, despite a natural caution, was to find himself in an unenviable positon.

After holding the warrant for five or six weeks, the Queen sent for Davison and signed it on February 1. She ordered him to have it sealed by the Great Seal immediately, telling him to also show it to Walsingham, saying satirically, "The grief thereof would go near to kill him outright."[57] Davison rather naturally told Burghley and took the warrant to the Great Seal. The following day, on learning of his action concerning the seal, the Queen was angry at the haste. Davison was well aware that the Queen was reluctant to take part in this matter and feared being isolated and blamed personally. He took the warrant and his fears to his old friend Hatton, explaining that he was not proceeding any further alone. Hatton's attitude was "as he was heartily glad the matter was brought thus far, so did he for his own part wish him hanged that would not join with Davison in the furtherance hereof, being a cause so much importing the common safety and tranquillity of her Majesty and the whole Realm."[58] The two men then went to confer with Burghley. They decided to call the whole Council together the following day. In the meantime Burghley planned to write the letters to accompany the warrant. When Burghley showed Hatton and Davison the letters the next morning Hatton disapproved of them, finding them "very particular, and such as, in truth, the warranty could not bear."[59] Burghley then offered to rewrite them by the afternoon and the Privy Council was assembled within the hour. Burghley explained the situation to the Privy Councillors telling them that he believed the Queen had done all that was required of her in signing the warrant. He described Davison's role and thought that since all the Council was concerned it should be made a common cause.

Each member agreed to take his share of responsibility and it was decided to send the warrant by a clerk of the Council, Robert Beale, to Fotheringay. The councillors present at this bold and decisive meeting were Burghley, Earl of Derby, Earl of Leicester, Lords Howard, Hunsdon, and Cobham, Sir Francis Knollys, Walsingham, Davison, and Hatton. Beale was ordered to ". . . use the utmost expedition in proceeding to Fotheringay."[60]

Thus without Elizabeth's knowledge Mary was told on the night of February 7 to prepare herself for death at eight o'clock on the following morning. When the news of her execution reached London on the afternoon of February 9, there was great rejoicing with church bells ringing and banquets in the streets with bonfires. This outpouring of joy on the part of the people of England lasted for a week. But Elizabeth did not join them.

The Queen's wrath was predictable when she heard of Mary's execution. Hatton was called at once and told that the execution was contrary to her orders. But her greatest anger fell upon Burghley and Davison. Elizabeth maintained that after signing the warrant she had ordered Davison to keep it in his hands until further word from her. Davison was interrogated by Hatton and Wolley on March 12 and again on March 14 and 16. Neither Hatton nor any other signatories of the warrant were part of the commission which tried Davison in Star Chamber on March 28. He was sentenced to a fine and imprisonment although the fine was later remitted. He never lost his fees as Council Secretary and was released from the Tower following the defeat of the Armada in October 1588. In 1594 Davison was given a lucrative land grant.

Walsingham remained discreetly absent at his country home of Barn Elms, alleging illness. Beale was sent to an inferior position in York while Burghley himself was excluded from the Court and Elizabeth's presence.[61] He remained at his country house for several months, appearing at the next session of Parliament only on the final day of the session.

There are differing interpretations which can be put on
these actions. Davison's biographer claimed that ". . . as it is
well known, Davison was sacrificed to the Queen's cruel and
selfish policy."[62] An earlier biographer of Hatton also thought
that Davison was the scapegoat in this situation and that
Burghley and Hatton must have known what was happening.
These two councillors certainly knew Elizabeth's habit of pro-
crastination and they were determined on Mary's death. The
Council had acted as a whole and each knew the danger of the
action. They were certainly in a difficult position with the public
aware of the sentence which they had no machinery for carry-
ing out. Hatton's biographer concluded:

> They had the warrant, and that was enough. Each must
> trust his own wits to fly the Queen's wrath should it explode in
> his direction. If Davison could not succeed in escaping from the
> danger zone, that was his look-out. So, consciously or uncon-
> sciously, argued the two elder statesmen, one of them Davi-
> son's friend and godfather to his son. It was not a very squeam-
> ish age.[63]

Following the concept that Davison was knowingly set up
as a scapegoat, then the grief displayed by Elizabeth was not
genuine. Certainly many Scottish and Frenchmen at the time
believed this. This could be explained by the political necessity
of providing an excuse so that relations between England and
Scotland and France could be maintained. Yet there is small
doubt that the emotion of grief and shock Elizabeth showed at
hearing of Mary's execution was genuine. Elizabeth felt very
deeply the problem of killing another queen. She was especially
concerned about having Mary publicly executed. She, as noted
earlier, had cast around for someone to secretly murder Mary
and this solution was the preferred option coming from the
rulers of Europe.[64]

The members of the Privy Council concerned were genuinely worried about the Queen's reaction. They wrote to her
on February 12, expressing ". . . with sobbing hearts our desire

to have your grief of mind to cease, and to give yourself to your natural food and sleep, to maintain your health."[65] There exists a letter from Burghley to an unknown person which defined his acute sense of danger and uncertainty. He wrote:

> I doubt not but you understand her Majesty's great displeasure for the execution of the Scottish Queen, though justly done and most profitable for her Majesty's surety. . . Poor Mr. Davison is . . . in the Tower, whose conscience does only comfort him; and though her Majesty has shown her offence to her Council that were privy to the execution, yet her offence is to me so further in some degree, as I, not having been able to appear before her with the rest, by reason of my hurt, am forbidden, or not licensed, to come to her presence to answer for myself. . . She . . . is informed that by her prerogative she may cause Mr. Davison to be hanged, and that we all may be so convicted as we shall require pardon.[66]

Burghley continued to describe the advice given to the Queen by Lord Chief Justice Anderson to the effect that her prerogative was absolute. Burghley asked his correspondent to warn other judges that the Queen might consult to be careful of their replies. He concluded, "I would be loth to live to see a woman of such wisdom as she is, to be wrongly advised, for fear or other infirmity; and I think it a hard time if men, for doing well afore God and man, shall be otherwise punished than law may warrant, with an opinion gotten from the judges that her prerogative is above her law."[67]

Perhaps the most considered opinion as to the responsibility for Mary's death and the true attitude of Elizabeth is that of Sir John Neale. He writes that although English foreign policy did require a scapegoat, Elizabeth was not merely playing an expedient role. She had spent many days searching for some other means to end this problem without a public execution, probably wishing that someone would murder Mary secretly. Neale's conclusions are that the ". . . Councillors must have been conscious that they were forcing her hand; a highly dangerous game, akin to touching the sceptre."[68] When Elizabeth learned of the irrevocable deed she was overwhelmed by a sense of tragedy and in unjust anger turned against her ministers.

When the storm of grief and anger died down England was in a much safer situation. The Catholic cause had indeed lost much of its focus and this itself had an impact on English Catholics. This group did not look favorably on Philip of Spain nor his daughter as rulers of England, as their actions would demonstrate on the arrival of the Armada. As the councillors had said, "the dead do not bite."[69] Mary's death secured the life of Elizabeth and the safety of Protestant England.

chapter ten

Hatton and
the Unruly Parliament

The Catholic problem of Mary Stuart may have been finished but the Puritans organized once again to achieve their goals as the Parliament reassembled in February, 1587. With Burghley absent from the whole session and other ministers less than vigorous in guiding the Queen, only Hatton remained to mediate between Elizabeth and a headstrong House of Commons.

The extremist Puritans had been getting documents, supplications, and bills ready for this session of Parliament but found the subject of Mary Stuart dominating the attention of the House of Commons in the earlier session. In February when Parliament was reassembled there was a group of men such as Peter Wentworth in touch with members of Parliament.[1] This group, led by Anthony Cope, planned to push their religious policies through Parliament.

Parliament had opened on February 15, but due to the absence of many members Hatton announced that it would be adjourned until February 22. On that day Hatton gave a speech:

>   That it was her Majesty's pleasure to have dangers dis-
> closed, and to have the House know that she thanked God for
> the goodness of the House, that she wished the meeting to be
> short, that men of government might go home . . . and to take
> another time for making laws, having such as be now of
> necessity.[2]

A list of dangers survived were ". . . of ancient malice, are to be
prepared for, and God called upon for aid. The principal heads of
the dangers were: the Catholics abroad; the Pope; the King of
Spain, the Princes of the League, the Papists at home and their
ministers."[3] The origin of these threats was described to be the
Council of Trent ". . . which agreed to extirp [sic] Christian
religion (which they term heresy) whereunto divers Princes
assented, and bound themselves in solemn manner."[4] From this
council had come the excommunication of the Queen, the
planning of the Northern Rebellion, and papal aid for Mary
Stuart. The various attempts to overthrow the "glorious gospel" by infiltration into Scotland and Ireland was described in
this recital of Anglo-Catholic relations and the Catholic machinations against England. A survey of naval and shipping
grievances England had against the Spanish was included. The
warlike preparations of Philip II were detailed with a list of his
forces: 360 sail of Spanish, 80 galleys from Venice and Genoa,
one galley with 600 armed men from the Duke of Florence, and
12,000 men maintained by Italy and the Pope.

   Then turning to defensive needs, Hatton highlighted English aid to the Low Countries and the common ties that bound
the two countries. He defended the Queen's intervention there
as being required by conscience and the defense of England.[5]
This emotional speech of Hatton's was followed by one by
Mildmay that pointed out the cost of the needed defenses.
There was a committee appointed to draw up the subsidy bill
required.

   The next day the emotionally charged atmosphere was
continued by the dramatic speech of Job Throckmorton, who
pointed to the iniquities of the foreign rulers, to which list he

undiplomatically added the King of France and ". . . the young imp of Scotland."[6] Hatton rebuked Throckmorton for speaking in such a manner about princes. Two days later Hatton made a motion to "admonish" Throckmorton because

> . . . he spoke sharply of princes and laid indignities on them. The reverence to princes is due by God. . . We are bound to obey good princes . . . We should use great regard of princes in free speech. . .[7]

Hatton continued to make the royal opinion clear. It was "hard and intolerable to use ill speeches of the King of France, continuing in league and friendship with us . . . . Matter nearer than this [was] glanced at also: yea; and touched a little against the King of Scotland, a prince young, of good religion, a friend, and in league with her Majesty. . ." It was ". . . a sin then to speak ill of him, and shame to detract him: rather to pray for him."[8] Hatton hoped that this motion of his might repair the damage done by Throckmorton's forthright speech, but this speech had already reached the ears of Archibald Douglas, the ambassador of James VI in London. It would not do now to further offend James, and Burghley later wrote to Douglas that Throckmorton was being punished ". . . for which cause he shall be committed tomorrow to the Tower as a close prisoner, and shall thereby, for the rashness of his tongue, feel smart in his whole body. His fault is not excusable, and therefore the sharplier to be punished."[9] Burghley hoped that this action would be immediately reported to James.

On February 24 the committee appointed to consider financial needs met to discuss the extent of English aid to the Netherlands. No one disputed that money was needed. A more difficult question concerned the acceptance of the Low Countries' offer of sovereignty to the Queen. Hatton made a major speech reported by Speaker Puckering whose presence was unusual. Hatton spoke most effectively, weighing the importance of the Low Countries in relationship to the control of the Channel and the economic importance of the Anglo-Dutch trade. He maintained a subsidy was not enough to assist them and considered the alternatives of English sovereignty or protectorship. In this meeting Hatton seems to have gotten carried away from his usually clear assessment of the Queen's reaction. "If we enter in strength, we shall have the sovereignty when it pleases us, or make such a peace as we ourselves desire."[10] He was obviously pleased with the conference, saying, ". . . these days' doings, well known and continued, will mightily further the enterprise. It is such a consultation as this Realm has not known these hundred years."[11] The Queen would certainly not agree with this assessment and Hatton had ignored the difficult political factors involved in the actions he advocated in his enthusiasm.

At the following committee meeting on February 27 Hatton more realistically stated: ". . . it is not fit to design and direct the Queen how she shall use. . ."[12] the money intended for the Netherlands. Despite being cautioned by these words the committee persevered, and in the afternoon meeting of March 6 Hatton received some news to the effect that the clergy had agreed to contribute a sum towards the Netherlands project. There followed a long debate concerning the amount of money to be offered and the conditions under which it was to be used, with Hatton reminding them ". . . we may not meddle with sovereignty."[13] After an attempt to work with the House of Lords had failed, it was agreed that a contribution would be raised similar to the Lords, half the subsidy rate.

At the conclusion of this difficult series of meetings an audience with the Queen was given to twelve members of the House of Commons as well as the Privy Councillors. Elizabeth refused the benevolences from Parliament altogether, accepting only the grant from Convocation. As Hatton had belatedly warned, she was unalterably opposed to accepting the sovereignty of the Low Countries and to having her foreign policy dictated by Parliament.

Other work of this Puritan Parliament concerned religious reform. On Monday, February 27, the attack began on Whitgift and the clergy of the established church. In a well-organized and planned maneuver Anthony Cope opened the debate by asking that a Bill and Book be read. The bill gave a review of the English Reformation and the reasons for Elizabeth's initial religious position, followed by a description of the "true church." This church was contrasted with the corrupt Anglican Church as it then stood. Cope spoke of the need for a learned ministry. In summation the purpose of the bill was to introduce the use of a newly revised *Genevan Prayer Book* combined with a Presbyterian form of church government. With this new order went a complete removal of the present church establishment, including the hierarchy, sacraments, church courts, and even the royal supremacy.

The Speaker recognized the revolutionary character of this bill and reminded the members of the royal command not to discuss the topic, but he was outvoted by the members of Commons who wished to hear the whole Bill and Book. When again reminded of the Queen's specific prohibition on meddling in religious matters, many members spoke in favor of hearing the bill regardless and of the urgent need for religious reform. Job Throckmorton made a lengthy speech which included mention of the need for freedom of speech and the great value of the Queen's safety if such a reformation were made. Unfortunately for the plans of these Puritans, the prolonged debate took all the time that day and they rose prepared to continue the following day. But when they met the next morning the Speaker had to explain that he had no documents, Elizabeth having sent for them from her residence at Greenwich.

Even this announcement of the everwatchful eye of the Queen did not deter these men. They began to discuss the sorry state of the church again, with many more speeches about the needed remedies. They spent the entire day debating this topic excepting only a period during which the subsidy bill was read.

On the following day, March 1, the stalwart Puritan Peter Wentworth made a carefully prepared speech concerning the liberties of the house. He began with the presentation of a series of questions for the Speaker to answer: Were not the members free to discuss any matter? Was it not against the rule for any member to make known to anyone what was being debated? Was it possible for the Speaker to rise without consent of the house or to overrule the house? Was it not against the law for the Queen or councillor to blame any member for words on the floor of the house? And there was a question which touched Hatton's role—was it contrary to the liberties of the house to receive messages either commanding or prohibiting discussion, or was it acceptable to inform the Queen of what was occurring in the house?

These provocative questions hit the vital point of Tudor management of the House of Commons. Hatton's relaying of information from the house to the Queen and returning with her prohibitions and admonitions was here brought under criticism. The Speaker tried to postpone the reading of these queries until he had heard from the Queen concerning Cope's bill, but the members would not allow it. The Speaker insisted on his right to read through bills and pocket the articles.

Then came a message from the Queen summoning the Speaker to Court. Since Elizabeth was at Greenwich she couldn't have been responding to this latest debate. She was either calling him due to the previous day's debate, or the councillors invented her summons.[14] In any case the Queen acted rapidly to queel the dissenters. Wentworth and Cope accompanied by three other Puritans who had spoken in favor of Cope's bill were put in the Tower forthwith. These men were accused of meeting to discuss government business outside of Parliament, an action for which they had no privilege.

On March 2 The Speaker reported on his meeting with the Queen, who had reminded him that members of the house had been specifically told not to meddle in religious matters. This was reinforced by Hatton, who told them they were hindering the orderly procedure of church reformation by their interference. The house returned to other business for the moment, but the Puritan leaders were probably planning their next move.

On March 4 Sir John Higham returned to the same matter, asking first for the release of Wentworth and his friends, since the house could not do their work without all the members present. Again he described the sorry state of the church in his county, where there was a great lack of ministers. At this point ". . . the invaluable Hatton rose to reply . . ."[15] He defined the difference between actions which were considered parliamentary privileges and those under Crown jurisdiction, and further indicated that he knew no particulars of this case. This last was not very likely. He advised that they wait to be further informed before they sent a petition for the release of the members. He also informed them

> . . . Touching the Book . . . that her Majesty had for divers good causes best known to herself thought fit to suppress the same without any further examination thereof; and yet conceived it very unfit for her Majesty to give any account of her doings[16]

Hatton then began a comprehensive attack on the Bill and Book which had been introduced by Anthony Cope. He said that the Queen had appointed himself, Milday, and Egerton to explain to the house her actions on the bill. Their aim was to define the bill's radical elements. Hatton claimed to have no deeper knowledge than that of the ordinary true Christian, but he asserted that much of the bill's content came within his knowledge of affairs of state. He, as had Cope, reviewed the English reformation's history and mentioned that the Church had many sectarian enemies and that this last Bill and Book surpassed them all. He asked ". . . will you alter the whole form and order of your service? Will you take the book from us which we have been persuaded to think both good and godly? . . . Might it not have sufficed to have reformed the errors? If you answer that there were so many, it could not be done, will any man believe you?"[17] He continued with a comparison of the Anglican service with the prayers which people could learn to their comfort, with the strange extemporaneous prayers advocated by the new book. He pointed out that the whole service in the new book is left to the minister's sermon, ". . . which is, indeed, the whole service

. . . Trust me you shall know it fitter to be suppressed than to be debated. And this I deliver you from her Majesty, that no further argument be used in it."[18]

Hatton continued to describe the effects of the new bill on various social groups such as the laity, the clergy, and the Queen herself. To the landholder he pointed out that the patronage of the church livings would be transferred from them to the new presbyteries. It ". . . touches us all in our inheritances."[19] Where was the money coming from to pay those clergy required for each parish by the new bill? There were to be ". . . one pastor, a doctor, two deacons at the least, besides I know not how many elders."[20] He also made clear that the Presbyterians expected the bishops and churches to be despoiled to pay for these offices and if this was not sufficient, which he assumed it would not be, then ". . . we are bound to surrender . . . our abbey lands and such other possessions as have at any time belonged to the church . . . they call us church robbers, devourers of holy things, cormorants. . ."[21] This point was certainly of interest to those gentry who had acquired former church lands.

Probably knowing that the fate of the higher clergy would not be of any great concern to the members, Hatton only mentioned them briefly before consideration of the effect of the bill on the Queen's estate. He said that the statutes concerning royal control of the church and religious matters would be ended, and this power would go to the ministers. Significantly the royal revenues would be severely cut and he made the point of the effect of this loss on the finances of others. "First fruits, tenths, subsidies, all gone; yet the Crown still bound to defend the Realm . . . It must all come out of your own purses."[22] This situation would lead to possible criticism of the Queen by the ministers and Hatton alluded to the disorder in the country this state of affairs would produce. He criticized the authors of the bill, ". . . whereas you pretend hereby to work wonders, you shall drive them [the people] by the thousands to become atheists or Papists. I tell you, there is an old note of schismatics or heretics, which is very rife among us,. . ."[23] Hatton concluded with a warning of the intentions of the writers of the bill. "For, I pray you, wherein differ these men in this case, from the Papists? The Pope denies the supremacy of princes, so do, in effect, these . . . The Pope . . . doth abrogate all such laws as any prince has made in church matters, to his dislike. And so would these men do with all the laws. . ."[24] Then as an appeal to those who may not have fully understood the import of the bill, "Out of my heart, I think the honest, zealous gentlemen of this House have been slyly led into this action."[25] So ended this effective speech defining the dangers to the church establishment and touching on areas of self-interest in land and purse, plus the last point about possible revolts and rebellion against a weakened Queen, a factor which always disturbed the Tudor gentry.

This important speech is printed in a biography of Archbishop John Whitgift and is to be found in the Lambeth Palace library. It indicates further the closeness with which Hatton and Whitgift worked to blunt the various attacks of the Puritans. This attitude separated Hatton in Whitgift's mind from other Privy Councillors, as he indicated in a letter concerning the Martinist tracts. In the prosecution of these secret writers Whitgift mentioned that

> . . . he had the certain allowance and countenance of the Queen therein; and the favor likewise of other great men of the Court; as the Lord Treasurer Burghley, the Earl of Leicester, Sir Francis Walsingham, and Sir Christopher Hatton, Vice-Chamberlain. And yet the three former had some kindness to such of the non-subscribers as were preachers . . . But Hatton was his fast and entire friend and confidant; and showed little or no favor to these wayward ministers, or any of them. To him therefore the Archbishop opened now his bosom. . .[26]

Whitgift, according to his biographer, John Strype, found it very strange ". . . that these great men should stand so variously affected as they did."[27] He complained that he had "received unkind speeches where he least looked for them; and that only for

doing his duty in that most necessary work. . ."[28] Whitgift also
found it strange that the same men who professed the wish for
peace and uniformity in the church ". . . yet could not abide
that anything should be done against them; wishing rather the
whole ministry of the land to be discountenanced and dis-
couraged, than a few wayward persons (of no account in comparison) suppressed and punished."[29] Whitgift maintained that
this attitude on the part of those in government made it difficult
to carry out the laws and that:

> Disobedient and wilful persons were animated, laws con-
> temned, her Majesty's will and pleasure little regarded, and
> executors thereof in word and deed abused, and though these
> overthwarts grieved him, yet he thanked God, they could not
> withdraw him from doing his duty in this case, which he was
> persuaded God himself, her Majesty, the laws of the State, of
> this Church and commonwealth, did require of him.[30]

Strype described the above letter as a secret one sent by
Whitgift on July 16, 1585, to Hatton in response to Hatton's let-
ter acknowledging the Archbishop's problems in this area.
Hatton had written that:

> perceiving what affronts the Archbishop endured, and what
> toils he underwent, he thought fit by the said messenger to
> assure him how sensible he was of his cares; and that he would
> take all opportunities to recommend him to her Majesty's favor
> and countenance; and signifying how well affected she stood
> unto him, and to the labors he sustained in her service towards
> the church; that he would always as occasion should serve solicit
> his suits unto her.[31]

According to Whitgift's biographer this letter greatly alleviated
the Archbishop's troubled mind and gave him great comfort. He
thanked Hatton in his return letter for the former's message
". . . and should think himself bound to him therefore, as long
as he should live. For it had not a little comforted him. . ."[32] He
added . . . that her Majesty must be his refuse. . ."[33] and

thanked Hatton for his assurances of his support with the Queen.

Mildmay followed Hatton's speech to the members of the House of Commons, again pointing out the disorder and change in laws the new bill would require. He appreciated the problems needing reform in the church but thought this attempt was too radical. His advice was to continue reforms ". . . with all humility, which is fit for us and is most like to prevail."[34] Egerton completed this threefold attack on Cope's bill by a speech showing concisely the legal changes it would require. Following this exposition of the government's stand on the bill, Hatton spoke again to give the members a list of Puritan tracts which the Queen wished them to read.

The irrepressible members tried still again when on March 8 Sir John Higham offered a two-part motion, one that was aimed at cutting some of Whitgift's disciplinary moves, and one to aid the development of a learned ministry. The house approved and a committee was appointed to organize a petition to the Queen.[35] Nothing is known about the petition but there is a letter from the Queen to Whitgift entitled "Why you ought not to deal with matters of religion," which seems to fit this period. This letter leaves no one in doubt as to the royal response to any future petition on this subject.

> Her Majesty is fully resolved, by her own reading and princely judgment, upon the truth of the reformation which we have already . . . Her Majesty thinks it very inconvenient and dangerous, whilst our enemies are laboring to overthrow the religion established, as false and erroneous, that we by new disputations should seem ourselves to doubt thereof.[36]

The Queen had considered the criticisms of the present church and found them frivolous and believed the new framework mentioned to be ". . . most prejudical to the religion established, to her crown, to her government, and to her subjects."[37] Elizabeth maintained that if there were matters requiring reform in the church the clergy should deal with them. To attempt to make new laws for each point ". . . were a means to breed great lightness in her subjects, to nourish an unstaid [sic] humor in them of seeking still for exchanges. . ."[38] Her statement concluded with her view of the royal prerogative:

> Her Majesty takes your petition herein to be against the prerogative of her crown: for, by your full consents, it has been confirmed and enacted . . . that the full power, authority, jurisdiction and supremacy in church causes . . . should be united and annexed to the Imperial Crown of this Realm.[39]

Stalemated on the religious reform so desired the members, led by Thomas Cromwell, turned to an attempt to get their imprisoned colleagues freed. An impressive committee was formed but nothing is known of its results. Hatton and other Privy Councillors were as usual included in the committee formed on Cromwell's motion and must have been uneasy about the actions of this truculent house. This was no time to approach the still angry Elizabeth with tactful petitions to release the dissenters in the Tower.

After other minor matters were debated Parliament was closed on March 23, 1587. Elizabeth had not been present at its opening and she did not attend its closing. Burghley, who had been absent all session, appeared on the last day but was not included on the commission to end the session. This must have been a deliberate act on the part of the Queen indicating how angry she still was on the matter of Mary's execution. And contrary to recent custom in which she had merely adjourned Parliament in order to have one available in such dangerous times, the Queen ordered this one dissolved. Relations had become so strained between the Queen and this body that perhaps she thought it best to remain absent and silent while she ended this disobedient parliamentary session.

chapter eleven

Lord Chancellor

After the death of Mary Stuart the problems faced by England and her Queen underwent some notable changes. Worries concerning the loyalties of English Catholics, for instance, were somewhat lessened. Although the Catholics might have favored Mary's claim to England's throne, they almost certainly would not fight for Philip of Spain and his similar but much more dubious claim. Worry about the actions and attitudes of Puritans, in contrast, increased steadily as these dissidents made themselves ever more a major domestic problem.

Elizabeth had long before seen that Puritan claims to an independent church organization ran counter to her ideas of royal sovereignty in both Church and State. The Puritans had advanced extreme demands in the last Parliament and had only been repressed by the Queen's taking part in the proceedings and refusing to allow debate on the Bill and Book to continue. Given this consideration and the excellent work done by Hatton in speaking against the Puritan bill and in dealing with Puritan dissenters, it was not surprising that Elizabeth chose to name Hatton to fill the post of Lord Chancellor vacated by the death of Sir Thomas Bromley in April, 1587. Hatton had over the years proved himself able and reliable in his supervision of both Puritans and Catholics who threatened the stability of the State. Hatton also worked in concert with Archbishop Whitgift on the all-important matter of religious uniformity. Given the recent threat by the Puritans in Parliament and the imminent arrival of the Armada, this naming of an able experienced politician to the office was a wise move.

This appointment was the pinnacle of Hatton's career. On April 29, 1587, Elizabeth presented the Great Seal to Hatton in a gallery of the palace of the Archbishop of Canterbury at Croydon, where the Court was in residence. The Queen took the Great Seal from its red velvet bag and put it into Hatton's hands, bidding him use it to seal a writ and then named him Lord Chancellor. Appropriate to the occasion was the presence of John Whitgift, the Archbishop, a longtime colleague of Hatton who had collaborated with him in actions to restrain the Puritans. It may well have have been the ability of these two men to work together against this primary danger to domestic security that influenced Elizabeth's choice of Hatton for a position normally held by a man of considerable legal training and experience. It was clearly a political appointment and as such it earned cautious criticism. William Camden reported that the appointment was ". . . advanced by the cunning Court-arts of some, that by his absence at Court, and the troublesome discharge of so great a place, which they thought him not to be able to undergo, his favor with the Queen might slag and grow less."[1] These forebodings seem not to have been substantiated by Hatton's actions in office, nor is there any evidence of a loss of the Queen's favor.

Although the appointment to this high post of someone not an eminent lawyer caused some astonishment and grumbling among the legal establishment, contemporary reactions have been somewhat exaggerated. Camden wrote that ". . . the great lawyers of England took very great distaste. . ."[2] to Hatton's appointment, believing that their professional rights to the office had been recognized ever since churchmen had ceased to hold the post. Thomas Fuller later continued the tale of the unhappy and envious lawyers, affirming that they considered ". . . his advancement their injury, that one not thoroughly bred to the laws, should be preferred to the place."³ The disgruntled attorneys did not fully take into account the Queen's evaluation of Hatton's recent work in her behalf in Parliament and her need for one of his fame and experience in this position at this time. She clearly would not have appointed him had she feared he would dishonor the office. Actually Hatton was not entirely inexperienced in legal matters at all, for as a Privy Councillor he had sat for more than ten years in Star Chamber cases.

That Hatton was well aware of the adverse comments and the effect they might have on Elizabeth is indicated by his statement to a member of Burghley's household who came to him with congratulations. The messenger reported that Hatton wished Burghley to know that he was disturbed by news received from the Court. The rumor was that the Queen repented of her appointment of Hatton because ". . an occasion was thereby given to the world to talk diversely thereof. . ."⁴ Hatton expressed his intention of going to Court to determine Elizabeth's attitude. If she continued to think in that vein he vowed that he would give up the Great Seal. Lady Burghley had sent best wishes to Hatton on April 30 by her son Robert, from whom we learn that Hatton had already changed his customary courtly hat and feather for a flat velvet cap similar to Burghley's own cap.⁵

If Elizabeth had any second thoughts about Hatton's appointment they were never translated into action, for he remained in office. On the first day of Trinity term, May 3, 1587, a stately procession made its way from Ely Place in Holborn to Westminster where Hatton took the oath of office. Before him in the procession went forty of his gentlemen in blue livery and chains of gold, plus Gentlemen-Pensioners and other gentlemen on foot. Also attending him were the officers and clerks of the Court of Chancery. Hatton rode in state behind them, having on his right hand Lord Treasurer Burghley and on the left the Earl of Leicester. Following him were nobles, judges, and many knights with their retinues.[6]

Regarding Hatton's appointment a recent author has written, "By a want of behaviour and competence, Hatton could have damned the Queen's decison, but in the circumstances his appointment must rank as one of her more complimentary achievements."[7] This modern view agrees with Camden's earlier assessment that although Hatton was criticized for his lack of legal training, "yet. . . he executed the place with the greatest style and splendor of any that ever we saw; and what he wanted in knowledge of the law he labored to make good by equity and justice."[8] Throughout his career Hatton had displayed abilities that advanced his role far above the level of favorite and courtier. He continued to maintain his widely acknowledged competence in this last and highest position. Indeed his personal contacts with the Queen made him impervious to many pressures. There is evidence of the essential impartiality and fairness of his decisions. He seemed especially concerned with poor litigants, one of whom lamented his death: "The old Lord Chancellor is gone that esteemed neither letters nor would be carried with any means of rewards."[9]

Dunkel pointed out that important qualities of Hatton's personality made him valuable in this position. He cited ". . . tact and intelligence beyond most men and he had a genius for getting men to work together with common purpose."[10] Dunkel believed that in the crucial year of 1587 men of goodwill such as Hatton were badly needed, ". . . who perhaps lacked nearly all the talents required in their important posts, except the supreme ability in gaining cooperation among men who had the necessary skills in abundance."[11]

In his new post Hatton could clearly rely on Burghley, Whitgift, and many others besides the Queen. That he felt the need of having men who had the necessary skills around him is evident. He brought to London from Cambridge his friend Richard Swale and appointed him a Master in Chancery. Hatton also ordered four Masters in Chancery to be in daily attendance on him in court or on the sessions held in his house. Thus he always had legal advice and guidance and was careful ". . . not venturing to wade beyond the shallow margin of equity, where he could distinctly see the bottom,"[12]

Little is known about his court work as only one case is preserved today. But it is recorded that he used a layman's common sense to achieve some order in areas of Chancery work. There had been few previous attempts to organize the daily handling of work, especially the allocation of hearings. In his first year in office Hatton assigned certain days of the week to hearings, reserving others for orders and interlocutory work. He now devoted Wednesdays and Fridays to the familiar Star Chamber work. On other days he sat in the Court of Chancery, holding court in Westminister Hall in the mornings and in his house in Holborn in the afternoons. He arranged his schedule efficiently and dealt with his new tasks with vigor.

Hatton took action against the encroachment of Masters Extraordinary who had been appointed to oversee work in remote parts of the country but who had recently begun to work near London. In 1588 he issued an order restraining them from acting within three miles of London and from doing any act or ". . . exercising any authority belonging to the office and room of a Master of Chancery."[13] These men were not regarded as part of Chancery but rather were viewed as interlopers in the work and fees of the Masters of Chancery.

The strengthening of the office of usher was central to Hatton's directive of 1590 in which he stipulated regulations for the conduct of court officials. The usher had a duty to attend the Lord Chancellor. He sat within the bar and was considered an official of the court. His earlier job of keeping the door was performed by a subordinate in Elizabethan times. The usher was now directed to see to it that the only persons allowed in court were the attorneys and officers whose attendance was necessary; all others were to be kept out.[14] It is possible that this order resulted from too many people crowding into the courtroom to see the famous Sir Christopher in action.

Hatton acted also to end the abuse of pleas in poverty in 1588. This practice allowed very poor people to bring cases to court without payment. Hatton maintained that the court had been abused by well-to-do persons who pretended extreme poverty and had been allowed to plead in *forma pauperis*. He ordered that no one should be allowed to plead in that manner henceforth without a certificate from a justice of the peace in the suitor's area stating that he had no alternative recourse in justice. This required the verification that the suitor had belongings of less than five pounds value or lands worth no more than forty shillings a year. Those who did not fit that standard of poverty were ordered to file their suits in the Court of Requests.

Hatton's attitude towards the law was expressed in a speech he gave on the occasion of Robert Clarke's appointment as Sergeant-at-Law in June, 1588. Hatton advised Clarke that "No man can live without Law, therefore, I do exhort you, that you have good care of your duty in the calling, and that you be a father to the poor; that you be careful to relieve all men afflicted."[15] He warned Clarke not to be ". . . carried away with the authority, power, or threatenings of any other."[16] Truth was to be his guide with regard either to friend or money. Hatton advised Clarke to use diligence as he had found ". . . by daily experience that diligence brings to pass great things in the course and proceeding of the law."[17] Hatton then addressed all present not to call men to the bar who were unworthy and said, "I find that there are now more at the Bar in one House, than there was in all the Inns of Court when I was a young man."[18] Hatton concluded by reminding Clarke that the ". . . law is the inheritance of all men . . . "[19] and prayed for God's blessing for him in his calling.

Hatton fulfilled other duties in addition to those of the courtroom. When the Armada came from Spain in 1588, an event which the English had been expecting for some time, Hatton, as Lord Lieutenant of Northamptonshire, was responsible for the mustering of troops from that county just as he had earlier levied men to be sent to Leicester in the Netherlands. He was also the Admiral of the Isle of Purbeck and had the same responsibility there. He had the authority to levy subjects for service in all of these areas, and to train, array, and muster them from time to time to be certain they were in readiness. He could also declare martial law and was responsible for the general peace of the county. He was not able to reside in the county at all times to discharge these duties, and as in the case with others holding these offices, he had deputies to act in his behalf. Hatton's three deputies were Sir Thomas Cecil, Burghley's eldest son; Sir Richard Knightley; and Sir Edward Montague.

Hatton had been specifically ordered by the Privy Council to enlist 1000 foot of substantial householders under captains who were ". . . the fittest gentlemen, best affectioned in religion. . ." to serve the Queen in 1586.[20] Each band of 100 men was to be equipped with forty shot, twenty armed pikes and forty bows. The soldiers and captains were required to take an oath of loyalty; all papists were to be disarmed, the largest towns were to be supplied with powder, and fire beacons were to be kept ready. Thus Hatton and his deputies helped put his county in a state of readiness for the approaching danger from the fleet of Philip II of Spain.

Apparently Hatton remained in London while Elizabeth and others of the Court were at Tilbury reviewing the troops on August 8, although some reports have placed Hatton at the Queen's side. The listing of those present does not include Hatton and Walsingham wrote to Hatton from the camp on that day, which indicates that he was at least some distance from Tilbury.

At dawn on the morning of July 20 the Spanish Admiral, the Duke of Medina Sidonia, had spotted the English fleet under Lord Howard of Effingham coming out of Plymouth harbor. Actual contact took place on July 21, and from then until July 30 when the battered Armada escaped into the North Sea, the battle was on. The English defensive strategy, which required a dispersal of the English fleet, had been ordered by the Council. These restrictions prevented Howard from actively attacking the Spanish fleet as it sailed into the Channel. He could only follow it and do what damage was possible. Therefore the Armada arrived at Calais in good shape, but Medina Sidonia's problems were soon to begin. In fact the dual nature of the Spanish plans brought them to a complete deadlock. The Spanish Admiral had serious doubts about advancing further without aid from the army of the Duke of Parma with whom he expected to make a rendezvous. Parma was very clear that he could not venture out without being attacked by the English and Dutch while the sea was not in Spanish control. Thus the army was contained in Flanders and the fleet at a standstill in Calais about a hundred miles away.

Howard was not slow to take advantage of this stalemate. On the night of July 28 he sent in eight fire ships which created tremendous confusion among the Spanish ships. The next day the decisive battle of Gravelines occurred with fighting taking place from daybreak to dusk. The excellent English gunfire was most effective as it was coupled with a shifting wind which threatened to drive the Spanish ships onto dangerous shoals. On July 30 five of the major Spanish ships were out of action and two others were wrecked on the shore. Another shifting wind allowed Medina Sidonia to pull his ships to safety from the threatening shoals but there was no recourse left to him but to flee from the English firepower and sail to the north. Howard of Effingham followed him as far as the Firth of Forth where lack of supplies and gunpowder made further pursuit useless. There was certainly no doubt as to the fact that the Spanish fleet had been defeated but Walsingham was not completely satisfied. No doubt nothing would have satisfied this devout Puritan short of the complete sinking of each Spanish ship within sight of the English viewers! He wrote to Hatton on August 8 from the Tilbury camp: ". . . your Lordship may perceive what is become of the Spanish fleet. I am sorry the Lord Admiral was forced to leave the prosecution of the enemy through the wants he sustained. Our half doings do breed dishonor, and leaves the disease uncured."[21]

In this judgment Walsingham was partly correct, not that the Armada had not been truly defeated but that a follow-up strike should have been made upon Spanish coast and islands at once. Therefore despite the loss of money and pride, Spain was able to revive and threaten England again, as Hatton was to warn in his speech to the next Parliament.

In August, 1588, Hatton showed his influence, character, and even temerity when he opposed the Queen's wishes because he thought they were illegal and unwise. The problem was especially delicate as it concerned the Earl of Leicester. Camden wrote that Leicester now ". . . began to entertain new hope of honor and power, by being put into the high authority of Lieutenancy under the Queen in the government of England and Ireland. Which indeed he had obtained, the Letters Patent being drawn, had not Burghley and Hatton prevented it and the Queen in time foreseen the danger of trusting too great a power in one man's hand."[22] Leicester's sudden death from fever on September 4 was to end this threat of his climbing to higher power on the wave of Armada glory. In 1587, Leicester had appointed his brother, the Earl of Warwick, Hatton, and Lord Howard of Effingham as executors of his will. To Hatton, whom Leicester called ". . . mine old dear friend. . .," was left one of his gilt ewers and basins and his best George and Garter medal.[23] As Hatton had been named a Knight of the Garter in April, 1588, he was able to wear that medal.

Celebrations of the Armada victory were held in London and reviews were held of the troops raised for the expected invasion. Elizabeth was entertained by Hatton at his house in Ely Place, and his company of 100 men-at-arms in uniforms of red and yellow was presented to her. Additionally, a joust was held in honor of the occasion.

The only case known to have been tried before Hatton as Lord Chancellor was that of a friend, Sir Richard Knightley, his deputy lieutenant for Northamptonshire and a Puritan. Knightley had become involved in the printing of the Martin Marprelate tracts, which were a source of great concern to the government. This case consequently put Hatton in an unhappy position for he had worked closely with Archbishop Whitgift to quell the Puritan effort to change the religious structure.

The appearance of the Martin Marprelate tracts spearheaded yet another attack on the bishopric system of the

Anglican Church. These anonymous writings began to appear
near the end of 1587 and with their bold, humorous criticism of
the bishops caught the immediate attention of the public, much
to the dismay of the government. Seven tracts which pointed
out the mistakes and bad practices of Anglican priests were
published by secret presses. The unusual style of these pamph-
lets with their unrestrained jocularity swept away much respect
for the religious hierarchy they attacked. The government
instituted a vigorous and successful search for the presses and
the spate of writings ended by 1589.

Richard Bancroft, who had been Hatton's chaplain and who
worked closely with Whitgift and Hatton, took the lead in
hunting out the secret presses and answering the attacks of the
tracts. Hatton, as Lord Chancellor and overseer of religious
uniformity, had very early been viewed with suspicion by the
Puritans. There is a suggestion that he may have chosen his
religious policy ". . . as a means of outpointing his principal
rival, Leicester, whose alliance with the most radical Protestant
elements in the country was an embarrassment at Court."[24] It
was said that no sooner was Leicester dead, ". . . but Sir
Christopher Hatton . . . bearing sway, Puritans were trounced
and traduced as troublers of the State."[25] Robert Beale, the
Puritan secretary of the Privy Council, wrote to Burghley that
Hatton and others ". . . earnestly went about. . ." to enforce
subscription to certain articles of the Anglican Church throughout the realm.[26] Indeed, Hatton's death in 1591 was said to have
led to a change in climate wherein ". . . Great comfort is to the
church by the death of the Lord Chancellor" as one Puritan
wrote to another.[27]

It is quite obvious that Hatton would not have acted in such
a manner were he not acquiring his strength and authority
from a close interpretation of the Queen's own mind and wishes
in such matters. He did not attack the Puritans viciously though
and, as will be seen later, tried to obtain a reprieve for one of the
imprisoned alleged Martinists, John Udall. Hatton no doubt
sincerely agreed with the Queen concerning the equal dangers
to the State and royal sovereignty from Puritans and Catholics,

as his speech in the 1589 Parliament would so eloquently demonstrate.

In the frantic search for the presses pouring out the Martinist tracts the authorities found evidence of the Puritan *classis* movement which was also broken up. These local ministerial organizations were abhorrent to Whitgift and the secular authorities as well as to the Queen. The leaders were sought out and imprisoned after refusing to take the *ex officio* oath before the Court of High Commission. Thomas Cartwright was the best-known of these leaders and Hatton had his case and those of nine ministers transferred to Star Chamber Court in May, 1591. Cartwright was imprisoned for eighteen months, being released in 1592. Hatton was not acting alone in these cases. The composition of the Privy Council had changed with the deaths of Leicester in 1588, Mildmay in 1589, and the Earl of Warwick and Walsingham in 1590. These men had all been sympathetic to the Puritan views and Leicester had been the patron of Cartwright. Leicester would have undoubtedly protected Cartwright from the actions of Whitgift and Hatton had he been alive. Only Francis Knollys, a Puritan friend, and Burghley remained although they were very old. Knollys was almost senile and Burghley had long since made peace with his conscience when it came into conflict with the Queen's orders or attitudes. He would not oppose her or Hatton now.

Sir Richard Knightley was accused of harboring the secret presses in his house in Northamptonshire. He was tried in Hatton's court of Star Chamber in February, 1590, along with John Hales, Roger Wigston, and Wigston's wife. Heavy fines were levied against the defendants—Knightley was fined 2,000 pounds, Hales, 1000 marks, Wigston, who was considered to be under his wife's influence, 500 marks, and Mrs. Wigston, 1,000 pounds. All were imprisoned during the pleasure of the Queen.

At the conclusion of the trial Hatton presented a pointed summary, saying that the prisoners were not the writers of the tracts and would have deserved greater punishment if they had been. He noted that Northamptonshire swarmed with sectaries and said that he hoped by these fines to make an example.

Moreover he wished the judges to make known his actions so that ". . . the people [would be] no more seduced with these lewd libellers."[28] It is apparent that as Lord Chancellor Hatton retained his compassion combined with a strong sense of duty even when a friend was involved.

Although Bancroft was extremely active in hunting down the sources of the printing the government did not positively identify the authors of these offensive tracts. John Penry, Job Throckmorton, and John Udall were suspected of their authorship and were imprisoned. Penry and Throckmorton were most closely associated with the printing and many authorities agree that Throckmorton seems the most likely author. The style of the tracts closely conforms to that of Throckmorton's speeches made in the 1586-1587 Parliament.[29] Penry died on the scaffold and Udall was pardoned, but he died in prison a few days later. According to the biographer of Whitgift, Hatton again showed his compassion by attempting to persuade the Privy Council to reprieve Udall if he would confess his errors. There is conflicting testimony that it was Whitgift who tried to obtain Udall's pardon and Hatton was against it. It is much more typical of Hatton's often demonstrated acts of charity that this reprieve was his idea and not that of Whitgift, who was not generally know for acts of compassion.

As Lord Chancellor, Hatton had not lost his wit and sense of humor, characteristics which must have brought him into favor with Elizabeth. These qualities were evidenced in a court case involving a land dispute. The counsels for both parties were setting out the borders of the disputed land and one said, "We lie on this side," and the other said, "And we lie on this side." Hatton responded with, "If you lie on both sides whom will you have me to believe?"[30]

He also continued to demonstrate one of his early abilities, that of dancing. In June, 1589, Hatton's nephew and heir, Sir William Newport, was married to Elizabeth Gawdy, whose father, Sir Francis Gawdy, was a Justice of the Queen's Bench. This marriage took place at Holdenby and Hatton joined in the festivities and displayed his skill at dancing. He allegedly left his judicial robes in a chair, saying, "Lie thou there, Chancellor."[31] Hatton was called away from the celebration by the news of the murder of the French King, Henry III. He had planned to remain at Holdenby for ten to twelve days but he ". . . was sent for . . . with all speed."[32] This murder was to usher in a chaotic time in France with the English policy favoring the accession of Henry IV.

With the death of Leicester the Chancellorship of Oxford University had fallen vacant and Hatton was quickly chosen to fill it. On October 3, 1588, Hatton received a large delegation from the university in his house at Ely Place. The delegation included the Vice-Chancellor, the Proctor, and twenty-four regents attired in scarlet gowns and hoods. Hatton met them in the great gallery where he greeted them and then sat down in his chair in the middle of the gallery where he was accustomed to receive guests. Several orations were made in Latin to the effect that they had chosen Hatton as Master of Arts and as Chancellor. He was asked if he would faithfully keep the privileges and orders of the university. The Vice-Chancellor announced the reasons for Hatton's choice as Chancellor. The qualities looked for in this post which they found in Hatton concerned faithfulness, justice, wisdom, and authority. These virtues were symbolized by handing first the keys of office to Hatton, second, the statute book for justice, third, the seals, and last, a staff for his authority. Hatton was given the staff to maintain learning and punish disorders. This concluded, the Vice-Chancellor thanked Hatton for accepting the responsibilities of the post.

Hatton responded with humility, claiming he was unlearned and unworthy of such office. He gave them thanks for the goodwill and favor done him and promised that what he lacked in ability he would supply by the use of all his authority to benefit Oxford's scholars. Bancroft, who described this ceremony, wrote that Hatton then began to act like a Chancellor, saying that if the reports were true he believed that the university had fallen a long way from the old and honorable reputation it had enjoyed. Hatton mentioned that students

were causing trouble, ". . . that colleges made havoc and
decayed their ancient revenues. . ."[33] He also referred to the
notorious laxity which prevailed in the wearing of gowns
appropriate to one's degree. Hatton claimed such abuses had
been unknown in his time there and he promised that since they
had laid the charge upon him he thought in conscience he was
bound to see redress of such grievances. He desired them to let
him know, from time to time, what abuses began to grow
amongst them, assuring them that as he would strive to
encourage, defend, and prefer the good and diligent students, so
he would be severe to the trouble-makers. Hatton maintained
that the quiet estate of the whole realm greatly depended upon
the good governance of the universities. He said that as the
Queen had made him a man of state it was his duty to ". . . be
careful for their good reformation."[34]

Hatton concluded by returning the keys, statutes, seals,
and staff to the Vice-Chancellor, keeping only the Letters
Patent naming him to the office. He asked for a copy of the
statutes and also to be authorized to make necessary reforms.
And with many thanks and promises that despite his many
other duties as Lord Chancellor he would consider their problems, he bade them farewell.[35]

As Lord Chancellor Hatton had thus successfully attained
one of the most respected positions in the Elizabethan government. Although not a lawyer, he performed ably in this important post despite some contemporary criticism. His administra-
tion of cases and streamlining of procedure reflected his
personal characteristics of moderation and soundness of judgment. He remained steadfast in his loyalty and service to the
Queen. His handling of the case of his friend Sir Richard
Knightley demonstrated clearly that he was a magistrate determined to supply justice with impartial dispatch. From his consideration for commonfolk troubled as Hamlet noted by the
"law's delay," to his unhesitant dealing with the rich and powerful, he honored the revered position he held.

If in 1587 Elizabeth departed from the usual custom of
appointing legally trained men to the office of Lord Chancellor,

she had an excellent reason. Following the execution of Mary Stuart in February, 1587, England expected foreign attack and internal conspiracies involving English Catholics. From another quarter came increasing pressure from the Puritans to reform the ecclesiastical hierarchy of the Church of England. An extremely steady hand was needed in this top position to aid the Queen in the delicate management of these diverse threats to the stability and security of the realm. After his many years of able devoted service it was apparent to the Queen that she could scarcely do better than to name Hatton.

It is to Hatton's credit that he did not disappoint her. While acting as a politican primarily due to the special needs of this unusual period, he capably handled the legal work required of him. After Hatton's death, with the national emergency over, Elizabeth appointed Soliciter-General Sir Thomas Egerton to the position, but it now carried with it the less impressive title of Lord Keeper. Hatton was a special person appointed for a special purpose.

chapter twelve

After the Armada

Very shortly after England's celebration of the defeat of the Armada in July and August of 1588 the government was forced soberly to consider its financial condition. Accordingly writs were issued summoning a new Parliament in September. Scheduled to meet on November 12, 1588, this Parliament was prorogued until February 4, 1589. As the major business of this new Parliament was to be finance, perhaps the fact that the final payment of the previous subsidy was then being collected prompted the delay.

Hatton, in his usual efficient manner, had made plans for the Crown's business to be expeditiously dealt with by using his new position as Lord Chancellor. On September 2, 1588, Hatton wrote to Sergeant Puckering, speaker of the previous House of Commons:

> Sir, I am to pray you to take the pains to repair unto this town about the latter end of this week, that I may have some conference with you concerning matters of Parliament to this purpose: because the use of the higher House is not to meddle with any bill until there be some presented from the Commons,

and so, by reason thereof, the first part of the sitting should be spent idly, or to small purpose, I thought it fit to inform myself what bills there were remaining since the last Parliament, of the which the Lords had good liking, but could not be passed by reason of want of time, and those I meant to offer to their Lordships till such time as there came some from the lower House.[1]

Hatton had been in touch with the clerk of the House of Lords on this matter and had been told that those bills were in the hands of Puckering. Hatton also informed Puckering "how the world goes here"[2] concerning the speakership of the new house. Elizabeth had decided to name Sergeant Thomas Snagge to that position.[3]

At the opening of Parliament on February 4, 1589, Hatton stood at the Queen's right hand. This occasion was undoubtedly the climax of the public career of Sir Christopher Hatton. A stunning triumph had been achieved over the dread Armada and now as Lord Chancellor he had the opportunity to speak to the assembled Lords and Commons in the awesome presence of the Queen.

A contemporary artist offers his view of the splendor and pomp of Parliament's opening ceremonies. The Queen's high-backed throne sits on a carpeted dais dominating the long stately chamber. Behind her a sumptuously draped panel carved with the royal coat of arms, lion and griffin rampant, rises to the tall beamed ceiling. The Queen is shown in her robes of state, wearing a crown and holding a scepter in her right hand and an orb in her left. When she was seated, Queen Elizabeth's head was appropriately (by at least three feet, it appears) higher than that of any other personage in the room.

The Lords Spiritual and Temporal sat on long padded benches which faced each other in the well of the upper house. Commons stood behind the bar at the far end of the chamber facing the Queen. Three officials of the lower house are shown in ceremonial robes, but other members are wearing the doublet and hose of normal usage. The only other people in view four scribes busily writing up the proceedings while on their knees behind a row of Lords.

All evidence indicates that the opening of this particular Parliament had special points of distinction. This was very likely the largest such gathering in Parliament up to that moment. No doubt a great majority of the 462 newly elected members of the Commons were present. Two factors would seem to add credence to this statement. Year by year steady growth of the House of Commons was taking place, and each new Parliament saw the election of additional members as more and more communities sought and received representation. The other circumstance that would tend to increase attendance in this instance was the understandable eagerness to experience a genuinely historic occasion, the unique opportunity to savor and celebrate an outstanding national victory.

The time, the place, and the Queen—they all were perfect for the right man to say the right words. And there is no record that any person who witnessed this event did not come away with a sense of profound and patriotic satisfaction. Hatton summarized the recent situation and his eloquent speech became in effect a State of the Nation address. Sir John Neale's recent evaluation of this oration is extremely positive:

> In the course of the centuries our English Parliament has listened to many famous speeches, and in our own time war has inspired oratory of immortal quality. For its eloquence, its emotion, and its stirring, confident patriotism, as well as a withering contempt for the enemy, Hatton's speech is not unworthy of place in the treasury of England's best.[4]

Even Hatton's Victorian critic, Campbell, granted that "this speech of the dancing Chancellor is in better taste than any performance of his predecessors, either ecclesiastical or legal."[5] Contained in the *Bardon Papers* is a collection of notes in Hatton's hand, evidently an abstract for this speech.[6]

Hatton began his effective address with a review of the dangers England had faced for many years from the papacy.

You cannot forget how Clement VII and Paul III, breaking out
into fury against her Majesty's father, spared not even then to
smite her honor. Afterward, her Majesty being possessed of the
Crown, what a raging bull did that monster Pius V bring forth,
whereby he labored every way to wound her: in her soul, by
denouncing her an heretic; in her honor by his slanderous
calumniations; and in her most royal dignity, by deposing her, by
absolving her subjects from their duties of obedience, and by
cursing of all such as should any way acknowledge their allegiance unto her. . .[7]

He noted that actions of succeeding popes fostered rebellion in Ireland and when that failed they sent a "litter of
seminary priests, from nine days old and upward, tag and rag,
sent hither, pell mell, thick and three-fold,"[8] to entice the
Queen's subjects from their obedience to her. While the priests
were preparing, the papacy encouraged conspirators such as
Parry, Savage, and Babington to murder the Queen. When
these plots failed:

The Pope that now is, Sixtus V, exceeding all other that went
before him in tyranny and cruelty . . . will needs have a bridge
of wood made over our seas . . . now he vows the utter subver-
sion and destruction of us all, Queen, people, and country, and
to make our land a prey to foreign enemies.[9]

To achieve the actual invasion of England, Hatton stated,
the pope solicited the princes and kings of the Holy League and
with promised financial support found a leader in the King of
Spain. "He came against us like thunder."[10] Hatton maintained
that the preparations and actions he had described are,

sufficient to show to all posterity the unchristen fury, both of
the Pope (that wolfish bloodsucker) and of the Spaniard (that in-
satiable tyrant) in that they never bent themselves with such
might and resolution against the very Turk or any other infidel,
as they have done against a Virgin Queen, a famous lady, and a
country which embraces corruption in doctrine the true and
sincere religion of Christ.[11]

As Hatton warmed to his subject he spoke of the actions of men with whom he dealt in Court:

> That which moves her Majesty most is this: to think that every any of her own subjects, mere Englishmen, born and brought up amongst us, should combine themselves—as some have done—with her so deadly enemies.[12]

The Lord Chancellor mentioned the names of English traitors beginning with Cardinal Reginald de la Pole in the reign of Henry VIII and ending with Babington and his co-conspirators. Hatton had special words for Cardinal William Allen, who had been the head of St. Mary's Hall at Oxford when Hatton attended there. Allen had established a Catholic seminary at Douai in 1568 and recently had written a scurrilous tract against Elizabeth in happy anticipation of the Spanish victory. Of him Hatton said:

> Of all the villainous traitors that I think this land ever bred or brought up, that wicked priest, that shameless atheist and bloody Cardinal Allen, he indeed excels. Look what late dangers have been anyway towards us, and you shall find him a chief dealer in them . . . He, like a proud and impudent varlet, dares by his letters to solicit the nobles and commonalty of England to join with the enemy. He is not ashamed to confess—and that in writing that the memory of his villainy may never die—how this Spanish hostility has been greatly furthered by his and the rest of these fugitives' endeavors. O savage and barbarous priest! It is much to have such cruelty attempted by any foreign enemies. It is more that priest should so delight in blood, but that English subjects, being priests, should take upon them to be the workers of such an extremity, and that against their own country![13]

The Puritan tracts of Martin Marprelate were coming into the hands of the people as Parliament met. Hatton did not ignore the danger from this quarter in his scathing denunciation of all enemies of England.

Hatton began this phase of this attack by stating that the

Queen had always known the Catholics were her enemies, that she had expected no better from them, and therefore that she was not so grieved at their actions. But she was much grieved that:

> There are divers, of latter days risen up, even amongst her friends, who, being men of a very intemperate humor, do greatly deprave the present estate and reformation of religion, so hardly attained to, and with such her danger continued and preserved; whereby her loving subjects are greatly disquieted, her enemies encouraged, religion is slandered, piety is hindered, schisms are maintained, and the peace of the Church is altogether rent in sunder and violated.[14]

Hatton warned the no doubt attentive members of Parliament assembled before him that these actions greatly troubled the Queen and that he was expressly commanded to present her firm attitude in relation to them. He reported that:

> Her Highness, upon certain trial, knows most assuredly that those kinds of platforms and devices which they speak of are most absurd, that they tend to intolerable innovation, that they want all grounds of authority.. . . that they affect an unspeakable tyranny, and that they are most dangerous to all good Christian government.[15]

The Queen, Hatton reiterated, was absolutely clear in her conscience that the present Church could be happily compared with any since Christianity began and that it conformed with the Scripture, with the Councils, the practice of the early Church, and opinions of former leaders. As Neale remarks, "A more direct and dogmatic refutation of the points of Presbyterian-Puritanism it would be hard to conceive."[16]

Hatton continued with words of both persuasion and threat:

> Her Highness therefore in respect of your loving affection towards her, does as a most gracious Lady very heartily desire and entreat you; but, if that will not serve, then does she, as your Prince and dread Sovereign, most straitly charge and

command you, upon your allegiance, that . . . you do not in this
assembly so much as once meddle with any such matters or
causes of religion, except it be to bridle all those whether Papists
or Puritans, which are therewithal discontented.[17]

The Queen also promised them, through Hatton, that reforms
would be made at a more appropriate time, which promise she
kept.

Having delivered these warning words Hatton returned to
his attack on the Catholics, with a shrewd look into the future:

> They will not cease to practice both at home and abroad . . .
> And concerning the Pope . . . may we look for any better
> dealing from him? It were madness to think so . . . with what
> villainous fury he is inflamed in his said Bull, how he rages, how
> he foams, how he lies, how he slanders, how he thunders against
> her Majesty and this estate . . . I am fully of opinion that, rather
> than this invasion should not go forward, if that might serve the
> turn, he would give his soul to the devil.[18]

Hatton assured his audience that certainly the King of
Spain could not accept a failure. His nature "is like a vessel with
the bottom upwards, and will never be full."[19] Hatton mentioned the high cost of these wars to Philip of Spain and that his
kingdom was in poor condition but "considering his oath in the
League, his promise to the Pope, his brags thoughout the world,
his peremptory distribution both of this crown and country," he
could not accept the shame and charges of cowardliness and
weakness which would be levied at him if he ended his war with
England in defeat. Spain's restive colonies would also take this
opportunity to "shake off the yoke of their servitude and sub-
jection"[20] if Philip were seen to falter. Hatton's prediction then
was that England should accept the situation that:

> what he is able to do, either by his friends, or his credit, by his
> money, or by his uttermost force, power and strength; what the
> Pope or any English traitor can any ways work by sorcery,
> cursing, practices, cruelty, or any manner of persuasions; what

they can severally, everyone of himself, or jointly all together, devise to bring to pass, all shall be employed to our invasion.[21]

This could not have been pleasant news for the nation to receive while celebrating the defeat of the combined forces of Spain and the League against England.

Hatton continued, taking special pains to point out that despite England's recent victory they were not completely safe, although:

> It is true that God has mightily defended her Majesty and this realm from the hands of her enemies by detecting their conspiracies and making the very birds of the air, as it were, to reveal them . . . Their bulls He has caused to gore themselves . . . But yet, notwithstanding we may not be secure. Means for our defense must diligently be cared for. An enemy is never so much to be feared as when he is contemned . . . We have lopped off some of his boughs; but they will sooner grow again than we think of.[22]

And in a final stirring plea for the English people to remain vigilant he urged:

> We are bound to defend ourselves, our wives, our children, our friends; it is by an instinct of nature. We are bound to defend our country, our prince, our state, our laws, our liberties: it is agreeable to the laws of all nations and touches us all in honor. We are bound to defend our possessions, our liberties, our goods, and our lands: it wholly concerns our profit . . . In times past our noble predecessors have been able to defend this Realm, when they wanted such means as we may have; and shall we now disable ourselves and through our negligence lose it? They . . . have been . . . most worthy conquerors; and shall we now suffer ourselves with all dishonor to be conquered? England has been accounted hitherto the most renowned kingdom for valor and manhood in all Christendom; and shall we now lose our old reputation? If we should, it had been better for England we had never been born.[23]

In urging defensive preparations he reminded his listeners that the enemy was making great preparations to invade by sea and the English navy must be made ready to encounter them. The enemy also had a large army and English forces must be strengthened. Since the enemy was continuing his offense England must consider means for its defense. "Our duties towards God, her Majesty, and our country requires all this at your hands."[24]

Hatton concluded with a final castigation of Spain and drew men of Parliament together for the defense of the Realm. He characterized them as an assembly "of the wisest and most prudent persons. . ." called together to organize plans for the safety and security of Queen and country. He especially pointed out the importance of sea power, saying that the navy is "the greatest bulwark of this Kingdom" and that it must be "repaired, manned, and fitted out for all events with the utmost expedition."[25]

It is clear from these extracts of this speech that Hatton brought into use all of his eloquence and dramatic abilities. The notes in the *Bardon Papers* demonstrate his careful preparation for this most important oration. We do not know the direct effect the speech had on his listeners but as a goad to action on the subsidy it was clearly successful. As had become common practice in Parliamentary strategy Mildmay took up a similar theme in the Commons after the formal opening, when he presented the government's statement of financial needs. Hatton had evidently impressed upon the members of Commons the need for money for military aid because an unusual double subsidy was granted, not without a preamble which noted this act need not become a precedent for the future.

Hatton's eloquence also achieved the effect of inspiring the House of Commons to include in the final speaker's oration a petition to declare war on Spain. But his cogent enumeration of future dangers did not panic the Queen into accepting the urging of either Hatton or the Commons to take precipitate action. Thus the English did lose the momentary advantage against the Spanish in favor of the usual Elizabethan policy of fighting the Spanish on land in alliance with the Dutch and on the seas by privateers. Due to this typical royal policy the Spanish fleet eventually did set forth again and the English

confidence inspired by the victory over the Armada soon dissi-
pated, followed by a general sense of uneasiness. The Jesuit
propagandists continued to add their disturbing efforts to this
situation as well.

In Parliament the Puritans in the Commons continued,
despite the clear and forceful warning from the Queen as trans-
mitted in Hatton's speech, to meddle in religion. After approving of the required tax bill and committing it to the councillors
to be drafted, the members' main goal was to prevent the too
rapid passage of the subsidy. They well knew that once the subsidy was provided for the Queen would rapidly send them home
before they could bring up their proposals on religion. They
succeeded in delaying the tax bill until March 10 and even then
they required some pushing. By this tactic some members were
able to bring up some topics which were viewed by the government as inflammatory because they attacked the prerogatives of
the Queen. For example, members of the Commons began to
debate matters of purveyance, a method of acquiring supplies
for the royal household at a cheap price, and the abuse of this
practice by the royal household officials. By February 25, Lords
had before them two bills sent by the members of Commons,
bills which they well knew would bring down the royal anger
upon them, and so they deliberately did not read them.

These bills definitely infringed upon royal prerogative and
the fact that they got to the Lords may have been due to the fact
that Hatton was not in the Commons to help quell their
proposers. One bill concerned process and pleading in the Court
of the Exchequer and the other concerned problems of purveyance. Both of these bills were introduced on February 14. Members had tried in 1571 to get reforms made in the procedures of
the Court of the Exchequer. A bill had gone to Lords where it
stopped, probably due to the Queen's orders. Changes had been
promised but the members of the Parliament of 1589 saw no
reforms achieved. So they tried again.

Sir Edward Hoby introduced the bill on the Exchequer
reforms. Hoby was a well-connected young man of twenty-
eight, hot tempered and often in trouble. He reported later in

the House that he was criticized for his actions. The critic was probably his uncle Burghley, who as Lord Treasurer was head of the Exchequer. Mildmay tried to head off the debate to follow by his report on the subsidy committee's work, but his interruption was brief; he was not able to quiet this group. Hoby's bill was given a second reading at once in a show of support.

By February 24 the bill had been rewritten and received Mildmay's support. On the following day it was passed and sent to Lords. The Lords had acted without the Queen, who had a complete aversion to the royal prerogative being limited in any way by statutory action.

Meanwhile the supporters of the bill on purveyance were also busy. The old dislike of the custom of purveyance and its abuses had been sharpened by the fact that the Armada threat had concentrated large numbers of soldiers in the area around London and the intolerable situation was more evident than usual. The topic was a sensitive one; blaming royal household officials could be construed as criticism of the Queen. By clipping the power of the household court, known as the Board of Greencloth, the bill threatened the royal prerogative itself.

This bill was read a second time at once, sent to a committee, and was reported on by Sir Thomas Heneage on February 19. Heneage had been appointed to Hatton's old position of Vice-Chamberlain and was also a royal favorite. He lacked most of the qualities of political understanding which had made Hatton so effective in the Commons. The bill had been amended and a proviso added in committee after consultation with some royal officers of the Greencloth. The bill was passed and sent to Lords on February 22.

These bills presented the Lords with a delicate political problem which they solved only by evasion. On February 27 the Commons heard that the Lords had received a royal message ordering a delegation of peers to an audience. The Queen's message was that in respect to any needed reforms of either bill she was able to deal with them herself. The bills were dead. There was to be no dilution of the royal prerogative.

Still the braver members of the House of Commons persisted and eventually obtained an audience with Elizabeth. They reported to the whole house that she would take matters into her hands, cause an inquiry to be made, and then advise them of the results. Naturally these repetitive and essentially negative remarks by the Queen were wrapped in words of loving concern for all of her loyal subjects. It must be added that Elizabeth did later report to the house with notice that four members were to confer with Privy Councillors and Household officials to make better regulations for the purveyors. In this she again displayed her wisdom in accepting the need for members of Parliament to be allowed to take part in decisions which concerned them.

Little beyond this was achieved in the Parliament of 1589, and Hatton seldom appears in its reports as his work was now confined to action in Lords, the proceedings of which were poorly recorded. Members of Commons had dawdled with their work, which necessitated a burst of last-minute activity. The Puritans put together a petition to the Queen complaining again of disorders in the Church. They were especially concerned about plural benefices and nonresidence of clergy in relation to the position they held. Charges were also laid against Whitgift and his aide Richard Bancroft for their severe use of the *ex officio* process against Puritans. A plea was made for restoration of the kind of religious toleration that had existed in the time of Edward VI. There was no time for a meeting between Elizabeth and the Puritan representatives and there is nothing known about what action, if any, was taken on this point. There is however a letter from a member of the house, Francis Alford, to a servant of Hatton in which he commented on Hatton's speech at the close of Parliament:

> My Lord, your master, gave us so good a lesson at our farewell that I trust will be remembered while any of us live which served in this council . . . You know how much I ever honored his Lordship for the great wisdom and natural excellency of speech that was in him; but in this conclusion I did wonder at him—wherein he surpassed himself and the best-learned men

that ever I heard in that place, which have been divers of great note and fame. For the service of God and preservation of His holy religion amongst us, his Lordship did with great zeal reprehend the fanatical humor of the Precision and the Puritan, most impure; whom he divided in his tender consideration of the Church, but, in truth, they be all one in faction and action. And, as he noted unto us her Majesty's benign inclination, in love of the peace of Christ's Church, to suppress them, and her clemency not to persecute them; so,if they be not utterly put down, and that with speed, I fear they will trouble the whole state.[26]

The point mentioned and approved in this letter concerning the content of Hatton's speech would seem to indicate that the Puritans had included their petition in the Speaker's last address. Alford's assessment of Hatton's speech is impressive, as he had no doubt heard the opening speech. If the closing one surpassed the first, it must have been deserving of acclaim. Apparently Hatton had sent his closing speech to Burghley for the latter's opinion. Burghley returned it on March 27 approving of its organization into three parts and noting that he had "unneedfully" made some suggestions to prove that he had read it. Unfortunately the whole speech is lost and all we know of its contents are those points mentioned by Alford.

This was to be the last Parliament for Hatton. Long before the next one convened in 1593, Hatton died.

It seems clear that Hatton was still busy with governmental work until his death. On September 2, 1589, he drew up a list of matters to be dealt with which was addressed to Burghley. These items concerned foreign affairs, particularly the problems in the Low Countries relating both to the government and the state of the English forces there, and also a consideration of the proper person to send to Scotland. Other points concerned English matters such as speaking with the Aldermen "touching money," and the "examination of Martin Marprelate to be thoroughly proceeded in."[27] Moreover the problem of seeing that released soldiers did not pillage the people on their route home was listed. Thus Hatton was obviously dealing with a broad range of foreign and domestic issues.

Little is known about Hatton's activities in 1590. Parliament did not meet and there are only a few surviving letters. He acknowledged the New Years's gift of the Earl of Shrewsbury by writing:

> My very good Lord, I have received that fair and honorable present, which it hath pleased you to send me at the beginning of this new year; for the which, and many other your honorable kindnesses towards me, as I must acknowledge myself much bounded and indebted unto your Lordship. . .[28]

In July he was in residence at Eltham where he was Keeper for the Queen. He wrote to Burghley:

> My very good Lord, We have received your honorable letters, and can well witness your endless travails, which in her Majesty's princely consideration she should relieve you of, but it is true the affairs are in good hand, as we all know, and thereby her Majesty is the more sure, and we her poor servants the better satisfied. God send you help and happiness to your best contentment. . . I hope the morrow to be at London, where if your Lordship will command me any service, I shall be ready for you.[29]

Hatton was concerned about the continuance of the wine trade in November, 1590. when he wrote to Burghley concerning the recent problems:

> My very good Lord, The times being now full of troubles, and our shipping and warriors diversely employed about reprisals, so as the trade for wines is like thereby to be very much hindered; and that the law inhibiting the bringing in of wines in strangers' bottoms doth not only withdraw all strangers . . . but also is a fear to our nation to lade home their wines in such strange vessels, as many time, for their better safety, they might and would do, if they were not subject to the danger of those statutes. . .[30]

Hatton asked Burghley to write to the Officers of Custom at the port of London, insisting that "no molestation be used" against those bringing in wines in strangers' ships contrary to the law.

Although Hatton's health was gradually declining in this period he continued to sit in the Court of Chancery and Star Chamber. On May 17, 1591, there was a letter from Hatton to Burghley concerning the approaching execution of the Puritan John Udall, who had been convicted of a felony in the Martinist case. Hatton hoped that Udall and others might still be persuaded to "acknowledgement of their faults, to be set down in such a submission as the Lord Chief Justice Anderson should draw up, then the Queen's mercy to be extended towards them; otherwise, that they might repair by the execution of justice on them, the harm they had done in sowing sedition."[31] According to Sir George Paule, the biographer of Whitgift, it was not Hatton but Whitgift who favored clemency for Udall.[32] In any case, Udall died in prison before any action was taken.

Hatton was involved with one other known case in this period, that of Henry Barrowe, who had been arrested with John Penry and John Greenwood in connection with the Marprelate tracts. Burghley, Aylmer, and Whitgift were questioning Barrowe with Hatton in Hatton's chamber in the Court. Barrowe insisted that "your church is not governed by the word of God but by the Romish courts," to which Hatton remarked that "he never heard such stuff in all his life." As he heard more he exclaimed "there must be straiter laws made for such fellows."[33] He also disputed with Barrowe the meaning of the word *presbyter*, which Hatton identified as the Latin for "a priest." Barrowe claimed it was of Greek origin and meant "an elder."

In September, 1591, Hatton wrote to his friend Sir Henry Unton, who was ambassador to France, concerning Unton's health. The letter is partially illegible, but it is clear that Unton and his wife had been ill. Hatton assured Unton ". . . how much her most excellent Majesty was perplexed to hear thereof."[34] Hatton wrote that ". . . I have been visited myself of late with some distemperature of body" and assured Unton that he would ". . . always be careful for your Lordship as a friend in anything which may concern your benefit, honor, or reputation. . ."[35]

Hatton continued working with both domestic and foreign

affairs until two months before his death. In another letter to
Unton on September 18 he wrote of the examination of certain
men ". . . who are found to be men distempered in their wits
and understanding, and are dealt with accordingly. . ." He
apologized to Unton for writing of trivial matters, "I must feed
your Lordship for the present with these trifles. It may please
you to accept all in good part. . ."[36]

A letter written by Walsingham's secretary, Thomas Phelippes, includes a report of Hatton's illness. On October 31
Phelippes reported that "The Chancellor is very sick with a
stranguary, and is not likely to recover."[37] Many years later
Henry Howard, in comparing the Earl of Shrewsbury's illness to
Hatton's, gave some indication of its nature. Shrewsbury was
described as being in such agony that "it is not possible that he
should live long in this torment, if it continue, for the neck of
the bladder is so raw as it should appear by excoriation (which is
the disease whereof Hatton, the Chancellor, deceased). . ."[38]

Little more than a month before his death Hatton wrote a
long letter to Unton concerning the complex situation in France.
With the assassination of Henry III in July, 1589, England's
policy towards France was necessarily changed. The heir to
Henry III, the Huguenot leader Henry of Navarre, was opposed
by the Catholic League, with Paris and Spain on its side. With
the possibility after 1590 of a Spanish encampment on the
Breton and Picardy coast within easy raiding distance of England, reaction was essential. The Queen sent prompt aid to
Henry of Navarre, lending him 20,000 pounds in September,
1589, and a further 15,000 pounds in October. A small military
force was also dispatched to Henry's aid under the command of
Lord Willoughby. Henry proved to be somewhat cavalier with
Elizabeth's money and troops, promising to pay back the money
lent in a short time, promising to pay the troops, and then
confessing that he had no money at all.

It is in this delicate situation that Unton earned the Queen's
displeasure in visiting a French general. Hatton advised Unton
"from henceforth to consider well upon . . . your commission
and in no wise to exceed it."[39] Hatton concluded with assurances of his goodwill:

My endeavors shall not fail—to do all good office, both to uphold and to increase her Majesty's gracious opinion of your Lordship, I assure you; and I nothing doubt of your Lordship's wise considerations upon these points; and that such amends shall be made by your discreet managing of this matter as shall be a full satisfaction and breed effect in her Highness of exceeding good liking towards you.[40]

Despite Elizabeth's fury at Henry's broken promises there was little she could do. A Spanish army had landed in Brittany and her support was even more necessary to prevent the Channel provinces of France from falling under Spanish rule. Although Henry of Navarre had failed to keep his promise to support the small English army already in France, he asked for a second army to be sent, again promising to repay his loans. Henry also had the temerity to suggest that the leader of this new army should be Essex, the new royal favorite. Essex was the stepson of Elizabeth's old favorite, the Earl of Leicester. He was now the new favorite of the Queen and exceedingly ambitious for glory and money. Elizabeth ignored this request for some time but finally gave way to the needs of the situation and to the fervent pleas of the Earl of Essex to be allowed to go.

This expedition justified all of Elizabeth's apprehensions. It had been sent with a specific purpose, to aid Henry in the siege of Rouen, and it was to remain for a limited time of two months. Henry was busy elsewhere and with the English army in France he had more extensive plans for it than those considered by the Queen. The glory-seeking Earl of Essex was not one to follow orders. He set off to meet Henry across enemy territory, where a festive time was had. On his return he had to be met by some of his infantry to safeguard his route and capped the whole foolish episode by a useless attack on Rouen in which his brother was killed. Despite hearing of Elizabeth's anger he went off to aid another unimportant town after which he was ordered home. Before he returned he committed one more indiscretion, making twenty-four of his followers knights. Despite these foolish actions Elizabeth was persuaded to allow Essex to return to France, for the siege of Rouen was finally about to begin.

Essex apparently saw Hatton as an obstacle to his ambitions. Thomas Phelippes, former secretary to Walsingham, mentioned in a letter to Thomas Barnes on July 1, 1591, that Essex was going to France because "he is impatient of the slow process he must needs have during the life and greatness of the Chancellor and Treasurer."[41] The Chancellor wrote to Essex a letter which is a characteristic blend of diplomatic reproof, an expression of personal concern for Essex's welfare, and a judicious helping of praise. Hatton noted that he had done his best to get permission for Essex to remain in France,

> but withal, I must advertise you that her Majesty has been drawn thereunto with exceeding hardness; and the chief reason that makes her stick in it is, that for she doubts your Lordship does not sufficiently consider the dishonor that arises unto her by the King's either dalliance or want of regard, having not used the forces sent . . . from so great a Prince . . . in some employment of more importance.[42]

Hatton further advised Essex, "that you have great care for the accomplishment of her Highness' instructions."[43] He alluded to the death of the brother of Essex in France and hoped that Essex would not "through grief or passions . . . hazard yourself over venturously."[44] He claimed that Essex's valor was well-known and required no proof. "I must pray and require your Lordship to have that circumspectedness of yourself which is fit for a General of your sort."[45]

Sadly for Essex he did not take Hatton's wise advice. On his return to France he acted as foolishly, as before, sending a challenge to the Governor of Rouen to a duel or tournament. Again Essex was recalled to England. The finances of England could not support his frivolous expenditures without anything to show for them. Essex's execution in 1601, as punishment for rebellion spurred by overweening ambition, demonstrated that he never learned the patience and wisdom of Hatton.

Clearly in his last days Hatton was still giving his good advice and mediating between the Queen and impatient Essex.

Soon after these letters were written Hatton became seriously ill with a kidney disease. As we have seen, earlier in his life he had had an illness of this same sort. According to the imaginative Camden, Hatton had become very worried about repayment to the Queen of a large sum of money amounting to over forty-two thousand pounds.[46] He was not alone in owing money to the Crown and it is unlikely that this debt seriously affected his health, as Fuller also alleges, ". . . it brake his heart that the Queen (which seldom gave boons and never forgave due debts) rigorously demanded payment of some arrears, which Sir Christopher did not hope to have remitted, but did only desire to be forborn. Failing therein in his expectation, it went to his heart, and cast him into a mortal disease."[47]

When the Queen heard of Hatton's illness all her concern and affection was evidenced in her several visits to him, staying overnight at Ely Place with him. She was at his house on November 11[48] and according to Fuller she brought "as some say, cordial broths unto him with her own hands, but all would not do. Thus no pulleys can draw up a heart once cast down, though a Queen herself set her hand therunto."[49] On November 20, 1591, Sir Christopher Hatton died at his home, Ely Place.

Hatton's funeral was one of extraordinary ceremony. The coffin was preceded by one hundred poor people wearing new caps and gowns given them for the occasion. More than three hundred gentlemen and Lords of the Council attended, in addition to a corps of the Gentlemen Pensioners.[50] Hatton was buried in old St. Paul's where an immense tomb was erected by his nephew and heir Sir William Hatton. Unfortunately this grand tomb was destroyed in the Great Fire of 1666, but a picture of it and the inscriptions on it were preserved in Dugdale's *History of St. Paul's Cathedral.* Hatton was depicted lying atop the tomb in armor with hands folded. The sarcophagus was placed within the arch of a canopy, which was built in three stages. On each side of the monument were detached obelisks reaching to the third stage of the canopy. The entire monument was encrusted with varicolored marbles. The third and top panel was filled with Hatton's coat of arms and above all was the golden hind.[51] This large monument designed by Maxmilian Colt seemed to outshadow the tombs of Walsingham and Sir Philip Sidney nearby, for according to some verses in Stow's *Survey of London:*

> Sir Philip, Sir Francis, have no tomb,
> For great Christopher takes all the room.[52]

Affixed to a tablet near Hatton's tomb was the epitaph written by Francis Flower, one of Hatton's followers. Flowers wrote this this eulogy which was inscribed on a tablet beside Hatton's tomb:

> Stay and behold the mirror of a dead man's house,
>   Whose lively Person would have made thee stay and wonder;
> Look, and withal learn to know how to live and die renowned,
> For never can clean life and famous Herses sunder.
> Hatton lies here, unto whose name Hugh Lupus gave
> (Lupus the sister's sonne of William Conqueror)
> For Nigel his dear servant's sake worship and land:
> Lo there the Spring; look here the Honour of his ancestry.
> When Nature molded him her thoughts were most on Mars.
> And all the Heavens to make him goodly were agreeing;
> Thence was he valiant, active, strong, and passing comely,
> And God did grace his mind and spirit with gifts excelling.
> Nature commends her workmanship to Fortune's charge.
> Fortune presents him to the Court and Queen,
> Queen Eliz. (O God's dear handmaid) his most miracle;
> Now hearken, Reader,—raretie not heard or seen,—
> This blessed Queen, mirror of all that Albion rul'd,
> Gave favor to his faith and precepts to his hopeful time;
> First trained him in the stately band of Pensioners.
> Behold how humble hearts make easie steps to clime.
> High carriage, honest life, heart ever loyall,
> Diligence, delight in duty, God doth reward:
> So did this worthy Queen, in her just thought of him,

And for her safety, make him Captain of her Guard.
Now doth she prune this vine, and from her sacred breast,
Lessons his Life, makes wise his heart for her great Councells,
And so Vice-Chamberlain, where foreign Prince's eyes
Might well admire her choyce wherein she most excells.
So sweetly temp'red was his soul with vertuous balme,
Religious, just to God, and Caesar in each thing;
That he aspired to the highest Subject's seat,
Lord Chancellour [sic] (measure and conscience of a holy King),
Robe, Collar, Garter, dead figures of great Honour,
Alms-deeds with Faith, honest in word, franke in dispence;
The Poor's friend, not popular; the Churches pillar,
This Tomb shews th' one; th' Heavens shrine the other[53]

Franciscus Florus ad memoriam heri sui defuncti, luctusq' sui
solatium, Posuit. Anno Domini 1593.

Many eulogies came into print soon after Hatton's death
and one of the most striking, by Robert Greene, is entitled "A
Maiden's Dream upon the death of my late Lord Chancellor."
Greene was one of the lesser authors of the time and had been
commissioned to write some of the answers to the Martinist
tracts and so had done some work under the direction of
Hatton. Greene praised Hatton's qualities of "amiability, integ-
rity and fairness and compassion," which are qualities almost
uniformly attributed to Hatton. That there were those who
held opposing opinons, perhaps motivated by envy, is indicated
by a sentence in the dedication to Lady Hatton, wife of Sir
William. Greene mentioned "base report who hath her tongue
blistered by slanderous envy begun as far as she durst, now
after his death, to murmur, who in his life time durst not once
mutter."[54]
    A second eulogy was "A Commemoration of the Life and
Death of the Right Honorable Sir Christopher Hatton" by John
Phillips, published in 1591. This poem was printed in "A
Lamport Garland" in 1881. Phillips also testified to Hatton's
"sense of duty, justice, loyalty, kindliness and helpfulness to the

poor, particularly in his solicitude for the rights of poor legal
suitors. . ."[55] Hatton is said by Phillips to have taken special
care of his men in the guard and to have persuaded the Queen
to raise their pay from 1 shilling 4 pence to 1 shilling 8 pence per
day to 2 shillings for three months of the year. Hatton was
apparently given most of the credit for the work on the
Babington conspiracy in this epic, and his method was described
in these dramatic lines:

> Those wily wolves untrusty to the Crown
> By justice he threw topsy turvy down.

Phillips described the death of Hatton and that

> He took his leave of his most gracious Queen,
> And praised God she had his comfort been.[56]

In a curious work written in 1595 Hatton was included
among such as Shakespeare and Spenser. The book is *Poliman-
teia, or The Means Lawful and Unlawful to Judge the Fall of a Commonwealth Against the Frivolous and Foolish Conjectures of the Age*. This
work was dedicated to Essex and written by William Clark.
It contains a eulogy of the universities and the Inns of Court.
After mentioning "sweet Shakespeare" Hatton was then
described:

> Then name but Hatton, the Muse's favorite, the Church's
> music, learning's patron, my once poor Island's ornament, the
> courtier's grace, the scholar's countenance, the Guard's Captain.
> Thames, I dare avouch, will become tears: the sweetest per-
> fumes of the Court will be sad signs: every action shall accent
> grief; honor and eternity shall strive to make his tomb, and after
> curious skill and infinite cost, engrave this with golden letters,
> *Minus Merito;* the fainting Hind untimely chased, shall trip to-
> wards Heaven, and *tandem si* shall be virtue's mot.[57]

Again the qualities stressed are those of kindliness, patronage
of music and learning, and support of the Church. Although

Hatton never married there is some evidence that he had a daughter. It was recorded of Sir John Perrot, Deputy of Ireland, that he had an illegitimate daughter by Elizabeth, daughter of Sir Christopher Hatton. Brooks suggests that Perrot had seduced Hatton's daughter thus providing the cause for the enmity between Hatton and Perrot which is factual.[58] Brooks extends his conjecture by assuming that an agreement made in 1583 between Perrot, Bromley, the Chancellor, and Arden Waferer, a lawyer known to work for Hatton, was a settlement made by Perrot with Hatton. This assumption is unproven.[59] No further evidence of a Hatton daughter is known to exist.

Hatton's estate was indeed in a bad condition on his death. From his office as Receiver of Tenths and First Fruits which he had held from 1578 he now owed nearly 42,000 pounds to the Queen, having failed to remit these revenues—a normal practice among Elizabethan officeholders. This entangled estate was inherited by his nephew Sir William Newport who had taken the name of Hatton. The estate's settlement was not completed in William's lifetime and the inheritance passed to another Christopher Hatton, the son of the Lord Chancellor's cousin. The new heir was underage and therefore became a ward of the Queen and was apparently kept short of money while he attended Cambridge. The Bishop of London, Richard Bancroft, who had at one time been Hatton's chaplain, wrote to Robert Cecil about the young heir's problems and asked Cecil to "favor the heir of mine old good friend and master, the late Lord Chancellor," writing "who would have thought that within seven years the Lord Chancellor's heir should have been brought to such an exigent?"[60] The heirs of Sir Christopher found it necessary to sell part of the furnishings of Holdenby and later some land. William is said to have sold most of Hatton's jewels to Elizabeth Hardwick, Lady Shrewsbury. This woman builder of great houses also bought a famous set of tapestries which Hatton had at Holdenby.[61]

In 1605, the second heir of Christopher Hatton, also named Christopher, got permission to sell part of his lands and in 1608 he conveyed Holdenby to the Crown. King James I was to give up the Crown's interest in other lands inherited from the Chancellor provided the debt was paid at the rate of 1,500 pounds a year. When James acquired Holdenby there were six bells which had been provided by the Chancellor in the steeple of the church. These bells weighed eleven thousand pounds and were worth about 166 pounds. They were removed as private property and two smaller ones substituted.[62]

This young Christopher was created Baron Hatton of Kirby by Charles I and his son was named Viscount Hatton of Gretton. These titles became extinct due to the lack of a male heir. The only daughter of the viscount married Daniel Finch, Earl of Nottingham and Winchelsea. Their younger son took the name of Hatton again and occupied Kirby. The present Earl of Nottingham and Winchelsea is descended from this man.

In this manner the fabulous Holdenby went to the Crown, a fact which accounts for its disappearance in the civil wars of the seventeenth century. It was sold and dismantled except for two huge arches that remain standing isolated in a field, lonely relics of a former "shrine" to Elizabeth built by her most devoted servant.

chapter thirteen

Hatton...On Balance

Christopher Hatton was valued by his Queen for a number of reasons. He was presentable and efficient at Court, taken for granted qualities which aided in his early work as Vice-Chamberlain in charge of progresses and major ceremonials. More important was that his views on religion—of all her courtiers—most nearly matched Elizabeth's. His letters prove that he was the refuge alike of Puritan and Catholic. The distressed, whether their troubles arose from offenses against the state, from having incurred the Queen's displeasure, or from sickness and poverty, always appealed with confidence to his humanity and compassion.

Hatton helped, with the Queen's support, to protect loyal Catholics from Puritan zealots. Elizabeth's favorite archbishop, John Whitgift, was his friend and ally. Whitgift's best lieutenant, Richard Bancroft, a future archbishop, began as Hatton's chaplain. It was perhaps at Whitgift's suggestion that Hatton became Lord Chancellor, his attitude being that the Queen was absolutely supreme in church and state, having two lieutenants, the Lord Chancellor, and the archbishop.

Hatton was in full accord with Elizabeth's taste as he performed ably in Commons to combine the rapid dispatch of government business with a tact and mildness that suited the Queen. She could rely on Hatton to interpret her wishes accurately and to pursue her policies loyally. He was admirably cast to be used on her confidential business, especially in religious matters. She admired his tact and invariable good temper. Burghley once complimented Hatton that of all the court and government Hatton was the least apt to bear resentment and pursue a quarrel.

As Lord Chancellor Hatton based his actions on the acquired experience in equity he had attained in Star Chamber and behaved with the circumspection and tact Elizabeth had foreseen.

He was no more high-minded than any courtier when it came to scrambling for money. Hatton was allowed more latitude to acquire Church lands than others in government. It is possible that his Church appointments were accompanied by simony.

In his costly building he was encouraged by Elizabeth, who knew he was building Holdenby at public expense, since all courtiers income came from the Queen's revenues which Hatton partially administered. His purchase of Kirby and building of Holdenby were done to exalt the Queen, to show his devotion to her, and to be worthy of her visitations. Although Hatton hardly ever visited Holdenby except in the company of the Queen, any gentleman traveling through the area could stop in and be fed and lodged. The house was an exercise in public relations conducted through a private individual. It can with Theobalds be described as a surrogate royal house. In these provincial houses the Queen could meet and impress the gentry of the area in suitable surroundings. Elizabeth was well aware that although she was the center of an elitist society, the apex of a hierarchical pyramid whose gradations she insisted on maintaining, her security rested upon the loyalty of the base. She was always concerned about the common people's view of her which she constantly sought to know through the progresses.

In maintaining his position with Elizabeth Hatton carried to exaggerated heights the homage paid by all courtiers. Hatton probably convinced himself that he was in love with Elizabeth and wrote to her accordingly, which undoubtedly pleased her. In his lifetime of loyal service to her he was the only one of the inner circle to remain a bachelor, being devoted, yet aware of the fact that his career would be advanced by remaining unmarried.

Hatton's letters to Elizabeth breathe such passion that at one time they were accepted at face value as evidence of physical intimacy. They were more likely only the passionate flattery that all courtiers knew the Queen liked to read, and Hatton excelled in it with credibility enhanced by his bachelor status. The only possible piece of evidence of the Queen's unchastity is the Dyer letter to Hatton mentioning that Elizabeth "had what she fancied" and of her being filled with "satiety and fullness." What Elizabeth no doubt got from Hatton was his company, witty attentions, his ingenious and thoughtful presents, his display of court accomplishments, and above all the purely verbal love making she enjoyed. It seems that she was once worried that Hatton might marry as Leicester had. Elizabeth lived a vicarious sex life and Hatton was a vital part of it.

Hatton's most important work for the Queen was done as a member of the House of Commons where he sat from 1571 until he became Lord Chancellor in 1587. He became one of the most influential men in the Court and was recognized as the Queen's spokesman in Commons. He acted as her intermediary, relaying the royal messages and prohibitions to the Commons members and guiding their actions. He was a front-bencher and government leader of the first rank. "That a man so long, and apparently so firmly, installed in legend as a Queen's plaything, should emerge with the stature he displayed in handling Parliament, is quite unexpected."[1] Hatton, according to all contemporary opinion, had an amiable, pleasant disposition which aided him in working with an occasionally irascible Commons and an obdurate Queen. He was well known for his successes in mediation. His voice was a reasonable and temperate one in

Commons and from contemporary accounts was respected by his colleagues.

The Queen delegated to Hatton supervisory powers in the all-important matter of maintaining religious conformity. This responsibility involved him in the most crucial policies of the reign, those concerning the position of the English Catholics and their enemies, the Puritans. Elizabeth maintained throughout the reign, even in the face of the Armada, that one faction was as dangerous as the other. Hatton adroitly carried out her policies in these matters.

Hatton played a major role in the examinations and trials of those accused of treason by the government, beginning with the investigation of the Duke of Norfolk in 1572. He was one of the commissioners who tried Mary Stuart and played a leading role in the trials of the many conspirators accused in plots revolving around Mary. His speeches in Commons concerning the dangers that Mary Stuart and the foreign Catholics represented, as well as his speech following the defeat of the Armada, are of such patriotic quality that they have been favorably compared with Winston Churchill's World War II speeches.

Hatton worked closely with John Whitgift, the Archbishop of Canterbury, to repress the dissident and radical Puritans who sought to convert the church hierarchy of the Elizabethan established church to that of a Presbyterian one. Although these Puritans proclaimed their loyalty to the Queen, in essence their plan attacked her sovereignty and the security of the state.

Engaged in a centrist role, Hatton's essential humanity and dislike of persecution in matters of religion were noted by contemporaries. William Camden wrote that Hatton believed that neither searing nor cutting should be used in religious matters. *"In religiousis causa non urendum non secandum."*[2] No doubt it was partly expedience that led him to follow the Queen's lead in maintaining a *via media*. But as demonstrated by Burghley, Leicester, Mildmay, and Walsingham, all Puritan sympathizers, it was not fatal to hold different views from those of the Queen in this regard. Hatton's much verified compassionate nature would seem to have allowed him honestly to agree with the

Queen in her religious policy of not "making windows in men's souls."[3] The danger from possibly disloyal English Catholics and foreign Catholic attacks was obvious. Less obvious was the danger to Elizabeth's sovereignty and the equilibrium of the state from the revolutionary Puritans. Hatton was the one Councillor who consistently supported and carried out the royal policy on this point.

Hatton's love of literature is well known. Letters and dedications show this was not merely an affectation. He gave his patronage to artists, musicians, geographers, and seamen. Although his formal education had been short, he wrote parts of plays performed in the Inner Temple and acted in others.

In an age of new men Hatton also wanted to establish his lineage and acquire the right to a coat of arms. In 1572, already well on his way to success, Hatton hired an agent to trace his ancestry, a practice followed by such sober men as Burghley. By 1580 the College of Arms agreed to a Hatton family tree going back to a Norman companion of William the Conquerer and descending through several generations of feudal lords. With this lineage Hatton acquired an impressive coat of arms.

Hatton emerges as a representative Elizabethan in many ways. He was ambitious, eager for place and wealth, and ready to play the love games required by Elizabeth. He was a courtier with other courtiers vying for position in the highly competitive Elizabethan political scene. Yet he was unique. Combined with his courtly graces were serious qualities which gave him depth of character. His compassion and concern for those caught in the delicate balance between religion and treason was both genuine and unusual. There is yet to be found a letter or reference from a contemporary that portrays him as indulging in any sort of mean or vengeful act. He seems to be that truly remarkable sixteenth-century person, a man of tolerance.

In the final analysis any evaluation of Christopher Hatton's accomplishments must rest on those of the Queen herself. He was her loyal resourceful lieutenant in many and varied royal matters ranging from revels to religion, from terpsichore to statecraft.

During his more than twenty-five years of personal and public service to Her Majesty Hatton proved himself again and again a fit companion to a fun-loving monarch, a valued counsellor to a most wise woman, and an eloquent spokesman for a highly articulate Queen. We can only sense a measure of Elizabeth's undoubted sorrow and personal loss when at his death she must have pondered where indeed she would see his like again.

Notes

Preface

1. Henry Harington, ed., *Nugae Antiquae* 3 vols. (London: T. Kadell, 1792), 2:136.
2. Ibid.
3. Neville Williams, *All the Queen's Men* (New York: Macmillan Co., 1972), p. 33.
4. Robert Naunton, *Fragmenta Regalia,* ed. by E. Arber (Westminster: A. Constable & Co., 1895) pp. 41–44.
5. Sir John E. Neale, *Elizabeth I and her Parliaments,* 2 vols. (New York: St. Martin's Press, 1958), 2:174.

chapter one / The Early Years

1. Anthony Wood, *Athenae Oxonienses,* ed. by Philip Bliss, 4 vols. (Oxford: Oxford University Press, 1813–1820), 1:582.
2. William H. Cooke, *Students Admitted to the Inner Temple, 1547–1660* (London: Clowes & Son, 1877), p. 35.
3. Thomas Fuller, *The History of the Worthies of England,* 3 vols. (London: T. Tegg, 1811), 2:165.

4. Lord John Campbell, *Lives of the Lord Chancellors and Keepers of the Great Seal of England*, 7th Ed. (New York: Cockcroft & Co., 1878), p. 138.

5. John Nichols, *The Progresses and Public Processions of Queen Elizabeth*, 3 vols. (London: Nichols & Son, 1823) 1:139.

6. William Camden, *Annales . . . of Elizabeth* (London: Benjamin Fisher, 1625), p. 127.

7. Henry Brackenbury, *The Nearest Guard: A History . . .* (London: Harrison & Sons, 1892), p. 60.

8. Great Britain Public Record Office, *State Papers, Domestic Elizabeth*, vol. 34, no. 52.

9. Nichols, *Progresses*, 1:276.

10. Sir James Melville, *Memoirs* (Boston: Small, Maynard, 1827), p. 85.

11. Ibid.

12. Great Britain Public Record Office, *Calendar of the Patent Rolls*, Elizabeth, vol. 4 (1566–1569), no. 986, p. 157; no. 1502, p. 252; no. 1377, p. 228; no. 2257, p. 386.

13. Ibid., vol. 5 (1569–1572), pp. 15, 207, 233.

14. Eric St. John Brooks, *Sir Christopher Hatton* (London: Jonathan Cape, 1946), p. 58.

15. Michael B. Pulman, *The Elizabethan Privy Council in the Fifteen-Seventies* (Berkeley: University of California Press, 1971), p. 51.

16. J.B. Black, *The Reign of Elizabeth*, (Oxford: Clarendon Press, 1959), p. 210.

17. Agnes Strickland, *Lives of the Queens of England from the Norman Conquest*, 8 vols. (London: George Bell & Sons, 1882), 6:336.

18. Nichols, *Progresses*, 1:276.

chapter two / Two Parliaments and Troubled Times

1. Sir John E. Neale, *Elizabeth I and her Parliaments*, 2 vols. (New York: St. Martin's Press, 1958), 1:150.

2. Ibid., p. 192.

3. Ibid., p. 237.

4. Ibid.

5. Sir Harris Nicolas, *The Memoirs of the Life and Times of Sir Christopher Hatton* (London: Richard Bentley, 1847), p. 9.
6. Neale, *Parliaments*, 1:244.
7. Ibid., p. 277.
8. Ibid., p. 280.
9. Ibid.
10. Ibid., p. 312.

chapter three / Renaissance Man

1. Sir Harris Nicolas, *The Memoirs of the Life and Times of Sir Christopher Hatton* (London: Richard Bentley, 1847), p. 21.
2. Ibid.
3. Ibid.
4. Ibid.
5. Ibid.
6. Ibid.
7. Ibid., p. 22.
8. William Murdin, *A Collection of State Papers . . . of Queen Elizabeth . . .* (London: Wm. Bowyer, 1740–1759), p. 558.
9. Ibid.
10. British Museum, Lansdowne MS. 15, Art. 43; also in Thomas Wright, *Queen Elizabeth and her Times,* 2 vols. (London: Henry Colburn, 1838), 1:440.
11. British Museum, Harleian MS. 787, fol. 88; also in Nicolas, *Memoirs,* p. 17.
12. Nicolas, *Memoirs,* p. 18.
13. Ibid.
14. Ibid., p. 19.
15. Edmund Lodge, *Illustrations of British History . . .,* 3 vols. (London: John Chidley, 1838), 2:17–18.
16. Ibid.
17. Ibid.
18. Nicolas, *Memoirs,* p. 25.
19. Ibid., p. 27.
20. Ibid., p. 26.
21. Ibid.
22. Ibid.

23. Ibid., p. 27.
24. Ibid., p. 28.
25. Ibid.
26. Ibid.
27. Ibid.
28. Ibid.
29. Ibid., p. 29.
30. Ibid., p. 30.
31. Ibid.
32. British Museum, Lansdowne MS. 17, art. 88.
33. Wright, *Queen Elizabeth*, 2:492.
34. Eric St. John Brooks, *Sir Christopher Hatton* (London: Jonathan Cape, 1946), pp. 130–31.
35. Nicolas, *Memoirs*, pp. 50–51.
36. Ibid., p. 36; Gentlemen's Magazine, vol. 79, pt. 1, p. 136.
37. Historical Manuscripts Commission, Salisbury MS., 2:120.
38. Ibid.
39. Ibid.
40. Nicolas, *Memoirs*, p. 36.
41. Public Record Office, Star Chamber, H 53–224; 49–38 (1583).
42. Brooks, *Hatton*, p. 116.
43. George Baker, *The History and Antiquities of the County of Northamptonshire* 2 vols. (London: John B. Nichols Co. 1822–1841), 1:201.
44. J. Alfred Gotch, *Old English Houses* (London: Methuen, 1925), p. 67.
45. Emily Hartsborne, *Memorials of Holdenby* (London: Hardwicke, 1868), p. 11.
46. A.L. Rowse, *The Elizabethan Renaissance: The Life of the Society* (London: Scribner's Sons, 1972), p. 118.
47. John Buxton, *Elizabethan Taste* (London: Macmillan, 1965), p. 49.
48. Brooks, *Hatton*, p. 160.
49. Buxton, *Elizabethan Taste*, p. 49.
50. Ibid., p. 195.
51. Brooks, *Hatton*, p. 142.
52. Buxton, *Elizabethan Taste*, p. 196.

53. Edmund Spenser, *The Faerie Queen*, (London: J.M. Dent, 1962), 1:9.
54. Brooks, *Hatton*, p. 143.

chapter four / A Leader Emerges: The Parliament of 1576

1. Sir John E. Neale, *Elizabeth I and her Parliaments*, 2 vols. (New York: St. Martin's Press, 1958), 1:312.
2. Edmund Lodge, *Illustrations of British History . . .*, 3 vols. (London: John Chidley, 1838), 2:75.
3. Neale, *Parliaments*, 1:329.
4. Ibid., p. 330.
5. Ibid.
6. Ibid.
7. Ibid., p. 361.
8. Ibid.
9. Ibid., p. 362.1 10. Ibid.
10. Ibid.
11. Ibid., pp. 366–67.
12. Ibid., p. 367.
13. Sir Harris Nicolas, *The Memoirs of the Life and Times of Sir Christopher Hatton*, (London: Richard Bentley, 1947), p. 38.
14. Ibid.
15. John Nichols, *The Progresses and Public Processions of Queen Elizabeth*, 3 vols. (London: Nichols & Son, 1823), 2:86.
16. Ibid., 1:114.
17. Ibid., 1:295.
18. Ibid., 1:324.
19. Ibid., 2:256.
20. J.R. Dasent, ed. *The Acts of the Privy Council of England*, New series, 32 vols. (London: Her Majesty's Stationery Office (HMSO), (1890–1907), 10:85 (1577–78).
21. Eric St. John Brooks, *Sir Christopher Hatton* (London: Jonathan Cape, 1946), p. 98.
22. Nicolas, *Memoirs*, p. 55.
23. Ibid., p. 56.
24. Ibid.
25. Ibid.
26. Ibid.

27. Ibid.
28. Ibid., p. 58.
29. Ibid.
30. Ibid.
31. Ibid., p. 59.
32. Brooks, *Hatton*, p. 200.
33. Nicolas, *Memoirs*, p. 61.
34. Ibid., p. 240.
35. Ibid.
36. Ibid.
37. Ibid.
38. Ibid., p. 69.
39. Nichols, *Progresses*, 2:94.
40. Ibid., p. 110.
41. Ibid., p. 111.
42. Nicolas, *Memoirs*, p. 57.
43. William Camden, *Annales . . . of Elizabeth*, 4 books (London: Benjamin Fisher, 1625) Bk. 2, p. 91.
44. Nicolas, *Memoirs*, p. 60.
45. Ibid., p. 63.
46. Ibid., p. 66.
47. Ibid.
48. Ibid.
49. Ibid.
50. Ibid., p. 67.
51. Ibid.
52. Ibid.
53. Ibid., pp. 72–73.
54. Ibid., p. 74.
55. Ibid.
56. Ibid., pp. 75–76.
57. Ibid., p. 81.
58. Ibid.
59. Ibid., p. 83.
60. Ibid., pp. 84–85.
61. Ibid.
62. Ibid., p. 91.

63. Ibid.
64. Ibid., p. 93.

chapter five / Marriage Diplomacy

1. Sir Harris Nicolas, *The Memoirs of the Life and Times of Sir Christopher Hatton* (London: Richard Bentley, 1847) p. 94.
2. Sir John E. Neale, *Queen Elizabeth I* (New York: Anchor, 1957), p. 245.
3. Eric St. John Brooks, *Sir Christopher Hatton* (London: Jonathan Cape, 1946), p. 170.
4. Ibid.
5. Ibid.
6. Ibid.
7. Neville Williams, *All the Queen's Men* (New York: Macmillan Co. 1972), p. 174.
8. Ibid.
9. Nicolas, *Memoirs*, pp. 91–92.
10. Ibid.
11. Ibid., pp. 133–34.
12. Ibid.
13. Ibid.
14. William Murdin, *A Collection of State Papers . . . of Queen Elizabeth . . .* (London: Wm. Bowyer, 1740–1759), p. 318.
15. Nicolas, *Memoirs*, pp. 113–15.
16. Ibid., p. 115.
17. Ibid., pp. 118–19.
18. Ibid., pp. 128–129.
19. Ibid., p. 135.
20. Ibid., p. 136.
21. Ibid., pp. 137–38.
22. Ibid., p. 145.
23. Ibid.
24. Ibid.
25. Ibid., pp. 152–53.
26. Ibid.
27. Ibid., pp. 153–54.

28. Ibid.
29. Williams, *All the Queen's Men*, p. 184.
30. British Museum, Harleian MSS. 416, fol. 200; also in Nicolas, *Memoirs*, p. 155.
31. Harleian MSS. 416, fol. 200.
32. Nicolas, *Memoirs*, pp. 156–59.
33. Ibid.
34. Ibid.
35. Ibid., pp. 158–61.
36. Ibid.
37. Ibid.
38. Ibid.
39. Ibid., pp. 166–67.
40. Ibid.

chapter six / Catholic Conspiracies and Parliament of 1581

1. A.O. Meyer, *England and the Catholic Church under Elizabeth* (London: K. Paul, 1916), pp. 269–71.
2. Sir John E. Neale, *Queen Elizabeth I* (New York: Anchor, 1957), p. 259.
3. Eric St. John Brooks, *Sir Christopher Hatton* (London: Jonathan Cape, 1946), p. 205.
4. Ibid., pp. 205–6.
5. Ibid.
6. Ibid., p. 206.
7. Sir Harris Nicolas, *The Memoirs of the Life and Times of Sir Christopher Hatton* (London: Richard Bentley, 1847), p. 242.
8. Ibid., p. 351.
9. Ibid.
10. Ibid., p. 352.
11. Ibid.
12. Ibid., pp. 351–53.
13. Brooks, *Hatton*, p. 213.
14. Ibid., p. 214.
15. Nicolas, *Memoirs*, p. 169.
16. Ibid., p. 181.

17. Ibid., p. 216.
18. Ibid.
19. Ibid., p. 217.
20. Ibid., p. 218.
21. Ibid., p. 219.
22. Brooks, *Hatton.*, p. 248.
23. T.B. Howell, *A Complete Collection of State Trials . . . to the Year 1783* 21 vols. (London: T.C. Hansard, 1816), 1:1111.
24. John Lingard, *A History of England,* 8 vols. (New York: Catholic Publishing Society, 1912–1915), 6:391–92.
25. Nicolas, *Memoirs,* p. 369.
26. Ibid., p. 377.
27. Ibid.
28. Ibid., p. 420.
29. Ibid.
30. Ibid., p. 427.
31. Brooks, *Hatton,* p. 257.
32. Sir John E. Neale, *Elizabeth I and her Parliaments,* 2 vols. (New York: St. Martin's Press, 1958), 1:377.
33. Ibid., p. 378.
34. Simonds D'Ewes, *A Complete Journal . . .* (London: Paul Bowes, 1693), p. 282.
35. Ibid., p. 284.
36. Ibid.
37. Ibid.
38. Neale, *Parliaments,* 1:382.
39. Ibid.
40. Ibid., p. 385.
41. Ibid., p. 388.
42. Ibid., pp. 390–92.
43. Ibid., p. 391.
44. Ibid.
45. William Camden, *Annales . . . of Elizabeth,* 4 books (London: Benjamin Fisher, 1625), book 4, p. 34.
46. Neale, *Parliaments,* 1:396-97.
47. D'Ewes, *Journal,* p. 301.
48. Ibid.

49. Neale, *Parliaments*, 1:402.
50. Ibid., p. 414.
51. Ibid., p. 415.

chapter seven / Parliament of 1584 — 1585

1. Sir John E. Neale, *Elizabeth I and her Parliaments*, 2 vols. (New York: St. Martin's Press, 1958), 1:17.
2. Ibid.
3. Ibid., p. 21.
4. John Strype, *The Life and Acts of John Whitgift*, 3 vols. (Oxford: Clarendon Press, 1822), 1:104–07.
5. Neale, *Parliaments*, 1:26.
6. Ibid., p. 28.
7. Conyers Read, ed., *The Bardon Papers*, Camden Third Series (London: Camden Society, 1909), p. 25.
8. Neale, *Parliaments*, p. 32.
9. Ibid., p. 34.
10. Ibid.
11. Ibid., p. 35.
12. Simonds D'Ewes, *A Complete Journal . . .* (London: Paul Bowes, 1693), p. 341.
13. Ibid.
14. Ibid.
15. Neale, *Parliaments*, 1:37.
16. D'Ewes, *Journal*, p. 340.
17. Ibid.
18. Neale, *Parliaments*, 1:42.
19. D'Ewes, *Journal*, pp. 343–44.
20. Ibid.
21. Ibid.
22. Ibid.
23. Ibid.
24. Sir Harris Nicolas, *The Memoirs of the Life and Times of Sir Christopher Hatton* (London: Richard Bentley, 1847), p. 411.
25. Ibid.
26. D'Ewes, *Journal*, p. 352.

27. Ibid., p. 356.
28. Ibid.
29. Neale, *Parliaments*, 1:50.
30. T.B. Howell, *A Complete Collection of State Trials . . . to the Year 1783*, 21 vols. (London: T.C. Hansard, 1816), 1:1105.
31. Ibid.
32. Ibid., p. 1107.
33. Ibid.
34. Ibid.
35. Ibid.
36. Eric St. John Brooks, *Sir Christopher Hatton* (London: Jonathan Cape, 1946), p. 241.
37. Ibid.
38. Ibid.
39. Ibid.
40. Ibid., p. 242.
41. Ibid.
42. Ibid., p. 243.
43. D'Ewes, *Journal*, p. 335.
44. Ibid., p. 339.
45. Ibid., p. 66.
46. Ibid.
47. Neale, *Parliaments*, 1:68.
48. Ibid., p. 69.
49. Ibid.
50. Ibid.
51. Ibid.
52. Ibid., p. 71.
53. Ibid., p. 74.
54. Ibid.
55. Strype, *Whitgift*, pp.391–92.
56. Neale, *Parliaments*, 1:99.
57. Ibid., p. 100.
58. Ibid.
59. Ibid.
60. Ibid.
61. Ibid.

62. Nicolas, *Memoirs*, p. 418.
63. Ibid., p. 426.
64. Ibid.
65. Ibid., p. 441.

chapter eight / Concerns of a Courtier

1. Sir Harris Nicolas, *The Memoirs of the Life and Times of Sir Christopher Hatton* (London: Richard Bentley, 1847), p. 153.
2. Eric St. John Brooks, *Sir Christopher Hatton* (London: Jonathan Cape, 1946), p. 224.
3. Nicolas, *Memoirs*, p. 144.
4. Brooks, *Hatton*, p. 184.
5. Ibid., p. 192.
6. William Murdin, *A Collection of State Papers . . . of Queen Elizabeth . . .* (London: Wm. Bowyer, 1740–1759), p. 539.
7. Brooks, *Hatton*, p. 303.
8. Nicolas, *Memoirs*, pp. 277–78.
9. Ibid.
10. Ibid., p. 415.
11. Ibid.
12. Ibid.

chapter nine / A Darkness of Conspiracies

1. Sir John E. Neale, *Elizabeth I and Her Parliaments*, 2 vols. (New York: St. Martin's Press, 1958), 2:103.
2. Sir Harris Nicolas, *The Memoirs of the Life and Times of Sir Christopher Hatton* (London: Richard Bentley, 1847), p. 443.
3. Ibid.
4. T.B. Howell, *A Complete Collection of State Trials . . . to The Year 1783*, 21 vols. (London: T.C. Hansard, 1816), 1:1131.
5. Ibid.
6. Ibid., p. 1127.
7. Ibid.
8. Ibid.
9. Ibid.

10. Ibid.
11. Ibid.
12. Ibid.
13. Eric St. John Brooks, *Sir Christopher Hatton* (London: Jonathan Cape, 1946), p. 290.
14. Howell, *State Trials*, p. 1141.
15. Ibid.
16. Brooks, *Hatton*, p. 295.
17. Nicolas, *Memoirs*, p. 444.
18. Ibid., pp. 450–51.
19. Howell, *State Trials*, p. 1171; also in Nicolas, *Memoirs*, pp. 451–52.
20. Howell, *State Trials*, p. 1171.
21. Ibid.
22. Ibid.
23. Ibid.
24. Antonia Fraser, *Mary, Queen of Scots*, (New York: Delacorte Press, 1969), p. 508.
25. Ibid.
26. William Camden, *The History of the Most Renowned and Victorious Princess Elizabeth*, ed. by Wallace T. MacCaffrey (Chicago: University of Chicago Press, 1970), p. 247.
27. Ibid., p. 508.
28. Neale, *Parliaments*, 2:104.
29. Simonds D'Ewes, *A Complete Journal . . .* (London: Paul Bowes, 1693), p. 393.
30. Conyers Read, ed., *The Bardon Papers*, Camden Third Series (London: Camden Society, 1909), pp. 82–84. doc. 18.
31. Ibid.
32. D'Ewes, *Journal*, p. 393.
33. Ibid.
34. Ibid.
35. Ibid.
36. Ibid., pp. 397–98.
37. Nicolas, *Memoirs*, pp. 453–54.
38. Neale, *Parliaments*, 2:114–15.
39. D'Ewes, *Journal*, p. 399.

40. Ibid.
41. Ibid., p. 402.
42. Ibid.
43. Ibid., p. 403.
44. Neale, *Parliaments*, 2:123.
45. D'Ewes, *Journal*, p. 404.
46. Ibid., p. 405.
47. British Museum Lansdowne MS. 94, fols. 86–88; also in Neale, *Parliaments*, 2:126-29.
48. Neale, *Parliaments*, 2:126-29.
49. D'Ewes, *Journal*, p. 406.
50. Sir Harris Nicolas, *The Life of William Davison* (London: John Nichols, 1823), pp. 86–87.
51. Neale, *Parliaments*, 2:134.
52. Ibid., 2:135.
53. Camden, op. cit. p. 279.
54. Neale, *Parliaments*, 2:136.
55. J.B. Black, *The Reign of Elizabeth* (Oxford: Oxford University Press, 1959), p. 386.
56. Camden, op. cit., p. 280.
57. Neale, *Parliaments*, 2:137.
58. Nicolas, *Memoirs*, p. 460.
59. Ibid.
60. Ibid., p. 461.
61. Thomas Wright, *Queen Elizabeth and her Times*, 2 vols. (London: Henry Colburn, 1838), 2:332.
62. Nicolas, *Memoirs*, p. 462.
63. Brooks, *Hatton*, p. 315.
64. Neale, *Parliaments*, 2:139.
65. Ibid., 2:141.
66. Ibid., 2:141-42.
67. Ibid.
68. Ibid., 2:143.
69. Ibid.

chapter ten / Hatton and the Unruly Parliament

1. Sir John Neale, "Peter Wentworth," *English Historical Review*, 34:50.

2. Simonds D'Ewes, *A Complete Journal . . .* (London: Paul Bowes, 1693), p. 408.
3. Ibid.
4. Ibid.
5. Ibid., p. 409.
6. Sir John E. Neale, *Elizabeth I and her Parliaments*, 2 vols. (New York: St. Martin's Press, 1958), 2:173.
7. Ibid. pp. 173–74.
8. Ibid.
9. Ibid.
10. Ibid., pp. 177–78.
11. Ibid.
12. Ibid.
13. Ibid., p. 181.
14. Ibid., p. 157.
15. Ibid., p. 158.
16. D'Ewes, *Journal*, p. 412.
17. Lambeth Palace, MS. 178, fols. 48–51.
18. Ibid.
19. Ibid.
20. Ibid.
21. Ibid.
22. Ibid; also in British Museum Harleian MS. 7188, fols. 96–103.
23. John Strype, *The Life and Acts of John Whitgift*, 3 vols. (Oxford: Clarendon Press, 1822), 3:188.
24. Ibid.
25. Ibid.
26. Ibid., 1:426.
27. Ibid.
28. Ibid.
29. Ibid.
30. Ibid.
31. Ibid.
32. Ibid.
33. Ibid.
34. Neale, *Parliaments*, 2:161.
35. D'Ewes, *Journal*, p. 413.

36. Lambeth Palace, MS. 178, fol. 88.
37. Ibid.
38. Ibid.
39. Ibid.

chapter eleven / Lord Chancellor

1. William Camden, *The History of The Most Renowned and Victorious Princess Elizabeth*, ed. by Wallace T. MacCaffery (Chicago: University of Chicago Press, 1970), p. 307.
2. Ibid., p. 306.
3. Thomas Fuller, *Worthies of England*, 3 vols. (New York: AMS Press, 1965), 2:507.
4. William Murdin, *A Collection of State Papers . . . of Queen Elizabeth . . .* (London: Wm. Bowyer, 1740–1759), p. 589.
5. Eric St. John Brooks, *Sir Christopher Hatton* (London: Jonathan Cape, 1946), p. 335.
6. John Stow, *The Annales of England* (London: Falfe Newbery, 1601), p. 741.
7. W.J. Jones, *The Elizabethan Court of Chancery* (Oxford: Clarendon Press, 1967), p. 40.
8. Camden, *History of Elizabeth*, p. 307.
9. Jones, *Court of Chancery*, p. 43.
10. W.D. Dunkel, *William Lambarde, Elizabethan Jurist, 1536–1601* (New Brunswick, New Jersey: Rutgers University Press, 1965), p. 103.
11. Ibid.
12. Lord John Campbell, *Lives of the Lord Chancellors and Keepers of the Great Seal of England*, 7th ed. (New York: Cockcroft and Co., 1878), pp. 149–51.
13. Jones, *Court of Chancery*, pp. 118–19.
14. George W. Sanders, *Orders of the High Court of Chancery . . .*, 2 vols. (London: Maxwell & Son, 1845), 2:612n.
15. Campbell, *Lives*, pp. 158–59.
16. Ibid.
17. Ibid.
18. Ibid.

19. Ibid.
20. Brooks, *Hatton,* p. 326.
21. Thomas Wright, *Queen Elizabeth and her Times,* 2 vols. (London: Henry Colburn, 1838), 2:385.
22. Camden, *History of Elizabeth,* p. 330.
23. Sir Harris Nicolas, *The Memoirs of the Life and Times of Sir Christopher Hatton* (London: Richard Bentley, 1847), p. 481.
24. Patrick Collinson, *The Elizabethan Puritan Movement* (Berkeley: University of California Press, 1967), pp. 166–67.
25. Ibid., p. 388.
26. Ibid., p. 408.
27. Ibid., p. 428.
28. Brooks, *Hatton,* p. 340.
29. Sir John E. Neale, *Elizabeth I and her Parliaments,* 2 vols. (New York: St. Martin's Press, 1958), 2:220.
30. Brooks, *Hatton,* p. 343.
31. Thomas Birch, *Memoirs of the Reign of Queen Elizabeth,* 2 vols. (London: A. Millar, 1754), 1:56.
32. Nicolas, *Memoirs,* p. 478.
33. British Museum Additional MS. 5845, vol. 44, p. 455.
34. Ibid.
35. Ibid.

chapter twelve / After the Armada

1. Sir Harris Nicolas, *The Memoirs of the Life and Times of Sir Christopher Hatton* (London: Richard Bentley, 1847), p. 482.
2. Ibid.
3. Snagge was a lawyer from Bedfordshire who had sat in two previous sessions.
4. Sir John E. Neale, *Elizabeth I and her Parliaments,* 2 vols. (New York, St. Martin's Press, 1958), 2:195.
5. Lord John Campbell, *Lives of the Lord Chancellors and Keepers of the Great Seal of England,* 7th ed., 6 vols. (New York: Cockcroft and Co., 1878), 2:153.
6. Conyers Read, ed., *Bardon Papers* (London: Camden Society, 1909), p. 107.

7. Lambeth Palace, MS. 178, fols. 75–81.
8. Ibid.
9. Ibid.
10. Ibid.
11. Ibid.
12. Ibid.
13. Ibid.
14. Ibid.
15. Ibid.
16. Neale, *Parliaments*, 2:198.
17. Lambeth Palace, MS. 178, fols. 75–81.
18. Ibid.
19. Ibid.
20. Ibid.
21. Ibid.
22. Ibid.
23. Ibid.
24. Ibid.
25. Ibid.
26. Inner Temple, *Petyt* MS 538/10, fols. 53-54.
27. Nicolas, *Memoirs*, pp. 485-86.
28. Ibid., p. 486.
29. Ibid., p. 489.
30. Ibid.
31. John Strype, *The Life and Acts of John Whitgift*, 3 vols. (Oxford: Clarendon Press, 1822), 2:97.
32. Eric St. John Brooks, *Sir Christopher Hatton* (London: Jonathan Cape, 1946), p. 341.
33. Ibid., p. 342.
34. Nicolas, *Memoirs*, pp. 490-91.
35. Ibid.
36. Brooks, *Hatton*, p. 352.
37. Ibid.
38. Historical Manuscripts Commission, Mar and Kellies MS., p. 53.
39. Nicolas, *Memoirs*, pp. 492-93.
40. Ibid.

41. Great Britain Public Record Office, State Papers, Domestic Elizabeth, vol. 174 (1591–1594), p. 65.
42. Nicolas, *Memoirs*, pp. 494–95.
43. Ibid.
44. Ibid.
45. Ibid.
46. William Camden, *The History of The Most Renowned and Victorious Princess Elizabeth*, ed. by Wallace T. MacCaffery (Chicago: University of Chicago Press, 1970), p. 34.
47. Thomas Fuller, *The History of the Worthies of England*, 3 vols. (London: T. Tegg, 1811), p. 165.
48. John Nichols, *The Progresses and Public Processions of Queen Elizabeth*, 3 vols. (London: Nichols & Son, 1823), 3:122.
49. Fuller, *Worthies*, p. 165.
50. John Stow, *The Annales of England* (London: Ralfe Newbery, 1601), p. 1270.
51. James Lees-Milne, *Tudor Renaissance* (London: Batsford Ltd., 1951), p. 90.
52. Brooks, *Hatton*, pp. 354–56.
53. Nicolas, *Memoirs*, p. 115.
54. Brooks, *Hatton*, p. 356.
55. Ibid.
56. Ibid.
57. Ibid., p. 358.
58. Robert Naunton, *Fragmenta Regalia*, ed. by E. Arber (Westminster: A. Constable & Co., 1895), pp. 41–42.
59. Brooks, *Hatton*, pp. 358–59.
60. Ibid., p. 361.
61. A.L. Rowse, *The Elizabethan Renaissance: The Life of the Society* (New York: Scribner's Sons, 1972), p. 118.
62. George Baker, *The History and Antiquities of the County of Northamptonshire*, 2 vols. (London: John B. Nichols Co., 1822–1841), 1:209.

chapter thirteen / Hatton . . . On Balance

1. Sir John E. Neale, *Elizabeth I and Her Parliaments*, 2 vols. (New York: St. Martin's Press, 1958), 2:438.

2. William Camden, *The History of . . . Princess Elizabeth*, 4 bks.
   (London: Benjamin Fuller, 1630), bk. 4, p. 34.
3. Neville Williams, *Elizabeth Queen of England* (London: Weidenfeld & Nicolson, 1967), p. 66.

Selected Bibliography

Manuscript Sources

The following manuscripts are located in London.

British Museum
Additional MS. 5,845. *Cole. MS.*
Additional MS. 15,891. *Hatton Letter Book.*
Cotton MSS. *Claudius,* CIII; *Titus* Fol. I.
Harleian MSS. 139, 787, 7188, 74, 993, 6843, 6991, 253, 6845,
    416.
Lansdowne MSS. 17, 22, 25, 15, 98, 41, 43, 94.

Lambeth Palace Library
MS. 178.

Public Record Office
Star Chamber. H. 53/24, 49/38 (1583).
State Papers, Domestic Elizabeth, Vols. 201, 140, 130–57, 186,
    142, 116, 54, 91, 174.

Printed Sources

Historical Manuscripts Commission
Ashburnham MS.
Buccleuch MS., vol. 3.
Finch MS., vols. 1–2.
Mar and Kellies MS.
Rutland MS., vol. I.
Salisbury MS., vol. 2.
Sidney State Papers, vol. I.
Various Collections, vol. 3–4.
Public Record Office, *Calendar of Patent Rolls,* Elizabeth Vol. 4
 (1566-69); Calendar No. 986 (April 19, 1568); Calendar No.
 1377 (July 27, 1586); Calendar No. 2257 (January 29, 1569),
 Calendar No. 1502 (January 29, 1569).
Public Record Office. *Calendar of State Papers, Foreign,* Elizabeth
 Spanish (1587-1603); 1568-79); 1591-94).
Public Record Office. *Calendar of State Papers, Domestic, of the Reigns
 of Edward VI, Mary, Elizabeth.* 1547–80. Vol. 34: Calendar No.
 52 (June 30, 1564). Calendar No. 45 (June 7, 1573).
Public Record Office. *Calendar of Scots and Mary, Queen of Scots.*
 (1584-85).
Dasent, J.R. ed. *Acts of Privy Council of England.* new series. 32 vols.
 London: Her Majesty's Stationery Office, 1890-1907.
Egerton Papers. London: Camden Society 13, 1840.
Leicester Correspondence. London: Camden Society 27, 1844.

Selected Secondary Sources

Aiken, Lucy. *Memoirs of the Court of Queen Elizabeth.* 2nd ed.
 London: Longman, Hurst, Rees, Orme and Brown, 1818.
Ayre, J., ed. *The Works of John Whitgift.* 2 vols. Cambridge,
 England: Parker Society, 1852.
Babbage, Stuart. *Puritanism and Richard Bancroft.* London: Church
 Historical Society, 1962.
Beckingsale, B.W. *Burghley, Tudor Statesman 1520-1598.* New
 York: St. Martin's Press, 1967.

_____ *Elizabeth I.* New York: Arco Publishing Co., 1963.

Bellot, Hugh. *The Inner and Middle Temple: Legal, Literary and Historical Associations.* London: Methuen Co., 1922.

Birch, Thomas. *Memoirs of the Reign of Queen Elizabeth.* 2 vols. (London: A. Millar, 1754).

Black, J.B. *The Reign of Elizabeth.* Oxford: Oxford University Press, 1959.

Brackenbury, Henry. *The Nearest Guard: A History of her Majesty's Body Guard of the Honourable Corps of Gentlemen-at-arms from 1509-1892.* London: Harrison and Sons, 1892.

Brooks, Eric St. John. *Sir Christopher Hatton.* London: Jonathan Cape, 1946.

Buxton, John. *Elizabethan Taste.* London: Macmillan, 1965.

Byrne, M. St. Clare. *Elizabethan Life in Town and Country.* rev. ed. New York: Barnes and Noble, 1961.

Camden, William. *The History of the Most Renowned and Victorious Princess, Elizabeth.* London: Benjamin Fuller, 1630.

_____ *Annales, the True and Royal History of the famous Empress Elizabeth—Queen of England, France and Ireland.* 4 books. London: Benjamin Fisher, 1625.

_____ *The History of the Life and Death of Mary Stuart, Queen of Scotland.* London: John Haviland, 1636.

Campbell, Lord John. *Lives of the Lord Chancellors and Keepers of the Great Seal of England.* 7th ed., 6 vols., New York: Cockcroft & Co., 1878.

Chambers, Edmund. *The Elizabethan Stage.* Oxford: Clarendon Press, 1923.

Churchyard, Thomas. *The First Part of Churchyard's Chips.* London: Thomas Marsh, 1575.

_____ *A Discourse of the Queen's Majesty's Entertainment in Suffolk and Norfolk.* London: Henry Bynneman, 1578.

Coker, John. *Survey of Dorsetshire.* London: J. Wilcox, 1732.

Collinson, Patrick. *The Elizabethan Puritan Movement.* Berkeley: University of California Press, 1967.

Cooke, William H. *Students Admitted to Inner Temple, 1547-1660.* London: Clowes & Sons, 1877.

Cross, Claire. *The Royal Supremacy in the Elizabethan Church.* London: Allen & Unwin, 1969.

Elton, G.R., ed. *The Tudor Constitution: Documents and Commentary.* Cambridge, England: Cambridge University Press, 1968.

D'Ewes, Simonds. *A Complete Journal of the Votes, Speeches and Debates Both of the House of Lords and House of Commons throughout the whole Reign of Queen Elizabeth of Glorious Memory.* London: Paul Bowes, 1693.

Dryden, Alice. *Memorials of Old Northamptonshire.* London: Benrose & Sons, 1903.

Dunkel, William D. *William Lambarde, Elizabethan Jurist, 1536-1601.* New Brunswick: Rutgers University Press, 1965.

Dunlop, Ian. *Palaces and Progresses of Elizabeth I.* London: Jonathan Cape, 1962.

Francis, Raymond. *Looking for Elizabethan England.* London: MacDonald & Co., 1954.

Fraser, Antonia. *Mary Queen of Scots.* London: Weidenfeld and Nicholson, 1969.

Frazer, N.L. *English History in Contemporary Poetry No. III, The Tudor Monarchy 1485-1588.* Cornwall, England: The Historical Association, 1970.

Fuller, Thomas. *The History of the Worthies of England.* 3 vols. London: T. Tegg, 1811.

Gladish, Dorothy M. *The Tudor Privy Council.* Worksop, England: The Retford, 1915.

Gleason, J.H. *The Justices of the Peace in England 1558-1640.* Oxford: Clarendon Press, 1969.

Gotch, J. Alfred. *Old English Houses.* London: Methuen & Co., 1925.

Harington, Henry. ed. *Nugae Antiquae.* 3 vols. London: T. Kadell, 1792.

Harrison, G.B. *The Elizabethan Journals, 1591-1603.* rev. ed. New York: Macmillan Co., 1939.

Hartshorne, Emily. *Memorials of Holdenby.* London: Robert Hardwicke, 1868.

Holmes, Martin. *Elizabethan London.* London: Cassell, 1969.

Howell, Roger. *Sir Philip Sidney.* Boston: Little, Brown & Co., 1968.

Howell, T.B. *A Complete Collection of State Trials and Proceedings for*

High Treason and other Crimes and Misdemeanors from the Earliest Period to the Year 1783. 21 vols. London: T.C. Hansard, 1816.

Hume, Martin. The Courtships of Queen Elizabeth. rev. ed. New York: Phillips & Co., 1904.

Hurstfield, Joel. The Queen's Wards. London: Longmans, Green & Co., 1958.

Jenkins, Elizabeth. Elizabeth the Great. New York: Capricorn Books, 1967.

Johnson, Paul. Elizabeth, a Study in Power and Intellect. London: Weidenfeld and Nicholson, 1974

Jones, W.J. The Elizabethan Court of Chancery. Oxford: Clarendon Press, 1967.

Knappen, M.M. Tudor Puritanism. Chicago: University of Chicago Press, 1939.

Lacey, Robert. Robert, Earl of Essex. New York: Atheneum, 1971.

Legh, Gerard. Accedens of Armory. London: R. Tottil, 1562.

Levine, Mortimer. The Early Elizabethan Succession Question, 1558-1568. Stanford: Stanford University Press, 1966.

Lingard, John. The History of England. 8 vols. New York: Catholic Publishing Society, 1912-15.

Lodge, Edmund. Illustrations of British History, Biography, and Manners in the reigns of Henry VIII, Edward VI, Mary, Elizabeth, and James I. 3 vols. London: John Chidley, 1838.

MacCaffrey, W.T., ed. The History of the Most Renowned and Victorious Princess Elizabeth. Chicago: University of Chicago Press, 1970.

McGrath, Patrick. Papists and Puritans under Elizabeth I. London: Blandford Press, 1967.

Melville, Sir James. Memoirs of his Own Life, 1594-93. London: A.F. Steward, 1929.

Murdin, William. A Collection of State Papers relating to Affairs in the Reign of Queen Elizabeth from the Year 1571 to 1596 left by William Cecil. London: William Bowyer, 1740-1759.

Naunton, Robert. Fragmenta Regalia. ed. E. Arber. Westminster: A. Constable & Co., 1895.

Neale, Sir John E. Elizabeth I and her Parliaments. 2 vols. New York: St. Martin's Press, 1958.

Nichols, John. *The Progresses and Public Processions of Queen Elizabeth.* 3 vols. London: Nichols & Son, 1823.

Nicolas, Sir Harris. *The Memoirs of the Life and Times of Sir Christopher Hatton.* London: Richard Bentley, 1847.

―――― *The Life of William Davison.* London: John Nichols, 1823.

Pearson, L.E. *Elizabethans at Home.* Stanford: Stanford University Press, 1957.

Pollen, J.H. *Mary Queen of Scots and the Babington Plot.* 3rd. series. Edinburgh: Scottish Historical Society, 1922.

Prest, W.R. *The Inns of Court under Elizabeth I and the Early Stuarts 1590-1640.* London: Longman, 1972.

Pulman, Michael B. *The Elizabethan Privy Council in the Fifteen-Seventies.* Berkeley: University of California Press, 1971.

Quennell, Peter. *Shakespeare.* New York: World Publishing Co., 1963.

Read, Conyers. *Mr. Secretary Walsingham and the Policy of Queen Elizabeth.* 3 vols. Oxford: Clarendon Press, 1925.

Read, Conyers, ed. *The Bardon Papers.* London: Camden Society, 1909.

―――― *Mr. Secretary Cecil and Queen Elizabeth.* New York: Knopf, 1961.

Riche, Barnabe. *Riche, His Farewell to the Military Profession.* London: Shakespeare Society, 1846.

Rowse, A.L. *The Elizabethan Renaissance: The Cultural Achievement.* New York: Scribner's Sons, 1972.

―――― *The Elizabethan Renaissance: The Life of The Society.* New York: Scribner's Sons, 1972.

―――― *The Expansion of Elizabethan England.* New York: Macmillan, 1955.

―――― *The England of Elizabeth.* New York: Macmillan Co., 1950.

Sanders, George W. *Orders of the High Court of Chancery and Statutes of the Realm relating to Chancery.* 2 vols. London: Maxwell & Son, 1845.

Spenser, Edmund. *The Faerie Queen.* London: J.M. Dent, 1962.

Stow, John. *The Annales of England.* London: Ralfe Newbery, 1601.

―――― *Survey of London.* London: John Windet, 1603.

Strickland, Agnes. *The Lives of the Queens of England from the Norman Conquest.* 8 vols. London: George Bell & Sons, 1882.

Strype, John. *The Life and Acts of John Whitgift.* 3 vols. Oxford: Clarendon Press, 1822.

Thomson, Gladys S. *Lords Lieutenant in the 16th Century.* London: Longmans, Green & Co., 1923.

Trinterud, Leonard. ed. *Elizabethan Puritanism.* New York: Oxford University Press, 1971.

Waldman, Milton. *Elizabeth and Leicester.* Boston: Houghton Mifflin, 1945.

Wernham, R.B. and Walker, J.C. *England Under Elizabeth.* London: Longmans, Green & Co., 1934.

Williams, Elijah. *Early Holborn.* 2 vols. London: Sweet & Maxwell, 1927.

Williams, Neville. *All the Queen's Men.* New York: Macmillan Co., 1972.

_____ *The Life and Times of Elizabeth 1.* New York: Doubleday & Co., 1972.

_____ *Elizabeth Queen of England.* London: Weidenfield & Nicolson, 1967.

Wood, Anthony. *Athenae Oxonienses,* ed. Philip Bliss. 4 vols. Oxford: Oxford University Press, 1813–1820.

Wright, Thomas. *Queen Elizabeth and her Times.* 2 vols. London: Henry Colburn, 1838.

Periodicals

Hinton, R.W.K. "The Decline of Parliamentary Government under Elizabeth I and the Early Stuarts." *Cambridge Historical Journal* 12, (No. 2), (1957): 116–32.

Neale, J.E. "Elizabeth I and her Cold War." In *Essays in Elizabethan History.* London: Jonathan Cape, 1958.

_____ "The Elizabethan Age." In *Essays in Elizabethan History.* London: Jonathan Cape, 1958.

_____ "The Elizabethan Acts of Supremacy and Uniformity." *English Historical Review* 65 (July 1950): 304–32.

_____ "Parliament and the Articles of Religion, 1571." *English Historical Review* 67 (October 1952): 510–21.

_____ "Peter Wentworth." *English Historical Review* 39 (January-April 1924): 36–54, 175–205.

———— "Proceedings in Parliament Relative to Sentence of Mary Stuart." *English Historical Reveiw* 35 (January 1920): 102–13.

Price, F.D. "The Abuses of Excommunication and the Decline of Ecclesiastical Discipline under Queen Elizabeth." *English Historical Review* 57 (January 1942): 106–15.

Smith, Goldwin. "Elizabeth and the Apprenticeship of Parliament." *University of Toronto Quarterly* (July 1939): 431–39.

Ward, B.M. "Queen Elizabeth and William Davison." *English Historical Review* 44 (January 1929) 104–6.

Wernham, R. "The Disgrace of W. Davison." *English Historical Review* 46 (October 1931): 632–34.

Index

As an assistant professor at the University of Dayton (Ohio), Alice G. Vines, Ph.D., specializes in the teaching of English history. She has contributed articles to various professional journals and has taught in the University's overseas program in London. Currently Dr. Vines is researching the life of Prime Minister Ramsay MacDonald's wife.